Tolstoy Remembered

Tolstoy Remembered

Tatyana Tolstoy

translated from the French
by Derek Coltman

with an introduction by
Professor John Bayley

LONDON
MICHAEL JOSEPH

First published in Great Britain by Michael Joseph Ltd
52 Bedford Square, London WC1B 3EF
1977

English translation © by Michael Joseph Ltd 1977
Originally published in France under the title
Avec Leon Tolstoi (souvenirs)
© 1975 Editions Albin Michel

ISBN 0 7181 1626 7

Set and printed in Great Britain by
Tonbridge Printers Ltd, Peach Hall Works, Tonbridge, Kent
in Garamond eleven on thirteen point, and bound by
Redwood Burn Ltd, Esher

The two pieces *Flashes of Memory*
and *I often think of my mother*
were originally written directly in French

The piece *My father's death* was first
published in 1928 in a special issue of
the magazine *Europe* dedicated to Leo Tolstoy.
Any previously published English translation
of this piece is not known

Contents

List of Illustrations

Introduction

by Professor John Bayley

As the family tree on the endpaper shows, Tolstoy always lived in the middle of a large family, even though both his mother and father died when he was a child. The youngest of four brothers, he was looked after by his aunt Tatyana, to whom he was greatly attached. He christened with the same name his eldest daughter, the author of this book.

Most of Tolstoy's children wrote about their famous father; the memoir of his second son, Ilya, is of particular interest. But Tatyana's book is by far the most remarkable. She is the only one of the family who exists in her reminiscences in parallel to Tolstoy, so to speak, illuminating him and the rest of the family by being herself. And it is a fascinating self, a distinct personality, full of its own sort of vitality and powers of perception.

She complements her father in another respect too: she was a far nicer person! She is never in the least self-important, whereas her father's obsession with himself, with every detail of his consciousness and behaviour, is the very key to his genius as a writer. The supreme importance of childhood for Tolstoy is that in it his self-absorption was most completely identified with his interest in the world around him. Childhood was not only the most important time of life but the thing that gave total meaning to *zhizn*—life—the most decisive word in all the great Russian novels, and the one most frequently emphasised. All his later preoccupations with the need for simplicity and truth can be seen as a desire, created with all the massive strength and earnestness of his mature powers, to reproduce the spontaneity of the happy childhood which he had had, which haunted him for the rest of his life.

He seems to have remembered much further back than most children. To his biographer, Biryukov, he claimed to recall a moment at two years old or less when he sat in a wooden tub, stroking its soapy and slippery sides, and waiting for his nurse to pour a jug of fresh water over him as she did at the end of his bath. All children recall such moments, but it takes a Tolstoy to identify them thus at the very beginning of life, and to comment on them as he did in his old age: 'As I was then, so am I now.'

His daughter Tatyana might have done the same. Not the least remarkable thing about this marvellous account of her childhood as Tolstoy's child is her own identification with the child she used to be. She does not appear to look back on those early experiences: we never have the feeling of two people, the child and the mature woman, but always of a single character of wonderful humour and transparency, through whose medium the early years come before us, as they do in her father's own writings.

Talents run in families, but genius is rarely transmitted. All the more remarkable that something of the paternal genius for conveying what it meant to be himself when young seems to have been rein-carnated in his daughter, whose reminiscences are nonetheless wholly original, and often quite unlike Tolstoy's own. Tolstoy had a passion, which his daughter naturally does not share, for analysis and 'placing', for putting people in different categories and thus, as it were, acquiring power over them—a compulsion of Tolstoy as creator and artist which is, of course, wholly at variance with Tolstoy as the exponent of Christian humility! But it must be admitted to be one of the chief sources of his extraordinary power over the reader. Nothing—himself least of all—escapes his penetrating eye, and his clarity and simplicity make him foremost of all great writers in moving the reader to see himself in the same way.

Do children see themselves thus? Tolstoy persuades us that they do, or at least that they have the power of doing so without being conscious of it themselves. In his own *Childhood, Boyhood and Youth*— the book that launched him on his literary career, and led Dostoevsky, in Siberia, to write off to a friend urgently requesting the identity of this marvellous new writer who signed himself L.N.—he makes us see how children *understand* each other, or fail to do so in a much more atavistic and absolute sense than do grown-ups. That *understanding* is not related, so Tolstoy assures us, to what is ordinarily thought of as intellect and intelligence: it is a primitive and instinctive sort of per-ception which in *War and Peace* he claims to be particularly Russian (as opposed to the *esprit* of the French) and which is an aspect of the directness, humour, and 'self-derision' so sovereign in childhood.

Most certainly this perception was characteristic of his daughter Tatyana. She 'understood' her father, so one feels from this book, as naturally as she breathed, and by the same method that Tolstoy had himself described. Indeed, it would not be too much to say that she understands him here a great deal better than any of his innumerable critics and biographers have done. She is not concerned, as they are, to pluck out the heart of his mystery, but instead invests all his vivid and fabulously contradictory qualities with a simple acceptance, almost as if he himself were a child, of a very fascinating kind, and she another.

This in itself would give these memoirs an incomparable value, quite apart from the absorbing charm and detail of her own recollections about herself and the world of Yasnaya Polyana, and the no less vivid ones of Samara, where Tolstoy went on the advice of his doctor to take the 'cure' of drinking fermented mares' milk and leading the simple life of the steppe nomads. There is in fact a remarkable irony in finding in his daughter's prose an echo, an almost exact example, of Tolstoy's own comments in *Youth*, the third part of his *Childhood* series, on how a family gets on together.

> . . . there exists a special capacity more or less developed in different circles of society—in families particularly—which I call mutual *understanding*. Two members of the same set or the same family possessing this faculty can always allow an expression of feeling up to a certain point beyond which they both see only empty phrases. Both perceive where commendation ends and irony begins, where enthusiasm ceases and pretence takes its place . . . To facilitate this common understanding the members of a family often invent a language of their own with expressions peculiar to them, or words which indicate shades of meaning non-existent for others . . . Dubkov fitted into our circle fairly well and *understood*, but Dimitri Nekhlyudov, though far more intelligent, was obtuse in this respect.

Most commentators on Tolstoy, though they may be 'far more intelligent' are, when compared with his daughter Tatyana, obtuse in precisely the same way! As I suggested in a study called *Tolstoy and the Novel*, it is almost impossible to exaggerate the importance of the way he interpreted the world and its values through this medium of the instinct and communication in a harmonious family group. It is significant that *War and Peace* ends with a kind of coda, as tender as

it is insouciant and unexpected, which takes us straight into the
consciousness of little Nicholas, the son of Prince Andrew, and into
the absurd and touching and delightful quality of his dreams and hopes
for the future, dreams of doing something which even his father
would be proud of, and yet suggesting the complete individuality of
this child in whom the future will in turn continue the rhythm and
cycle of time.

And yet Tolstoy could also say that 'Family life was hell'. This too
his daughter understands and accepts with serene equanimity. In 'My
Father's Death' it is clear that she 'understood' by instinct the nature of
his difficulties with his wife, Sofia Andreyevna, and she deeply sym-
pathised with her mother while not possessing any idea or wish to
judge between them. Tolstoy's wife was not an 'understander': indeed
one may feel she could never have stood it if she had been one—and
moreover that Tolstoy would never have married her if she had been
one. In his wife he required a worshipper; only in his daughter could
he go back, as it were, to find a childhood style of friend. But most
men—and in this respect Tolstoy was as fully human as we might
expect—have an instinct for the kind of wife who would suit them in
fact, however much they are prone to protest later on that she doesn't
understand them, that she tries to take them over, that she makes the
home a place to get away from at all costs.

Tatyana could, and did, understand, where her mother could not.
And it is illuminating to compare the daughter's recollections of the
father with those of the mother. The Countess Tolstoy portrayed her
husband in her recollections in such a way as to make him seem an
indefatigable crank, dragging his reluctant family behind him through
fad after fad, whim after whim, permitting them no life or opinions
of their own. Her image of her husband is all the more inadvertently
deadly for being so hagiographical by intent: every earnest sentence
makes the great man's feet of clay larger and more obtrusive. Napoleon
said that no one is a hero to his valet; and Hegel retorted that this
was because valets were valets, not because heroes were not heroic.
The same may necessarily be true of wives. Could Countess Tolstoy
have possibly read *War and Peace* and *Anna Karenina* as we do, when,
after a busy day of housekeeping and looking after the children, she
addressed herself to copy out the day's draft of the current novel, so
that her husband might have a clean manuscript to go to work on in
the morning? In what she read and copied she would necessarily
recognise not only the general *ambiance* of family and house, her own,

that of her parents, and the Tolstoy friends and relations, but also traits drawn from herself and her sister, their ways and remarks, and insights—often too piercing to be at all comfortable—into their mind and thoughts.

The great novels that seem to us so majestic, so lucid and so calm, must have seemed to her swarming and pullulating with daily emotions and crises, painful and joyful events—scenes they were living through. No wonder her genuine reverence for her great husband must also have contained an incredulity that all this was hailed with awe and admiration by the reading public when it was turned into art and published. Her daughter was not of course on such immediate terms with her father's daily 'leaving a little flesh in the ink-pot', as he called it. As a little girl she would run to him, as she tells us, to play and be talked to; and like her brothers and sisters she was aware of some mysterious activity that went on in the study. When she grew up she felt a certain emulation to 'write', as papa was doing, to fill notebooks with thoughts and aspirations, to be a 'Tolstoyan'. Her brothers Sergei and Ilya were doing the same. But here again one has the feeling that of all Tolstoy's family, Tatyana was the one who most instinctively 'understood': who was closest to her father himself in being least a 'Tolstoyan', and least concerned with the image of the great sage and teacher who attracted disciples from all over the world.

Where his daughters were concerned Tolstoy was, as we might expect, a possessive father; and the girls were not above vying with each other in the flirtatiousness with which each in her own way sought to attach herself to the great man. But here again Tatyana was different, and certainly as different as possible from her youngest sister, Alexandra, who became a particularly slavish Tolstoyan to her father in his old age, and the only one of the family—so gossip reports—who made up to and got on well with the faintly sinister guards officer, Chertkov, the most influential and strong-minded of Tolstoy's following, who tried to secure the rights of his books away from the family to a foundation. Tatyana, and to a lesser extent her sister Masha, intuited how much appetite and nostalgia for the world and its ways still remained in their father. After they had been to balls and parties in Moscow they found themselves being questioned, confidentially and with a sort of avid relish, about who was getting off with whom, what the girls were wearing, how it was the fashion for the young men to behave. The passionate interest in society which is open in *War and Peace* and filled with irony and disapproval in *Anna Karenina* (but the relation of Anna and Vronsky is wrecked because they are starved of society and excluded from it) lay dormant in Tolstoy all his life, as did the aristocratic pride in himself and his social position that went with it.

Not so unlike her father in this respect, Tatyana could play the *grande dame* as easily as she could run a kitchen or help the women in the fields; and both kinds of activity drew her equally. Her father fought a ferocious battle against any suitor, and when she married Sukhotin, a blameless and amiable widower with six children, he growled to his journal: 'Tanya has left—God knows why—with Sukhotin. Pitiful and humiliating.' But Tatyana herself wrote that though she was sorry to have 'betrayed papa' she didn't 'feel any remorse'. She was wholly capable of independence. She led her own life, with its own family happiness—including the birth of her own daughter Tanya, who contributes the final section to this book—and shortly before the first war she began to write down her recollections. Except for a few extracts these have never been printed before, even in Russia, and they come to us now from France. Destitute at Yasnaya Polyana after the revolution, and with her family dead or scattered, Tatyana emigrated with her daughter to Paris, where she came to know and talked with French men of letters, and writers whose interest in her father was not that of 'Tolstoyans' but of fellow-authors and fellow-craftsmen. When her daughter married an Italian, Signor Albertini, she went to live in her son-in-law's house in Rome, where she died in 1950.

'My father's death' is a moving and compelling meditation, which seems to rise out of a central Russian tradition of recall, at once tranquil, humorous and elegiac. Like many other things in the book it may remind us of Aksakov, who wrote about his childhood at the time Tolstoy himself was young; and even of Mandelshtam's *The Noise of Time* and of some pages of Pasternak. 'Flashes of Memory', short vignettes about her father, are as vivid and as moving. But more uncanny almost, because so closely related to what most pleased or fascinated Tolstoy himself, are many of the earlier scenes in 'Childhood' and 'Adolescence', like the horse-race in Samara, the visit to the hermit, the game of strength Tolstoy used to play with the Bashkirs and at which he was eventually beaten by an enormous Russian soldier. (He did not look at all pleased.) When the coachman loses his way on the steppe with a thunderstorm coming up we may be reminded of a similar sort of episode in Tolstoy's own *Childhood*; and Tolstoy's superstition at seeing a black cat as he set out on a journey is quaintly similar to that of his great forerunner (and, incidentally, fellow-sceptic) Pushkin, who always turned home if a hare crossed his path. A remarkable portrait is that of Agafia Mihailovna, stalwart nurse and kennel-maid; and the record of childhood illness is written with unique detail and practical sense. Most remarkable of all, to me, are the occasions when Tolstoy's own perception of things seems to be involved, the kind of perception in his art which the critics have called 'making it strange', when we are made to see something with a kind of naïve intensity: Thus Tolstoy describes driving on a journey out of Moscow, and passing through streets which he feels are 'never seen except by those who are going on a journey', as he is.

His daughter had the same power, shown in such a memory as this one:

Suddenly I spied a strange figure on the steppe, just off the road and standing quite motionless. I pointed it out to mamma.

'Look, what is that near the road over there?'

'It must be one of the local children. Lost like us I expect.'

Strain my eyes as I might I simply couldn't make out for sure what it was. It was true that it did look rather like a child, perhaps wearing a dark caftan, but the head was so small, and such an odd shape. Abruptly the figure broadened, as if it had lifted a big cape with its arms. Then, waving its cape, what I had taken to be a little boy rose slowly into the air.

'An eagle! An eagle!' we all cried.

This is the kind of moment, and the kind of vision, that we have in tales like 'The Cossacks', at the beginning of Tolstoy's writing life, and in 'Hadji Murad', at the end of it.

Childhood at Yasnaya Polyana

I

Recalling my childhood stirs up deep feelings, above all feelings of warmth and gratitude toward those around me in those happy days.

I was fortunate enough to grow up surrounded by people who loved one another and who loved me. I assumed then that such loving relationships were only natural, an inherent characteristic of human nature. And despite a long existence during which I have since encountered cruelty and hatred between men, that is still my belief. I am truly convinced to this day that such behaviour is no more normal than illness is. And that, like illness, it is produced by transgressing the fundamental laws of life.

After his marriage on September 23rd 1862, my father lived with his family at Yasnaya Polyana for eighteen years. He was absent only on rare occasions, when his presence was required in Moscow on business.

Life in the country gave me a taste for solitude and tranquillity, as well as the habit of observing and loving nature; but when I turn my inner gaze back to that happy time I see it illumined above all by the presence of three human beings, all of whom I remember with inexpressible gratitude: my father, who directed and guided our whole life; my mother, who strove perpetually in every way she could to make it beautiful; and Hannah, our English governess, who spent six years as a member of the family, surrounding me with love and care while imbuing me with solid moral principles.

It was with these three people, who occupy a special place in my memory, that my early years were spent.

Hannah left us when I was almost nine. Her departure marked the end of my childhood and of the cloudless happiness I had enjoyed until then. My girlhood was about to begin. But I shall come to that in the second part of these memoirs.

2

I was born at Yasnaya Polyana on October 4th 1864.

Several days beforehand my father had been thrown in a riding accident. Still a young man then, he loved hunting, especially for foxes and hares in the autumn. So on September 26th 1864 he took his pack of borzois and rode out to hunt on a young and spirited mare named Mashka. Some distance from the house he started a great russet hare in a field and immediately set on his hounds. 'Follow! Follow!' he yelled, and urged his mount after the bounding hare. Whereupon Mashka, an inexperienced hunter but only too eager to go, was soon launched into an all-out gallop. A dry water-course appeared across her path. She failed to clear it, stumbled, and fell on to her knees. Then, instead of pulling herself to her feet again, she toppled heavily over on to her flank. My father fell with her, and his right arm was trapped so that it took the mare's full weight.

Without giving her rider time to collect his wits, Mashka then scrambled to her feet and set off back to her stable, leaving my father in the ravine.

He was unable to walk, and it was almost a verst [about two-thirds of a mile] to the road that was his only hope of finding help, but he did somehow find the strength to drag himself that far.

Later, my father said that during the whole of that time he was almost unconscious, and under the impression that his accident had in fact occurred at some time in the distant past.

Once the long, agonizing struggle to the road was over, his strength completely deserted him, his head began to swim, and he lay down. From then on he made no attempt to move, but simply lay there waiting for someone to pass by.

At length a cart with some peasants in it appeared along the road. My father summoned up his last ounce of strength and hailed them:

'Stop! Help me!'

The peasants, either not hearing or not wishing to stop, continued on their way.

My father went on waiting. At last a passer-by recognized him.

'Saints in heaven, if it isn't the count from Yasnaya Polyana! What can have happened to him?'

The man stopped the next telega that came along, had the driver help him lift my father into it, then told him to take the injured man to

Yasnaya Polyana. My father was in terrible pain.

'Don't take me to the house,' he told the driver, 'go to one of the isbas in the village.'

He thought that if he appeared without warning in his present condition it would be too great a shock for my mother.

Meanwhile, at home, lunch had been served, and my young mother— she was twenty at the time—, together with her brother-in-law Count Sergei Nicolayevich Tolstoy [the second of the four Tolstoy brothers] and her mother Lyubov Alexandrovna Behrs, was waiting for the arrival of her husband and his sister, Countess Marya Nicolayevna Tolstoy [Tolstoy's younger and only sister].

So far neither of them had appeared, and the soup was getting cold.

'Oh, these Tolstoys,' my mother grumbled, 'always eternally late for their meals.'

But the idea had already sowed itself in her mind that something might have happened to my father. She was beginning to be worried.

Suddenly Marya Nicolayevna walked in and went over to Lyubov Alexandrovna. She whispered something in her ear and both women left the room.

Before long Lyubov Alexandrovna returned. No sooner was she inside the room than she began talking, in a rather strained voice and apparently addressing herself to no one in particular:

'One should never allow oneself to become upset. Whatever may befall us in life we should always behave sensibly and . . .'

My mother didn't even allow her to finish the sentence. She knew at once that something had happened to her husband.

'Where is Lyova? . . . (1) Tell me! . . . Is he dead?' she cried.

As soon as she had learned the truth from the two older women she hurriedly dressed and rushed down to the village. There she found her husband seated on a bench undergoing what looked like a form of torture. His injured arm, bared to the shoulder, was firmly locked in the grip of the peasant whose isba he'd been brought to, while a woman, the local bonesetter, was vigorously massaging it. A former serf of the Tolstoy family, Agafia Mikhailovna, and my father's aunt, Tatyana Alexandrovna Yergolskaya [born in 1795, died June 20th 1874], were also there. It was almost impossible to breathe in the room, which was tiny, dark, and full of yelling children.

My mother sent at once for a doctor from Tula [a town 9 miles from Yasnaya Polyana and 115 from Moscow] and had my father carried up to the house. The doctor made eight attempts to get the arm back into place, twisting it this way and that completely in vain. After putting my father through the most excruciating agony he left again without having achieved a thing. My father spent an appalling night, and my mother didn't leave him for a second. Next day she sent in to Tula for another doctor, a young surgeon, who gave my father chloroform then finally managed to reseat the arm in its socket and set it. But still my father's fever did not abate and there was no lessening of the pain.

By the time I came into the world my father had still not recovered from his fall.

My parents already had a son, eighteen-month-old Seryozha (2), and they were delighted to have a daughter. One of my father's friends, Dmitri Alexeyevich Dyakov [1823–91], stood godfather to me, and as godmother I had my grandmother, Lyubov Alexandrovna Behrs.

My father decided he would like me to be christened Tatyana, in honour of the aunt I have just mentioned, Tatyana Alexandrovna Yergolskaya, who had brought him up [together with his four brothers and sisters after his mother's death in 1830] and of whom he was extremely fond. As for my mother, her younger sister was also named Tatyana, so she was delighted to give her daughter the same name as her favourite sister.

Apparently I was a healthy, active baby, and no trouble at all to raise.

All those around me in those early days were much preoccupied with my father, who was still suffering a great deal with his arm, and even afraid he might remain a permanent cripple. He spent night after night without sleep. The devoted old Agafia Mikhailovna had to remain at his bedside for six weeks on end, never permitting herself more than an occasional doze in an armchair.

After some while, when the use of his arm still hadn't returned, my parents decided my father must go and consult a first-class surgeon in Moscow, where it was discovered that his arm had been incorrectly treated.

While in Moscow, papa stayed with his parents-in-law. My grandfather, Andrei Behrs, was the court physician, and lived with his family in one of the Kremlin buildings.

My father's letters to my mother make it clear that he consulted quite a number of doctors. The advice they gave him varied. Some were of the opinion that his shoulder ought not to be tampered with, that given time and suitable exercises it would settle back of its own accord. Others said an operation was essential if the continuing dislocation was to be remedied.

My father began by following the advice of the first group, which included my grandfather Behrs, and diligently performed all the exercises they had prescribed. But the arm only got worse and worse. For a healthy, active young man, as my father was at that time, the prospect of losing the use of his right arm permanently was a black one indeed, so he decided to have the operation. It was successful.

Nevertheless, because of the constant need for his dressings to be changed, my father was obliged to remain in Moscow for some while longer, and he made use of this enforced stay to negotiate terms for the publication of *War and Peace*. Then at last, in December 1864, he returned to Yasnaya Polyana.

3

I was four months old. My mother was wholly absorbed in her home life. At that time she had no other interests but her husband and children, and it was her fervent desire that all those she loved should also love one another. Unfortunately, however, my father had never felt any particular fondness for very young children, and apart from that he also had other things on his mind at that time. For one thing he still wasn't absolutely certain of recovering the use of his arm, and that was causing him a great deal of anxiety. In addition, he was then deeply immersed in the most monumental of all his works, and that entailed a vast amount of reading, research, and reflection.

As a result, when informed that his baby daughter was laughing, had succeeded in grasping some object or other in her tiny fist, or was actually able to recognize her mother and her nurse, he displayed very little reaction.

Mamma was desolate. 'He pays not the slightest attention to Tanya,' she wrote to her sister Tatyana Andreyevna (3), referring to my father. 'I do find it most odd, and it upsets me. Because she's such a darling little thing, so healthy and good-tempered. She's already five months now, is going to have her teeth through in no time, and will soon be walking and talking. And she's going to grow up without anyone taking the slightest notice of her. So you must pay a great deal of attention to her, Tanya, and love her, I beg you. I think she will have dark eyes, but it's still hard to say for sure. At all events they're very big, and so merry and shining.'

A year later, mamma was writing to her sister in a very different vein:

'Tanya never stops wishing everyone "Googorning" (good morning) and can already say "Shesha" (Seriozha). Lyovochka (4) is quite wild about her.'

In another letter she writes: 'Tanya my dear, if you could only see what a funny little thing Tanyusha has become. She can say anything now, in her own way of course. She fairly skips along when she walks, dances as though she's had lessons, can get up and down stairs, and adores her father.'

4

As we grew a little older my father began to insist that we should all live as simply as possible. He himself always displayed the greatest simplicity in his tastes and needs.

Mamma used to tell me that before they were married papa had always slept with his head on a leather cushion without even a pillow slip over it, and that on her arrival at Yasnaya Polyana she had found the house only very basically furnished to say the least.

Papa was against expensive toys, so while we were little mamma used to run up playthings for us herself. She had made us a golliwog that we quite doted on. He was made of black cambric with white linen eyes, black lambswool hair, and lips cut out of a piece of some red material.

Papa always wore a grey flannel smock, and never changed into European clothes except when he went to Moscow. He had requested that my brothers and I should always be dressed in smocks just like his. But then, very gradually, mamma began introducing changes that fitted in more with her own view of things. For a start, she persuaded papa to let her give us toys at Christmas. For Seryozha *just the one* little rocking horse, she begged, and for Tanya *just the one* doll.

As Christmas followed Christmas, however, so the gifts grew in number, and the grey smocks were replaced by more varied and elegant attire. Little by little we began leading the same kind of life as other landowners of our class.

On the big religious feast days it was the custom for a priest to come in and hold an evening service in 'Auntie' Tatyana Alexandrovna's rooms. Her companion would light candles in front of the two ikon windows, and their silver frames, freshly polished for the occasion, would glitter with bright reflections of the wavering flames. Axinia Maximovna, Auntie's old maid, went bustling to and fro without a sound, arranging tiny lamps and candles everywhere, crossing herself as she settled each one in place. All the rooms had just had their floors scrubbed, so that everywhere smelled of the mint and kvas [a peasant drink made from fermented malt or rye] that were always burned in the passages and stairwells after any big housecleaning. This is how it was done: you placed a red-hot brick in a brass bowl with some dried mint on top, then you sprinkled the brick with the kvas, which hissed as it vapourized, leaving a very agreeable smell of malt and mint all over the place.

All sorts of odd people lived with us in those days.

There was a monk named Voyeykov who was in the house for years. He was a brother of my father's guardian, and he wore his monk's habit all the time, even though it often seemed a little unsuitable considering his passion for drink.

There was also a dwarf. His main job was to chop wood for the house, but he also played an important part in all the festivities and fancy dress parties at Yasnaya Polyana.

Then there was Marya Gerasimovna, an old woman who always dressed as a man and spent her life making one pilgrimage after another. She was my aunt Marya Nicolayevna's godmother.

I was told that after giving birth to my father—her fourth son—my grandmother longed increasingly for a daughter. So she made a vow that if her wish was granted she would take the first woman to appear along the road as the child's godmother. Shortly afterwards she did in fact give birth to a daughter. Someone was sent out on to the high road, which was a pilgrim route, and the first person to come along was a simple-minded girl dressed as a boy. It was Marya Gerasimovna, who as a result became my aunt Marya Nicolayevna's godmother.

Later, my grandmother arranged for her to be taken in by the convent in Tula, but she still used to come and stay with us quite often at Yasnaya Polyana.

One day she told everyone about a rumour circulating in Tula that strange creatures, either animals or birds, had started appearing in the air. They were supposed to be carried in by the 'zephyrs', and people were calling them 'zephyrotes'.

Shortly afterwards, my two young cousins Varya and Lisa Tolstoy arrived back from abroad with their mother. 'Ah, now here are our real "Zephyrotes",' papa declared. It became a family joke, and that's what they were always called from then on.

When Christmas came round, the villagers and the servants all put on fancy dress and came up to the house, which was turned quite topsy-turvy for the occasion. Here is a description of these junketings from a letter mamma wrote to her sister in January 1865:

'In the morning we set to making masks and crowns and so on. Then we sent Arina Frolkovaya to tell the servants—you remember what a character she is—and in the evening we were inundated with a whole horde of people, all in fancy dress. Here is how we were all got up: Varya as a French Zouave, red jacket, red trousers, cap with bobbles on, also red. We spent the whole day cutting and sewing the costumes. Varya walked arm-in-arm with Seryozha (Sergei Arbuzov, who later became a manservant), who was dressed as a *vivandière*. Then came Lisa and Dushka (mamma's lady's maid), Lisa as a marquis with Dushka as his marquise, stockings and court shoes, hair in powdered roll curls, tricorn tucked under one arm, they looked ravishing. Then came Grisha (son of my uncle Sergei Nicolayevich) dressed as a clown with humps back and front, and Anna (wife of our cook, Nicolai Mikhailovich Rumyantsev), our little German, also as a clown. At the head of the procession a dwarf I'd taken on specially for the occasion, absolutely tiny, leading Mashka the cook's daughter. They were got up as savage chieftains, with gold and silver crowns, bangles round their wrists and ankles, barefoot and blackened all over with soot, carrying huge staffs and wearing red cloaks that were really shawls lent by Auntie and Mashenka [wife of Sergei Nicolayevich Tolstoy]. Auntie had delved into her most secret trunks and drawers to find things we needed for our costumes. And then all the servants and village girls were dressed up too, all in their own way.

'There was such merriment, such high jinks, I just can't tell you. Serezha [Sergei Nicolayevich Tolstoy, Tolstoy's older brother] arrived during the course of the evening, couldn't recognize a soul, and was helpless with laughter. The dwarf had us all splitting our sides. He used to be employed by Auntie's nephew once as his fool, and he really is the genuine article. We took round liqueurs, apples, gingerbread, and tea for the servants; everyone was very gay and delighted with everything. As for Grisha and the Zephyrotes, they were quite simply in their seventh heaven. Varya was so excited that when they began a round dance to "Malina Kalina" [the first words of a folk song] she just couldn't keep still and started jumping up and down. She was absolutely radiating delight, as though she had attained the very peak of human happiness.

'Later in the evening, when everyone had quietened down, Serezha suddenly announced that it had all been such a success we must do it again. And he was quite prepared for it to be the very next day. But I insisted on having time to get my breath back, so we decided to organize a magnificent masked ball for Twelfth Night, *le jour des Rois*, with a proper cake and fancy dress again. Serezha promised to appear with all his party in costume. What a pandemonium the house was in all that day, such a hustle and bustle everywhere. Lyova and I organized a throne for the king and queen. We put the two big armchairs with the golden eagles' heads up on the dining-room table; then everything, the walls, the tables, the benches, was draped with green cloth, and over the chairs we had a sort of palanquin fitted up. It was made out of a white bedspread with red flowers all over it, and on top there were crowns and decorations. On either side we had flowers arranged, plus bay trees and orange trees in pots, it was really quite superb. All this was set up in the drawing-room in front of the big glazed doors. The other furniture had been taken out to make room. Varya was dressed as a page, her hair all in curls, with a little black velvet cap stuck with a red feather and edged with gold braid, a white tailcoat, a raspberry-coloured waistcoat, white breeches, and boots with raspberry tops. She looked ravishing. Lisa was dressed in Algerian costume: it was so complicated and befurbeloved I really couldn't tell you exactly what it was any more. Lyova had dressed Dushka up as an old major, and she looked quite the thing. Seryozha was the wife. We also had a man dressed as an old nurse, and he'd been given Vaska-byelka (the cook's son) to carry, all swaddled up in a shawl. Then someone had the idea of two people being dressed up to make a horse, and Dushka clambered up on top. Everyone was ready, it was past six o'clock, and still no Serezha.

'We were just about to despair when we heard the bells on their sleighs, and Serezha burst into the house with all his band. We took them up into my room to put on their costumes. Lyova was dressing up his lot in the study, Mashenka hers in Auntie's room. Meanwhile I was seeing to the lights, the food, and above all the children. Then the musicians arrived, a fiddle, a trombone, and a huge round guitar thing that made a lovely big noise. Grisha was dressed as a harlequin, with cymbals and bells, there were two Pierrots—the little Brandts from Kaburino (5)—, the lady's maid and the coachman's wife were got up as a great lord and his lady, and a little boy had come as a shepherdess. The whole procession entered to a deafening noise of little bells, crackers, and cymbals; and bringing up the rear a giant, really very well done, almost reaching up to the ceiling. Inside the giant was Keller (6), who made him dance. The effect was extraordinary. A whole crowd of servants had come too, and Arina was dressed up as a German peasant. Then we had to pick our king. It was Brandt who got the bean, whereupon he chose Varya as queen and we installed them on their thrones. After that the racket we set up was indescribable. Songs, dances, games, bladder fights, firecrackers, ring-around-the-roses, refreshments, a collation, and to end up with, Bengal lights. After which we all had headaches and tummyaches the whole of that night and next day.

'Most of the time, of course, I was downstairs with the children . . .

'Next day, since everyone was still here, we took out two troikas and went for an outing, playing at racing one another and all getting very excited. That evening the children played various games, and the morning after that it was time to say goodbye . . . Lyova and I set out in the carriage to accompany our guests a little of the way, but as soon as we turned out on to the road the wind got up, so everyone turned around and came back to the house for lunch. Then Mashenka and the two girls set off back to Pirogovo [Sergei Tolstoy's estate], though Serezha didn't leave us until later that evening.'

We younger children took no part in those particular fancy dress parties, and I myself have no recollection of them. Most of what I have recounted so far has been culled from the personal reminiscences or letters of my parents and relations.

5

I can remember myself when I was still very little. But what comes back to me of my very early childhood is often confused in my mind with what I have been told about it, and with the memories of others.

My father, in his *First Recollections,* tells how he remembers the time when he was still in swaddling-clothes, struggling to free himself from his wrappings and suffering acute distress at his own impotence.

Whenever I read that passage I always feel that I can recall that state too; I see myself again tightly wrapped in swaddling bands, a stiff doll that people pick up with its head cradled in the crook of one arm—since the only place it can bend at all is at the neck—and then lay down again on something hard.

Yet it is possible that this memory doesn't really apply to me, that it has remained so vivid simply because I spent so much time looking after my many brothers and sisters, because it was so often I who swaddled them and nursed them in my arms.

The first memory that is beyond doubt really personal to me is one of my nurse, Marya Afanassyevna Arbuzova. I remember her kindly face, all round and wrinkled, the black silk cap on her beautifully smooth hair, the white kerchief around her neck, and her forefinger—so horrible to look at because it had a segment missing.

It is in the evening, just before bedtime. We are sitting at a square table made of pale birchwood in one corner of the nursery. I am sitting on her lap while she spoon-feeds me buckwheat and milk, and I am enjoying the taste and smell very much.

The buckwheat and milk of those days seemed so much nicer than what we get today, as though it was some completely different kind of buckwheat, another kind of milk altogether. When my nurse couldn't find any buckwheat meal in the kitchen she would crumble rye bread into the milk and feed us that simple fare. And it was just as good as the buckwheat and milk, if not better. Probably my two brothers were eating with me, because we were brought up together, but I don't remember them on that particular occasion.

With a child's intuition I was aware that nurse was feeding me without my parents' knowledge. That was an idea she'd got firmly into her head: that we didn't get enough to eat.

My second memory is that of the journey we all made to Moscow to see our grandfather Behrs when he was dying (7). That was the first time I left Yasnaya Polyana.

As far as Serpukhov we travelled in a sleigh, since in those days the railway from Moscow only reached that far. It was about a hundred versts [just over sixty miles] from Yasnaya Polyana to Serpukhov, and for that part of the journey we had to use horses.

I am with my nurse in a closed sleigh, and it is stifling. My mother and father are behind in an open sleigh.

Seryozha, who is about three and a half (8), is with me and fretting about his friend Nikolka, a little boy from the village he often plays with. Seryozha wanted Kopka, as he called him, to come with us. To keep him quiet he is told that Kopka is behind, in the other sleigh. Seryozha is reassured, but every now and then, as though to convince himself it's true, he smiles and says:

'Kopka's behind . . . Kopka's behind . . .'

I vaguely remember stopping at an inn in Serpukhov. Delighted at being set free again after so long sitting still, I am running along a corridor with such impetuosity that no one can catch me. Later we are put to sleep on the floor, and that seems to me a great game.

In Moscow I remember my grandfather Andrei Yevstafyevich Behrs, paralyzed. I can see myself, frightened and overawed, being led into his study in the Kremlin. My grandfather is in a bed at the end of a long narrow room. He is an old gentleman with a white beard and pale blue eyes. He tries to show me that he can no longer move his left arm, and lifts it up with his right hand. The arm is lifeless, with no strength in it. I am intrigued, and very impressed too.

Grandmother is also there, she is tall and beautiful. All her gestures are calm and full of nobility. She is my godmother and I love her extra-specially.

6

Neither our stay in Moscow nor the journey home has remained in my memory. My memories begin again back at Yasnaya Polyana.

It is no longer Marya Afanassyevna who is bringing us up but an English girl, Hannah Tracey (9). My father had written asking her to come over from England to take care of his three children. He felt that English literature was the finest of all, especially the books for children, and he wanted us to learn English so that we could read these books in the original.

Hannah was brought to Yasnaya by her sister Jenny, who was already governess to the Lvov princes, whom we knew. The two sisters arrived while papa was away in Moscow, and mamma, who knew almost no English, was extremely put about by this unexpected arrival.

'Just imagine,' she wrote to my father on November 12th 1866, 'just before lunch today the tall English girl from the Lvovs appeared with her sister, our English governess. It put me in such a state my head is still spinning, and the upset has left me with a headache. How shall I describe her? Well, she is just what I expected. Very young, on the whole charming, a pleasant face, in fact very sweet. But our reciprocal ignorance of each other's tongue is frightful. Her sister is spending the night with us. For now she's acting as interpreter, but what will happen after that, heaven alone knows. I am totally at sea, especially without you, my friend . . .'

For a while we children still remained in the nursery with our old nurse. Hannah slept alone and only looked after us during the day.

I know from what my mother told me later that it took me some time to take to Hannah. I didn't want to be parted from Marya Afanassyevna, even though I did make efforts to please my new governess.

Mamma wrote to my father: 'The children are growing used to the idea: Tanya is on her (Hannah's) lap looking at pictures and explaining them to her . . .' But in the evening I went back to the nursery and behaved in a silly way, making fun of Hannah and mimicking the way the 'gooverniss' talked. Marya Afanassyevna laughed, and I could tell my silliness pleased her.

'Tanyusha isn't letting herself be passed on to someone new all that quickly and easily,' my mother wrote to my father two days after Hannah's arrival. 'She starts arguing with her as soon as I leave them together. I hear Tanya weeping, and then she comes to me and complains that "the 'gooverniss' is being nasty to me" . . .'

In fact, our sweet Hannah was quite incapable of being nasty to anyone. But the effort required to understand her was very tiring for me, so that after a while I became depressed and listless. I felt she was responsible for my tiredness so I complained about her to my mother. And our old nurse was missing us a lot too.

'If you only knew,' my mother wrote in the same letter, 'what a sadness it is for nursey having the children taken away from her . . . She told me: "It's just as though I've lost something all the time. I just don't know what to do with myself".'

Little by little, however, we grew accustomed to Hannah, and with my customary desire to please everyone I did try my best to satisfy the gooverniss. Eventually I came to love her with all my heart.

In another letter to my father, mamma recounts how I spent a whole day conscientiously repeating all the English words Hannah spoke to me, and how pleased Hannah was with my progress. I became so carried away by my own enthusiasm that I even began repeating what my mother said in Russian. But by the end of the day I got tired of the game and wanted no more of the gooverniss.

My mother did all she could to amuse Hannah and make life pleasant for her. She succeeded totally.

Several days after the young English girl's arrival mamma took us all out for a sleigh ride, which she described to my father. 'It was a lovely day . . . Hannah was so delighted that she bounced up and down in the sleigh the whole time, saying "so nice", which I presume means she was enjoying it. And there in the sleigh she explained to me that she liked me so much and that she liked being in "the country", and was "very happy" . . .'

7

Hannah and her sister Jenny, who had travelled with her to Yasnaya Polyana, were the daughters of one of the gardeners at Windsor Castle, near London. They were respectable and excellent creatures, both of whom spoke and wrote their own language extremely well. They were never downhearted when it came to work, and there was no task that daunted or repelled them. On the contrary, they considered hard work to be a necessary precondition of happiness . . .

At the time Hannah left her own country for strange and far-off Russia she was nineteen. She didn't speak a word of Russian. We couldn't speak a word of English. As for me, I could scarcely talk properly in my own tongue at that time. So we had to communicate in other ways. Smiles, caresses, kisses, gestures, tears, they none of them require knowledge of any tongue, and signify the same things among all peoples. So in the early days such wordless means of communication were what we had perforce to use. The love that grew in my heart for her, and has always remained there, was neither English nor Russian but universal, and it bound me to her for the rest of my life.

Once she had settled in, Hannah took to life at Yasnaya Polyana as though she had said goodbye to her past for ever, as though her entire interest was now directed exclusively to our family.

I remember her as always gay and alert, her hands never without some piece of work, dressed invariably, winter and summer alike, in a pale frock protected by a perpetually spotless apron.

It never entered my head that this young and pretty girl might sometimes feel a desire for diversion in the company of young people of her own age and nationality, that it might be dispiriting for her having to live year in year out in a Russian village. I was too small to understand such things, and if she did think such thoughts she was too proud ever to let it show.

We never saw her a prey to boredom, never heard her complain of a way of life so very foreign to her. On the contrary, she always tried to extract as much profit and pleasure from it as she could.

The first innovation she introduced at Yasnaya Polyana was daily baths for the children. She had a bathtub specially sent over from England, and you can still see it at Yasnaya Polyana to this day. Then she turned her attention to the floors, which she had decided no one in our house knew how to keep properly clean. She ordered—again from England—a special set of brushes, with which she personally got down and scrubbed the nursery floor.

Again from England, she had iceskates sent over for us to learn to skate on. In those days skates were made of wood, the only steel parts being the actual blade and the screw that fixed them into the heel of your boot. Then there were two sets of straps that held the wooden sole firm against the sole of the boot.

Before long we children had succumbed to her influence totally. We acquired an unquestioning belief that whatever she told us to do was for our own good and happiness.

And it was.

I don't recall any naughtiness, any sullenness, any tantrums with Hannah. We did kick over the traces occasionally, I admit, simply because Ilya and I sometimes got so excited that it was difficult to control us.

And I did, every now and then, twist the truth just a little, which was something that grieved Hannah terribly. She herself was an exceptionally veracious person, and Seryozha, my eldest brother, was likewise a remarkably frank and open child. But to my great shame I cannot say the same for myself. However hard I tried never to tell lies I was such a fidget, so mischievous and feather-brained, that sometimes, despite myself, caught up in my own excitement, I said things I would have known I shouldn't if only I'd stopped to think a moment,

In addition, my lively imagination often carried me away into the realm of fiction, and I would tell made-up stories as though they were real ones.

I remember Hannah once beginning to cry when she realized I'd lied to her. Those tears made a far deeper impression on me than any punishment could have done. I am over sixty now, and I still haven't forgotten them . . .

Because I had such trust in Hannah, and because it made me happy too when I succeeded in my efforts to be honest, I gradually cured myself of that bad habit.

I did try to tell the truth, even though I was not always believed. That vexed me and hurt me.

One day when we were doing lessons with mamma she sent me up to her room for some medicine she was supposed to take at a certain time.

'Tanya, run and bring me the dark drops in the little bottle on my dressing-table.'

I ran up to her room, but I couldn't see any little bottle, either on the dressing-table or the bedside table. I came back down and told her I couldn't see the medicine.

'You can never find anything,' mamma said as she got up to look for it herself.

That hurt me, so I waited with my heart full and my eyes brimming with tears. Mamma came back with the drops, which she had found in her chest of drawers.

'Was it you who nibbled that fig and left it on the dressing-table?'

'No, I didn't even see any figs on the table.'

'Then how is it there's a piece of fig with teeth marks in it just beside the fig bag?'

I didn't answer.

'Come over here. Open your mouth. If you have been chewing a fig there are bound to be pips in your mouth still.'

Burning with shame, bitterly resenting the wrong being done me, I went over to her, forcing back indignant tears, and opened my mouth.

Naturally there wasn't a single pip to be seen, since I hadn't touched the figs.

I crowed with malicious triumph.

Is it really worth while telling the truth, I asked myself, when no one believes me anyway?

But another, inner voice told me that if I told the truth it was not really for mamma's or Hannah's sake, or even in order to be believed; it was because once one has come to love the truth any betrayal of it becomes repugnant to oneself.

8

It may seem strange that in evoking my childhood I have begun by talking about the people who looked after me and said very little about my relations with my parents. The reason is that my father and mother, as they exist in my very early memories, are almost indistinguishable from the texture of life itself, so that I was in a sense almost unaware of them. We do not really notice the air we breathe, even though it is so indispensable to our existence. And I did not really notice my parents in much the same way.

It is mamma, even more than papa, who was indistinguishable from existence itself in those days. She rarely appears in particular, remembered scenes. She was perpetually busy at some household task, tending a baby, supervising our schoolwork, organizing the cleaning, whirring away at breakneck speed on her sewing-machine, or mixing medicine for some peasant woman who was ill.

Sometimes, in the evenings, papa and mamma used to play duets together on the piano. But most of the time my picture is of mamma over in a corner of the drawing-room busy at her little work-table.

In the mornings, Marya Afanassyevna would come in, hands clasped over her belly, head cocked a little to one side, to receive mamma's instructions for next day's menus. (Since Hannah's arrival our old nurse had been fulfilling the functions of housekeeper.) Then they would settle down to discussing how many eggs, or chickens, or boiling fowl needed to be bought down in the village. Sometimes they decided that a shopping expedition to Tula would have to be made, and nurse would go and bring in the order books. Then mamma would write out all the items and quantities needed, some in the grocer's book, some in the butcher's.

'Sofia (10) Andreyevna, we shall have to have five pounds of those Kaletovs,' nurse would say.

It was only much later that I eventually found out what these mysterious Kaletovs were. There was a factory at a place called

Kaletov that manufactured stearin candles, and nurse always called them by the name of the town on the packet to distinguish them from ordinary tallow candles.

'And we shall have to have some candles too,' Marya Afanassyevna went on after a pause. 'There's not a taper left to light the maids' rooms, and if one of the children goes getting a sore throat . . . Well, I handed out the last candle end only yesterday.'

I listened to those last words with horror, nausea rising at the very thought of the remedy that was regularly applied when one of us had a sore throat or cough. Nurse would melt a tallow candle in a silver spoon, remove the wick, then make us drink the liquid fat. A second spoonful was then used to rub one's chest, throat, and the soles of one's feet. After that the poorly throat was swaddled in a woollen stocking—but you had to make quite sure it was a left one!

Once nurse had departed with her order books, mamma settled down to her daily grind as father's copyist. Did it go on for a long while? I have no idea, since as soon as I had wished my parents goodnight I had to go off to bed. But as my mother hunched over the sheets of paper covered in papa's big handwriting it was plain, just from the expression of concentration on her face, that for her the most important time of her already well filled day was just beginning. We had scarcely finished wishing her goodnight before that pretty head, its hair so black and smooth, was already bent over the table again, her short-sighted eyes peering to decipher my father's manuscript, those pages crammed with writing, scrawled with erasures, the lines of script sometimes criss-crossing in every direction.

In the morning, my father would find the sheets back on his desk, plus a neat and legible fair copy, which he then proceeded to work over again, adding whole new pages black with his vast, illegible scrawl, sometimes deleting other pages completely with a single stroke of the pen.

In the evening, mamma copied everything out once more in her neat hand, next morning papa rewrote and pruned. And added further sheets . . .

He spent days, months, sometimes years on a book, never sparing even the minutest effort to make sure he had expressed his conceptions as exactly as possible. Until I grew up and took over, it was my mother —except for very rare interruptions—who copied out all my father's manuscripts. Later, as I say, I took over the task, and after me it was

B

my sister Masha's (11) turn, then finally, until my father's death, that of my youngest sister Sasha (12).

Sometimes I saw papa go over to mamma and look over her shoulder. Then my mother would take his big hand and kiss it with love and veneration, while he tenderly stroked her dark, shining hair, then bent to kiss the top of her head.

My child's heart brimmed over at those moments with such love for them that I wanted to weep and thank them for loving one another, for loving us, and for impregnating our whole life with love.

My brother Ilya (13) has described his feelings toward our mother in his *Reminiscences* as follows:

'Mamma was the most important person in the house. She had to decide everything. It was she who told Nicolai the cook what the meals were to be, she who gave one permission to go out, she who mended our shirts. She was always feeding a baby, she spent all day running upstairs and downstairs all over the house. You could be a little naughty with her sometimes, but every now and then she got cross and punished us.

'She knew about everything better than anyone else.

'She knew that you must wash every day, that you must eat your soup at dinner, speak French, work hard, not crawl about on the floor, not put your elbows on the table. If she said you mustn't go outside to play because it was going to rain, then you could be sure that was exactly what was going to happen, and you had to obey. When I had a cough she gave me licorice pastilles to suck, or a dose of "the King of Denmark's drops", so I was always very glad when I coughed. When mamma had put me to bed and gone away to play the piano with papa I couldn't get to sleep. I was unhappy because I'd been left on my own, so I began coughing, and I went on coughing till nurse went to fetch mamma. I would get furious because she took such a long time coming. Until she'd appeared again, until she'd poured out my ten drops into a little glass and held it for me while I drank, nothing on earth would have got me to go to sleep.'

9

Our father was really the controlling influence in our home. We were all aware of that.

We saw our father less often than our mother, and his appearance in the nursery was always an event.

I remember him when he was still young. His beard was auburn, almost red; he had black, slightly wavy hair and pale blue eyes. Those eyes were sometimes gentle and caressing, sometimes merry, sometimes severe and inquisitorial. He was tall, broad-shouldered, well-muscled, yet very quick and dexterous in all his movements.

At that time his hair had not yet turned white and his face was still unmarked by the suffering and the scalding tears that furrowed his features later on, during that period when he was searching so fervently and in such loneliness for the meaning of life.

As he grew older so he went white, began to stoop, and shrank in size, while his pale eyes became gentler, and sometimes sad.

We rarely heard reproaches from his lips, either as children or when we grew up, but when papa said something you didn't forget it, and you did as he said without fail.

In his leisure moments he was the merriest man I have ever known. Life was always entertaining when he was with you. He only had to appear for something interesting to happen at once. You felt a life force radiating from him.

He used to call me 'Choorka' [a small piece of wood], and I loved that nickname because he always used it when he was in a good mood and wanted to tease me or be nice to me.

The extraordinarily strong feeling of love and veneration I felt for my father never faded. From what I remember, and also what I have been told, he too always felt a particular affection for me.

I also remember climbing up on to his lap and tickling him under the arms and chin. Since he was very ticklish he always started laughing, making funny noises, and wriggling about. I thought it very funny that a man as strong as he was, so important and indeed omnipotent in my eyes, could be so much in my power.

When I was only two he went away to Moscow and stayed there for some while. I fretted at his absence, and mamma wrote to him:

'Tanya's just come in and said to me: "Take papa down off the wall, I want to look at him . . .'."

And again, two days later:

'They (the children) talk about you often; Tanya, suddenly acting about, started looking under the bench and calling "Papa! Papa!"'

In 1869, when I was four, papa went to Penza to look over a property he was thinking of buying. I missed him badly.

'You'd be delighted to hear the way Tanya keeps asking about you at the slightest opportunity,' mamma wrote to him. 'She talks about you non-stop. "What can papa be doing there in Penza?" or "I think papa must be in that train"—the passing trains were visible from the windows of the house—"Perhaps he's already got to Tula now." Yesterday, when they were all playing, she pulled the horse in front of an armchair and said: "Now I'm going to fetch papa back from Penza, because he's much too long coming home." Even when her brothers had stopped playing she still didn't budge, sitting up there very solemnly, slapping her horse with the reins and telling us: "It's still a long way to Penza, and I have to bring papa home . . ." '

At last papa did come home, and we were happy again.

There was one game he played with us that we loved extra-specially. He'd invented it himself.

This is how it went: without any warning papa suddenly looked terribly frightened, began shooting glances all around him, grabbed two of us by the hand, and then, walking on tiptoe, lifting his knees up ever so high, trying not to make a sound, he went and hid in a corner.

'There it is . . . There it is . . .' he whispered in a frightened voice.

The one of us he hadn't pulled with him would hurl him or herself into the corner too and clutch his smock. Huddled there, hearts thumping, we waited for 'it' to go by, while papa pretended to be watching some imaginary being with the most tremendous intensity. He followed it with his eyes, while we clung together and kept as quiet as mice for fear that 'it' would notice us.

My heart used to beat so hard that I was sure 'it' was going to hear and be attracted by the noise.

At last, after some minutes of tense silence, papa would suddenly adopt a jaunty, carefree air and announce:

'It's gone!'

Delighted at this news, we all leapt up from our corner and followed papa as he wandered off through the house. Then suddenly his eyebrows would shoot up, his eyes would open terribly wide in a most scary expression, and he would freeze where he stood: 'it' had come back.

'It's coming! It's coming!' we all whispered as we scattered looking for somewhere to hide. Once again we took refuge in some corner and waited with dread while papa followed 'it' with his eyes. Eventually 'it' went away without discovering us, we got up again, and so it would go on until papa had had enough and sent us off back to Hannah.

It was a game we all felt it was impossible ever to get tired of.

We also loved a certain story papa used to tell us. It was called 'the Seven Cucumbers', and its fascination lay in the extraordinary variations of pitch and volume papa worked into his telling of it.

He told it so often, to me and to other children, that I know it by heart. It went like this:

'A little boy went into a garden. He saw a cucumber. A cucumber as big as this (holding up his two forefingers to demonstrate the length). He picked it, hup!, and ate it. (The voice quite matter of fact so far, and pitched fairly high.) The little boy continued on his way and saw a second cucumber, a cucumber as big as this. Hup! He ate it. (The voice now slightly louder and deeper.) He went on, he saw a third cucumber, a cucumber as big as this (the forefingers indicating a length of about eighteen inches), and hup! He ate it. Then he saw a fourth cucumber, a cucumber as bi-i-i-g as this. Hup! He ate it.'

And so it went on until the seventh cucumber, with papa's voice getting louder and louder, deeper and deeper.

'The little boy went on and saw a seventh cucumber. A cucumber as bi-i-i-i-g as this (papa's arms were stretched as wide as they would go). The little boy picked it, hup! And ate it!'

When papa showed how the little boy ate the seventh cucumber his mouth with its missing teeth opened so wide it was frightening to see. And he seemed to be having the most awful difficulty pushing that seventh cucumber inside . . .

As we watched, so all three of us involuntarily opened our own mouths as wide as they would go, just like him, and we stayed like that, mouths gaping and eyes riveted on his fearful struggle.

Another amusing thing, in the morning, when he was getting dressed, was going into his study to do gymnastics with him. There was a room there then, which doesn't exist any more, where he'd had a special bar fixed up between two pillars. Every morning we did exercises on it with him.

He also made us do Swedish drill.

One, two, three, four, five. Stretching our muscles as far as they would go we did all the movements in time with him: arms out, to the sides, up, down, back.

Papa was remarkably strong and nimble, and all his children inherited his exceptional physical strength (14).

After our gymnastics papa would go and work, and during that time no one was allowed to disturb him. Or rather, as I was told later, no one but myself, since I was the only one papa ever allowed to come in and watch him while he wrote. I don't remember that, but I know that to the end of his days I was always fearful of disturbing his thoughts while he was at his work, which I always respected, and thought necessary and important.

As a child, I understood instinctively that a man like my father could not possibly be indulging in any futile occupation. As an adult, helping him with his work, I understood and recognized all its significance.

'Papa was the most intelligent man in the world, he knew everything but with him one could never be naughty,' my brother Ilya wrote in his *Reminiscences*. 'When he was doing "work" in his study you hadn't to make a noise, and it was forbidden to go in and see him. What he actually did when he was "working" we had no idea. Later on I discovered that papa was a "writer".

'This was how. I had read some poetry I'd liked, so I went and asked mamma who'd written it. She told me that it was by Pushkin, and that Pushkin was a great writer. I was put out because papa wasn't someone like that too. So then mamma told me that my father actually was a famous writer, and I was delighted.

'At the dinner table papa sat facing mamma, and he had his own special round spoon made of silver. When Natalya Petrovna, the old lady who lived downstairs with Auntie, poured herself a glass of kvas, he picked it up and drank it all down in one go, then said: "Oh dear, I'm so sorry, Natalya Petrovna, I just wasn't thinking." We all thought it terribly funny and laughed, but it did seem very odd to us that papa wasn't the least bit afraid of her. When we had kissel [fruit jelly thickened with potato flour] for pudding, papa said that it was terribly good for glueing things, so we went and fetched some paper and he made boxes for us. Mamma wasn't at all pleased, but he wasn't afraid of her either.

'Sometimes we had great fun with him.

'He could ride better than anyone, run quicker than anyone, and there was no one in the world stronger than he was.

'He almost never punished us, but if he looked me in the eyes he knew everything I was thinking, and that made me afraid.

'I could tell fibs to mamma, but not to him, because he knew straight away. And none of us ever told him stories.'

Like Ilya, I too was convinced that papa was the most intelligent, the most just, the best person in the world, and that he could never ever be in the wrong.

Only once, just for a moment, did I doubt his infallibility. But even then I immediately backtracked, telling myself that there must be reasons for his acting as he did that I just didn't know about. Here is the story:

One day I saw him coming back from Chepizh, an old oak wood near the house. He had his shotgun over one shoulder, his game-bag over the other, and was wearing topboots.

I ran to meet him, caught hold of one of his fingers and skipped along beside him. But he seemed preoccupied and tried to pull his finger away.

'Wait, Choorka, just wait a moment,' he said, and stopped.

I watched as he put his hand inside the game-bag and pulled out a woodcock that was still not quite dead . . . The bird fluttered in his hand . . . Papa pulled out one of its feathers and drove the point of it into the bird's neck just behind its head. The woodcock became quite still, and then papa put it back in the bag.

I thought what he had done was horrible and disgusting. I gazed at my father in shock . . . How could he have done such a thing?

Papa didn't even notice the look I was giving him and began chatting away just as though nothing had happened. My doubts lingered.

But if it was papa who did it, I told myself, then it can't have been very bad . . .

(Later on my father gave up hunting of any kind. He even came to wonder how he could ever conceivably have killed mammals and birds like that without being aware of the cruelty in his pastime.)

10

Sometimes my father had visitors. Most of them were very educated people with whom papa would converse about matters that were way over our heads.

For instance there were P. F. Samarin, A. A. Fet-Shenshin, Prince B. S. Urussov, Count A. P. Bobrinski, and I can't think how many more. They scarcely ever paid any attention to us children; but we enjoyed watching them and sizing them up.

Where Samarin (15) was concerned we were on the whole indifferent.

Papa always talked about very serious things indeed with him, and they got into arguments we found totally incomprehensible. We referred to these conversations as 'talk on the higher plane', and we knew it was no good our even trying to follow them.

There was only one occasion when we took a very active part in an argument between papa and Samarin. It was over racehorses. Papa had insisted that his horses from the steppes were just as fast as English horses. Samarin, however, contemptuously denied this claim. So papa challenged Samarin to a wager: they would race his Russian horse against Samarin's English horse and see who won.

Naturally we were all absolutely on papa's side, but to our great chagrin Samarin's horse outstripped ours easily.

Fet we didn't care for much (16). For one thing we didn't think he looked very nice. He had little black eyes like nailholes, with red rims and no lashes, a big, rather purple, hooked nose, white and very carefully kept hands with long nails, like a doll's hands, very tiny, and also equally tiny feet, encased in little boots that would have fitted a woman. Plus a great paunch and a bald head. In short, a by no means attractive figure.

In addition, when talking Fet was given to dragging out his words and interspersing them with strange grunts. When he was telling some supposedly amusing anecdote he would take so long over it, and interrupt the words so often with his inarticulate noises, you just hadn't the patience to keep listening, so that in the end his story never managed to be funny in the slightest.

My parents were very fond of him. There was a time when papa held him to be the most intellgent of all his friends and said that Fet was the only person capable of understnding him and pointing out the defects in his work.

'If we love one another,' my father wrote to Fet on June 27th 1867, 'it is because we think alike, with the intelligence of the heart, as you put it.'

'Sometimes I am almost choked by the unsatisfied yearning I feel for a fellow soul like yours,' he wrote in another letter on August 30th 1869, 'so that I can speak all that is here inside me.'

In a letter written on April 29th 1878, my father told Fet that when the time came for him to leave for 'the beyond', in other words to die, he would send for him, Fet. 'No one could be more necessary to me in that moment than you and my brother. Before dying, one values, one rejoices in the conversation of beings who keep their eyes fixed in this life beyond its frontiers . . . Suddenly, hitherto unperceived details of your nature, so profoundly akin to my own (particularly where death is concerned) have come before me so vividly that I find myself abruptly attaching much more value than hitherto to our relationship.'

Ilya and I remained puzzled by our father's opinion of his friend. And on one occasion we even conspired together to poke fun at the respectable Afanassi Afanassyevich Fet.

One evening we were both in the drawing-room, playing at glueing something or other, seated at a table on our own while the grown-ups drank tea and talked.

We could hear Fet telling everyone in his drawling voice how modest his tastes were, and how little he needed to satisfy him in life.

'Give me a good bowl of soup and some buckwheat kasha . . . hm-mmmmmm, that's all I need . . . Give me a nice piece of meat . . . Hmmmmm . . . and that's quite enough. Give me . . . mmmmmm . . . a good bed to lie on, that's all I ask . . .'

And so it went on, with Fet enumerating at great length, interrupting himself with interminable grunts and groans, all the various items indispensable to his well-being, while Ilya and I at our table were nudging one another, doing our very best to stifle our giggles, and making whispered additions to his list of demands.

'Just give me a big box of chocolates every day, and that's all I ask,' Ilya said, choking with laughter.

'Just give me some good caviare and a bottle of champagne,' I chimed in, 'that's all I really need.'

Fet used to come over and visit us with his wife, the goodhearted and charming Maria Petrovna. We liked her a great deal more than we did her famous husband. Friendly to everyone she met, she was all modesty, kindness, and goodness.

We remained on friendly terms with Fet and his wife until the end of their lives. Speaking for myself, when I grew up I learned to love Afanassi Afanassyevich's true poetic gift, and to appreciate his vast intelligence.

Whenever Count A. P. Bobrinski (17) came papa always got into heated arguments with him on religious questions.

I remember one occasion when papa became so passionate, as the two of them sat on a bench outside the house arguing religion, that it really got me very worried. Naturally I was on papa's side, not because I understood or consciously approved of what he was saying but simply because I assumed that he was incapable of being in the wrong; but I was nevertheless very distressed to hear him laying into Bobrinski with quite such gusto. The fact was that Bobrinski had told me, only a short while beforehand, that he had a daughter named Missi, more or less my age, and that he wanted me to meet her. I was very excited by this prospect, and I was terrified that after this awful set-to with papa Bobrinski might change his mind.

Papa's guests were not all great intellects and did not always sit discussing incomprehensible subjects. We also had visits from our neighbour N. V. Arsenyev (18), whose conversation was simpler and more approachable. For that reason, or perhaps because Nikolenka Arsenyev took notice of me, I was very fond of him. He was young, good looking, and gay. When he came over from Sudakov, his estate, I always tried to stay on in the drawing-room with the grown-ups so that I could listen to him and watch him.

One day he arrived just as papa was about to go out planting birches. He suggested that Nikolenka go with him. And to my great joy the visitor asked permission for us children to go as well, so we all set off to plant birches together.

Those birches are old now. The plantation is called Abramov's wood. Whenever I happen to pass it or walk through it now I still see myself that day, diligently following papa's and Nikolenka's exact instructions as I held saplings in place with their shiny, sticky leaves that smelled so fresh and nice.

'When you're grown up you'll come gathering mushrooms here,' papa told me.

I remember one day when Nikolenka had come over and we were all in the drawing-room. It was evening, and at our usual bedtime Hannah came in to fetch us. I was most put out at having to leave Nikolenka, but there was nothing to be done about it, one never disobeyed Hannah.

Bathing went by order of seniority, so I was second, after Seryozha. Having soaped my head, Hannah left me for a moment to fetch a jug of clean rinsing water. A bold plan flashed into my mind. I took advantage of Hannah's back being turned to flee from the nursery as fast as my legs would carry me. Unadorned as God made me I hurtled back to the drawing-room, leaving a trail of wet footprints as I went.

I burst into the room and came to a halt in front of Nikolenka. Then raising my arms in triumph I cried:

'Here's Tanya!'

I've no idea what he thought when he saw that little naked body streaming with water, its soapy head covered with what must have looked like whipped cream, but I do remember that mamma, appalled and very distressed, seized me round the middle and hurried outside to hand me over to Hannah, who by that time had become aware of my flight and followed my tracks.

II

As young children we lived with Hannah in a room on the ground floor. When my father was a child the house we lived in had been one of two smaller pavilion blocks flanking the big house where he was born. In those days our ground-floor room wasn't used for living in. It had been a store-room where all sorts of provisions were kept.

There were big iron rings, which are still there to this day, fixed to the vaulted ceiling. And in the old days they had been used for hanging up hams, dried herbs, mushrooms, fruit, and so on.

The big house itself, where my grandmother was born and where my father spent his childhood, had been sold long before his marriage. It was dismantled, carted away to an estate twenty-five miles from Yasnaya Polyana, and rebuilt there exactly as it had been before. In 1913 the estate on which it stood was sold off to the peasants, who demolished the house and shared out the materials to build themselves isbas.

After my father had sold the house, he, Auntie Tatyana Alexandrovna, and all the other occupants, moved into one of the flanking pavilions.

It was in this same pavilion that my father took up residence with his young wife after their marriage. And it was there that my brothers, my sisters, and I were all born and spent most of our childhood.

Papa enlarged the building by adding a hall, a study, and the big drawing-room upstairs.

Years later, mamma had the little wooden annexe at the other end of the house demolished and replaced it with a big room of the same dimensions as the one my father had built.

We three eldest children spent our entire childhood in the vaulted downstairs room, which was divided in two by twin stone arches. Hannah had the smaller section, Seryozha, Ilya and myself the larger.

Seryozha was the eldest. He was a serious, quiet little boy, trusting and very honest, goodhearted and sensitive. For some reason I have never fathomed he found all demonstrations of affection repugnant, as if such things were criminal, and always did his best to conceal his feelings.

He wasn't as much fun to play with as Ilya. He had less imagination and could never catch the spirit of a game with the same lightning alacrity as Ilya and myself. As soon as I had an idea, Ilya would not just understand it but immediately improve on it. And it was the same the other way round: he had only to throw some new notion in my direction for me to catch it in mid-flight and toss it back to him.

Seryozha played on his own most of the time. He had a doll, with shiny black porcelain hair and painted blue eyes, that he called Génia, in honour of Hannah's sister Jenny, whom he loved very much. Seryozha always played alone with this doll, and sometimes Ilya and I caught him talking to it in a very quiet little voice.

'Ilya, go and listen to what he's saying.'

'He'd only notice,' Ilya answered. And it was true: as soon as Seryozha became aware that we were watching him he stopped talking, looked embarrassed, and put the doll down as though it were of not the slightest interest to him.

I was the next oldest after Seryozha. It's difficult to describe what I was like. According to what I've heard from people who knew me as a child, I was very lively, bright and gay, very full of fun, sometimes rather a show-off.

When I was still a baby my cousins used to amuse themselves by banging my head very gently against the wall, because I used to put my hand over my eyes and pretend to be hurt and cry.

'Oh, oh, oh!' I would mew, very piteously.

My cousins thought it was very funny, and went on playing the game until one day one of them banged my head too hard and I really howled.

I have also been told that on one occasion, when I was playing hide-and-seek with Seryozha, I pretended I couldn't find him when in fact he was completely visible. He crouched under the piano, gazing out at me with wide eyes, while I walked around the room, hands behind my back, giving him sly glances out of the corner of my eyes, and saying:

'He isn't here! He isn't here!'

Ilya, the third oldest, eighteen months younger than me, was a veritable force of nature, bursting with health, merry, playful, and impulsive. But laziness, and a certain weakness of character, made it impossible for him to make himself always do what he ought to, or refrain from doing things he knew he shouldn't.

When we were out for walks he always lagged behind, and quite often Seryozha and I, immersed in our own games, forgot about fat Ilya bringing up the rear. Suddenly we would hear terrible howls. It was Ilya.

'I'm left behi-i-i-nd! I'm left behi-i-i-nd!' he wailed.

We would turn and run back, looking for him, then hold his hand for a while. But before long we were always off again, looking for berries or mushrooms, and the same thing would happen again.

'I'm left behi-i-i-nd! I'm left behi-i-i-nd!' the despairing wail would come.

Three years after Ilya came Lyova (19), then Masha. They lived upstairs with their nurse and were always referred to, in English, as 'the little ones'. They played almost no part in the life of us three older ones (20).

12

While we were living downstairs in the big vaulted room with Hannah, a very strange incident occurred. It impressed itself so deeply on my memory that I can still recall all the details even now.

One night, when we were all in bed and everyone had gone off to sleep except me, I saw the door at the far end of the room swing open and a wolf came in. It was on its hind legs, half walking and half slithering in a sort of squatting position. I remember it was wearing trousers, and perhaps a jacket too, though it must have been open because I could see its furry chest. My eyes were wide with terror, but I didn't dare call out in case I attracted the wolf's attention. Inside I was wishing as hard as I could for someone to wake up . . . But they all kept on sleeping, I could hear their quiet, regular breathing.

The long, dark room, the stone vaulting with its heavy iron rings, the shadows, the sleepers' breathing, the wolf's silent approach, everything filled my soul with terror.

'Perhaps it isn't me he's come for,' I said to myself. But something told me it wasn't true. I knew it was me and me alone he'd come to find.

Slithering noiselessly over the floor, the wolf got nearer and nearer. Icy, paralyzed with terror, I closed my eyes. Then suddenly—oh, the horror of it—I felt him picking me up out of my bed and carrying me off in his arms.

As silently as he had come, he made his way back toward the door, past the sleeping figures of Hannah, Ilya, and Seryozha. I wanted to cry out, but I couldn't make even the tiniest sound.

In my mind, however, I kept begging him to leave me alone and take me back to my bed.

'Be a nice wolf, please be nice,' I said. 'Do please take me back and go away . . .'

We slithered on, nearer and nearer to the door, and then suddenly, oh the relief, the wolf did turn back. He carried me back past the sleepers, reached my bed, and laid me down again.

What happened then, how he left, how I went to sleep again, I have no recollection . . .

Of course there was never any wolf. I had dreamed it or imagined it. But the vision was so clear that I can still see all the details of the scene even now, just as though it did really happen to me.

My wolf looked very like Goethe's *Reinecke Fuchs* as illustrated by Kaulbach. There was a most beautiful edition of it in papa's library, and I was very fond of looking at the pictures in it. Probably that is why the vision is so clearly engraved in my memory.

13

It was while we were living down in the vaulted room that we all three had scarlet fever.

The fear of infection that nowadays leads people to commit foolish and sometimes cruel acts scarcely existed at that time.

In our case the infection was brought into the house by some peasant children who had been invited up to the house to share our Christmas tree. There was a big epidemic in the village that winter, and many of the children came to the party while they were still contagious. Some of them were actually still peeling, and we all three thought it great fun pulling the skin off their hands in great strips.

So it was hardly surprising that we all went down with scarlet fever. The infection struck so quickly that we didn't even have time to eat all our Christmas treats or play with the toys we'd been given.

Ilya wasn't really all that ill, Seryozha rather more seriously, and I almost died. Mamma told me later that I was unconscious for several days, and that they were afraid I'd become too weak to throw the infection off.

I had two different sorts of drink put beside my bed: water with white wine in, and water sweetened with jam. I would sit up in bed and say very decisively 'the white', or 'the red.' For several days I was able to take nothing else.

At that time there were no clinical thermometers, and no one had ever heard of medical tests. There were fewer doctors, so they were called in less often. One simply waited for the illness to run its course, rubbed the patient with warm olive oil, made sure he had plenty to drink, and left the rest to the will of God.

I remember the day when I felt better. I am in bed, and I have a sensation of being soaked with well-being. Next to my bed is Ilya's, and on the far side of that Seryozha's. They are both in bed too. Papa comes in and sits down by me.

'Well, Choorka? Are you still pretending to be ill?'

There is tenderness in his eyes, and I feel I could ask him for anything I liked. But there's nothing I want. Taking his big, strong, dry hand I pull off his wedding ring. He goes on looking down at me, smiling benevolently, putting up no objection. I play with the wedding ring until it slips from my fingers and rolls away where we can't see it. Papa doesn't scold me and waits patiently for Agafia Mikhailovna to retrieve the ring from a crack between the floorboards.

When we were all much better we were allowed to have our Christmas presents and treats. We played sometimes on one bed, sometimes on another, we had our dear Hannah lavishing attention on us, mamma often popped in to see us, and papa himself came sometimes. We were very happy.

14

During our scarlet fever we were nursed by a woman I want to say something about, because she was very important in the lives of us children and occupied quite a considerable place in the family's life generally.

This was Agafia Mikhailovna—my great-grandmother Pelageya Nicolayevna Tolstoy's lady's maid—who when we were children was what we always called 'the dogs' governess'. She was tall and spare. Her proud, stern face, with its thoroughbred features, still retained the traces of a remarkable beauty.

She had remained unmarried, presumably because she had not wished to subject her life to another's control. When young she had been obliged, since she was a serf, to submit to her mistress and acquit herself diligently of all her duties willy-nilly. But when my father became master at Yasnaya Polyana, doubtless out of respect for her pride of spirit, he gave her a room of her own in the servants' building, allotted her a pension, and imposed no obligation of any kind on her in return. He told her she could work at whatever she felt would suit her.

As an old woman she liked telling how on one occasion, when she was still a serf, someone had wanted to buy her from papa and had offered him a brace of hunting dogs in exchange. But my father had refused the offer.

'And you know, they were first-class dogs,' she would say, with the confident air of an expert in the field.

Agafia Mikhailovna began by taking charge of the sheep-pens, then later switched to the kennels, which she continued to manage until the end of her life.

Her love was not confined to just dogs however. To her mind every living creature was worthy of love and compassion. She even refused to kill nasty insects like fleas and cockroaches, and flew into a rage when other people did so in her presence. And not content with sparing their lives she even fed them. As for eating mutton, from the first day she took charge of our sheep she was quite unable to touch it.

'She had a mouse,' my brother Ilya writes in his *Reminiscences,* 'which used to come out on to the table when she was drinking her tea and nibble the breadcrumbs.

'One day we went picking strawberries, and by clubbing together we managed to raise the sum of sixteen kopeks, bought a pound of sugar, and made Agafia Mikhailovna some jam. She was very pleased and thanked us. This is what happened:

' "When it came time to have my tea," she told us, "and I wanted some of my jam to put in it, suddenly I saw the mouse there inside the pot. I hoiked her out, gave her a wash in warm water, and that took some doing I can tell you, then let her go."

' "And the jam, what about the jam?"

' "Oh I threw it out. A mouse, eugh! they're dirty creatures. I couldn't have brought myself to eat it after she'd been in it like that." '

In winter, when the family went away to Moscow leaving papa alone at Yasnaya Polyana, or when he came back alone to have a rest from the stresses of city life, Agafia Mikhailovna used to come and visit him, and they would sit chatting together beside the samovar. My father mentions her frequently in his letters to my mother, always with affection.

'Today Agafia Mikhailovna entertained me hugely with stories about you,' he wrote in a letter on March 2nd 1882. 'It was most enjoyable. Her dog and cat stories are so amusing, but usually when she talks about people it's all so depressing. So-and-so is begging for a living, so-and-so has St Vitus' dance, so-and-so has tuberculosis, so-and-so is bed-ridden now, so-and-so has abandoned his children . . .'

In various other letters he wrote: 'The tea is made, Agafia Mikhailovna is here.' 'Agafia Mikhailovna came to see me, we had a chat and she's just left.' 'Agafia Mikhailovna has been reminding me of old times, interesting stories about me I'd forgotten, what an appalling barchuk [young master, the landowner's son] I was . . .' 'I had lunch, received a visit from Agafia Mikhailovna, a pleasure always fresh . . .' 'I spent my evening making the shoes for Agafia Mikhailovna . . . D.F. [Dmitri Fedorovich, the village schoolteacher] and Agafia Mikhailovna were here, we read *The Lives of the Saints* aloud.' 'It's six in the evening, Agafia Mikhailovna is with me.' 'Today I got up at eight, put my affairs in order, and went to visit Agafia Mikhailovna.'

Papa's last mention of her was in 1890: 'It's nine o'clock, I've been out for a walk. There's snow, the weather mild, everything so still. I looked in on Agafia Mikhailovna . . .'

As a little girl I too used to look in on Agafia Mikhailovna quite often, to chat with her and see the dogs, which I loved dearly. Agafia Mikhailovna would tell me about the old days, about my great-grandmother when Agafia Mikhailovna had been her 'lady-in-waiting' (which was how she herself always referred to her duties). 'I'm ugly now, but you mustn't let that fool you; when I was young I was a beauty,' she told me. 'Sometimes milady the countess would go out on to the balcony with her guests. When she needed a handkerchief she would call me out there: *'Fambre-de-chambre, apportez mouchoir de poche.'* And I'd answer: *'Toute vite, matame la comtesse.'* And all those ladies and gentlemen gave me such looks!'

As we chatted the dogs would amble round the room. And there was almost always one of them, for some reason, in particular need of Agafia Mikhailovna's care and attention just then, lying in one corner on a bed of fresh straw.

I asked her a lot of questions about my grandmother Marya Nicolayevna, my father's mother; but she could never tell me very much, because she had been a Tolstoy serf and my grandmother was born Princess Volkonski. Agafia Mikhailovna could only tell me that she was very stiff and formal in her manner and incapable of ever being angry.

The reason I tried to find out as much about my grandmother as possible was that I knew my father had such love and veneration for her memory. Agafia Mikhailovna said that I was like her physically, and that gave me great pleasure, even though she was said to have been a plain woman. In fact, it is impossible to know whether what she said was true or not, since no portrait of my grandmother has survived, apart from one tiny black silhouette.

'Papa didn't remember his mother,' my brother Ilya wrote in his *Reminiscences*. 'She died when he was two and he only knew about her from family accounts.

'She had a marvellous talent for telling children's stories, and papa said that it was from her that his older brother Nicolai inherited his gifts as a storyteller.

'Papa spoke of his mother only rarely, but when he did it was always wonderful to listen to, because at those times he was always in a very particular mood, a mixture of tenderness and gentleness. There was so much respectful love, so much piety toward her memory in all he said that we had the impression our grandmother must have been a saint.

'Papa's father did not die until he was nine, and he remembered him well. He loved him too, and always spoke of him with respect, but all the same one felt that the memory of his mother, whom he had never known, was even dearer to his heart.'

But I must come back to Agafia Mikhailovna.

One day I went to her room and saw Milka, papa's favourite greyhound bitch, lying in one corner. Her body was completely covered by the quilted dressing-gown mamma had only just finished making for Agafia Mikhailovna. Milka, as though aware that she had been made the object of excessive honour, stretched out her slender muzzle in my direction with a slightly shamefaced look in her magnificent dark eyes. Just where her tail should have been there were strange movements going on under the dressing-gown, and as I looked it slipped, revealing a whole litter of puppies with their eyes still not open. Some were feeding, some sleeping, others wriggling and nuzzling in the straw around their mother's body. Milka turned her head and contemplated her offspring with an anxious gaze.

I thought sorrowfully of all mamma's labours. I had seen her sewing away for hours, bent over the table and peering down at the stitches with her shortsighted eyes. And now here was her handiwork on the back of a dog! In fact, mamma was used to it. This was by no means the first time. Any number of skirts, waistcoats, dressing-gowns had already been sacrificed in just the same way. As for Agafia Mikhailovna herself, she was wearing a tunic-jacket so torn, and so threadbare, that there was almost nothing left of it but the padded lining, with the filling sticking out all over in great lumps. Her old woman's neck and throat were uncovered: the neck long and scraggy, the skin of her chest aged to the colour of old parchment and sprinkled with snuff. Her thick white hair stuck up every which way, and beneath the thick white eyebrows her eyes were piercingly bright.

'Come now, little countess,' she said when I expressed my sorrow, 'do you really think a dressing-gown worth more than one of God's creatures?'

I was obliged to admit that she was right and made no further objections. But all the same I decided I would conceal the fate that had befallen her intricate labours from mamma.

Agafia Mikhailovna's care and attentions were not lavished on the dogs alone. She was the perfect nurse, and whenever anyone in the house fell ill she was always sent for. Calm, patient, she would remain for nights on end keeping watch beside her patient, nursing him or her with skill and eager devotion. It was she who looked after our steward, Alexei Stepanovich, papa's former valet, when he fell ill. And when he lay dying at Yasnaya Polyana she spent whole weeks by his bedside. She was very fond of him and they had long heart to heart conversations together.

Simple people are not embarrassed to talk openly about death, and one day Agafia Mikhailovna had a long talk with her dying friend about the nature of this end that comes to us all. They wondered together whether the transition to the next life is a painful one, and Alexei Stepanovich promised to tell her the answer before he died. When it was obvious that the end was very near, Agafia Mikhailovna reminded him of his promise and asked him if he felt easy about it now.

'And how!' Alexei Stepanovich replied without a hint of hesitation.

After his death Agafia Mikhailovna missed him terribly.

'Yesterday Agafia Mikhailovna spent a long time weeping,' my father wrote to my mother, 'and as usual her grief expressed itself in a bizarre but nevertheless sincere way. "Lev Nicolayevich, tell me, what should I do? I'm afraid I'm going to go mad. I go in to see Shumikha [one of the Yasnaya Polyana dogs], I take him in my arms, and I start crying and talking to him: Our dear Alexei Stepanovich is dead, Shumikha," and so on. And then she weeps some more.'

As far back as I can remember I was always hearing Agafia Mikhailovna complaining about a birch tree that was growing in her insides. Whenever I asked after her health she would always shake her head, pull a face, and answer: 'That birch tree in there, little countess, it's still growing away . . . It's making it hard for me to breathe . . .'

I didn't know then, and I still don't to this day, whether she really believed in that birch tree, but as a child I certainly did, and I imagined that if it kept on growing then it would certainly have to come out somewhere in the end. So I was perpetually waiting, half in curious anticipation, half in terror, for the birch tree to finally emerge.

During the long autumn and winter nights this old woman, alone in her room tormented by her birch tree inside, used to twist and turn in bed with her mind beset by strange thoughts.

'One time I remember, I was in my bed,' she once recounted, 'and everything was very quiet. There was only the tick-tock of the clock, and it kept saying: "Who are you? Who are you?" Well I began thinking about that, and I really started asking myself: "Who am I? What am I?" And I went on thinking about that all night long.'

My father always enjoyed telling that story. And another one too, also about this strange woman.

One day, Tatyana Andreyevna Behrs, mamma's younger sister, fell ill while on a visit to us. As usual, someone was sent out to fetch Agafia Mikhailovna.

'I'd just had a bath,' Agafia Mikhailovna used to recount, 'I'd had my tea, and there I was tucked up snugly on the stove. Suddenly I heard someone tapping at the window. "What is it?" "It's Tatyana Andreyevna. She's been taken ill and she's asking for you to come and look after her." Well there I was all cosy up on my stove, I certainly didn't want to go clambering down, getting dressed again, and going out into the cold. So I answered: "You just say that Agafia Mikhailovna can't come, that she's just got out of the bath." When the fellow had gone I began telling myself: "Well now, this isn't at all a nice way to behave. Here I am pampering myself up here and not caring a jot about that poor thing who's ill." I sat up and began pulling on my boots. Then the tapping on the window came again. "What is it now?" "Tatyana Andreyevna sent me to say you really must come, and she'll buy you a new frock if you do." "Ah, so she'll buy me a frock will she? Well just you go and tell her I'm not coming, that there's no question of my coming!" I took off my boots again, tucked myself back on top of the stove, and after a long while I managed to get off to sleep. It's not for frocks I look after people when they're poorly . . . I was very fond of her, that Tatyana Andreyevna, but she properly got my dander up that night.'

Agafia Mikhailovna knew and was very fond of a number of our visitors, but her favourite was M. A. Stakhovich (21). It has to be admitted that he on his side lavished so much consideration and attention on her that it would have been amazing if he hadn't won her heart. He never came to see her empty-handed; but what old Agafia Mikhailovna with her proud heart appreciated far more was the fact that he always treated her with as much respect and courtesy as if she had been a lady of the very highest rank. When he went to see her she offered him tea. The room was rank with the smell of dog. There were cockroaches running all over the walls and table. Because of the dogs, fleas were legion, Agafia Mikhailovna herself was dirty, and her tea service not much better.

But Mikhail Alexandrovich would bravely pour a little of his tea into his saucer and sip at it, then nibble at a rather suspect lump of sugar that had every appearance of having been used before.

I remember that one day Agafia Mikhailovna offered him some of her snuff, and he took a pinch from the birchbark box without even flinching, placed it on his left thumbnail, and dutifully sniffed it up.

The 6th of February was Agafia Mikhailovna's birthday, and we never missed wishing her many happy returns. Only once did the distractions of life in Moscow make us forget to write to her. And even papa, though he had stayed behind at Yasnaya Polyana, had failed to finish the shoes he'd been meaning to give her. In a letter to mamma he wrote: 'The children have forgotten to wish Agafia Mikhailovna a happy birthday, and my shoes aren't going to be ready in time either.'

But Stakhovich hadn't forgotten. On February 5th, a biting cold day with a blizzard blowing, a man arrived from Kozlovski-Pasyeka and handed Agafia Mikhailovna a telegram from Stakhovich wishing her a happy birthday. 'This evening Agafia Mikhailovna came in with her telegram, she's as pleased as punch,' my mother wrote to mamma on February 5th 1881.

Agafia Mikhailovna went round showing off her telegram to every-one, absolutely radiant with joy. But when she showed it to papa he laughed and said: 'Aren't you ashamed that a man had to trudge through weather like this for three versts and more just on your account!'

That upset Agafia Mikhailovna, and she flew into a huff: 'Trudge! So that's all you can think of to say! My patron saint came carrying it to me and you say he trudged! He trudged!' And the old woman's fury took a long time to abate.

When we got back to Yasnaya Polyana next spring, the first thing Agafia Mikhailovna told us was that Stakhovich had sent her a telegram and that papa had said that the man who brought it had 'trudged' from the station . . . 'Trudged. When you have a message brought to you at the house that's a different thing altogether. But when it's me then it's 'trudged', isn't it? And with my patron saint carrying it too . . .' she kept saying. And she was in the right. Rarely can any greetings telegram have brought such joy to its recipient.

Agafia Mikhailovna died while we were all of us away from Yasnaya Polyana. She faded away quietly, without a murmur and without fear. Before dying she left a message for the whole family telling us how grateful she was for the affection we had shown her. I was told that when they took her to the graveyard to be buried her dogs followed the procession for a long way out of the village, all howling. Without Agafia Mikhailovna life at Yasnaya Polyana certainly became duller.

15

There were other people living with us at Yasnaya Polyana too: Tatyana Alexandrovna Yergolskaya, or Auntie, who had brought up my father, his brothers, and his sister; Natalya Petrovna, her companion; and Axinia Maximovna, her old maid who lived with her.

Our actual kinship with Tatyana Alexandrovna was a very distant one. Papa called her Auntie 'from habit', as he says in his *First Recol-*

lections. 'Our kinship was so tenuous that I have never been able to remember exactly what it was,' he goes on, 'but because of her love for us, as with Buddha and the wounded swan, she occupied the primary place in our upbringing. And we were aware of it.'

'I experienced explosions of tender and ecstatic love for her,' he writes further on. 'I remember once, when I was about five I should think, I tumbled down behind her on the divan in the drawing-room. She stroked me with her hand. I seized that hand and covered it with kisses, weeping with tenderness and love.'

I believe that until his marriage there was no one in papa's life he loved and esteemed as much as that sweet-natured old lady.

'Tatyana Alexandrovna,' he wrote elsewhere in his reminiscences, 'had the greatest influence of all on me. She influenced me firstly in the sense that she taught me the moral delights of love. Not with words, but because the love that emanated from her was contagious. I could see and feel her happiness in loving, and I came to understand the felicity of love. That was the first thing. The second was that she taught me the charm of a quiet and solitary life.'

Tatyana Alexandrovna devoted her entire life to her wards and totally renounced all thoughts of personal happiness for herself. Among her papers, my father recounts in his *First Recollections,* a note was found, tucked inside a little pearl-embroidered wallet. It had been written in 1836, six years after his mother's death [which took place shortly after the birth of her daughter Marya], and it read:

'August 16th 1836. Nicolas [my grandfather N. I. Tolstoy] today made me a strange proposition, that of marrying him and of acting as a mother to his children and never leaving them. I refused the first proposition, I promised to carry out the second for as long as I live.' 'That is what she had written,' my father comments, 'but she had never mentioned a word of it to anyone.'

From that day onward the life of the Tolstoy children became the same thing as her own.

I have the impression that she felt an especial love for my father. At all events she remained with him after his only sister's marriage, the death of two of his brothers, and his brother Sergei's move to Pirogovo, the estate which fell to him as his share of the family inheritance. An orphaned and lonely adolescent, my father switched all the love he would have felt for his parents to her alone. He always knew that there was someone living in that half-empty house at Yasnaya Polyana who loved him, who was concerned over his ardent and passionate nature, and who lived in anticipation of news from him.

I believe that this knowledge prevented him on more than one occasion from allowing his passions to get the better of him.

Wherever my father went he continued writing to his dear Auntie and waiting impatiently for her letters to him. If a long time went by without his receiving one he began to worry, got terribly upset and reproached her for not writing. 'It is not pleasure your letters bring me,' he wrote to her in 1855 from Simferopol, in French as usual, 'they are for me the supreme good, I become quite different, I become better when I receive one of your letters, which I re-read a hundred times: I'm so happy to get them I can't keep still, I want to rush out and read them to everyone; and if before they arrive I have allowed myself to be led astray by some temptation, then I call a halt and begin making plans to become a better person.'

It was she who spurred my father on to write. When he was twenty-three he wrote to her from Tiflis: 'Do you remember, dear Auntie, how one day you advised me to write novels? Well I've followed that advice! And when I wrote telling you about being so busy it was literature I was busy with. I don't know whether what I'm writing will ever be published, but the work fascinates me, and I've gone too far with it now not to finish.' What he was writing at the time was *Childhood,* which was to appear in September 1852 in the magazine *Sovremennik* [one of the most famous Russian literary magazines, started by Pushkin in 1836 and at this time under the editorship of Nekrassov].

In 1852 he wrote to her from the posthouse at Mosdok, 'halfway to Tiflis' as he himself puts it in his letter, confiding his dreams of future happiness to her, looking forward to the day when he would have returned from the Caucasus, to a time when he would be back with her at Yasnaya Polyana again, married, with Tatyana Alexandrovna sharing his life and his family's, all united in their love.

'If I were to be made emperor of Russia,' he wrote in French, 'if I were to be given Peru and all its gold, in a word, if a fairy came with her magic wand and asked me to name my heart's desire—then hand on that heart I would reply that my one wish is for this dream to become reality . . . Again I weep. Why do I weep when I think of you? They are tears of happiness—I am happy at the knowledge of loving you. If every misfortune were to befall me, I should never think myself unhappy as long as you existed.

'Do you remember our parting at the Iverskaya chapel (22) when we were leaving for Kazan? That day, as the moment came to leave you, I understood as though by inspiration all that you were to us, and although still a child I managed with my tears and my incoherent words to make you understand what I was feeling.'

In 1852, while at Pyatigorsk, in the Caucasus, he thought often about their next meeting. 'In a few months,' he wrote to her, 'if the Lord does not upset the plans I am making, I shall be with you and in a position to prove to you by my attentions and my love that I have deserved, at least in some small measure, all that you have done for us. You are so present in my memory that having written those lines I sat for a while not writing, busy envisaging the happy moment when I shall see you again, when you will weep for joy at seeing me, and when I too shall weep, like a child, as I kiss your hands.'

Loving her as much as he did, papa would have liked someone in his family to perpetuate the image of his aunt. He had named me Tatyana on her account, and he used to tell me—and also wrote to me—that he would very much have liked me to live a life like hers. Alas, neither my character nor my life bear any resemblance to those of his beloved Auntie.

The day my only child was born, my daughter Tatyana—to whom this book is dedicated—, papa came in to see me, very moved and tender, and told me that the previous night he had seen Tatyana Alexandrovna in a dream. He added that he would like my daughter to bear her name. Needless to say, both my husband and myself acceded to this wish without hesitation. Tanya was only five when her grandfather died, and he was therefore unable to judge whether or not she was worthy of bearing his dear Auntie's name.

When papa married, Tatyana Alexandrovna welcomed my mother with every mark of affection. And mamma, appreciating all the older woman's greatness of soul, always surrounded her husband's aunt with respect and solicitude.

Tatyana Alexandrovna, Natalya Petrovna, and Axinia Maximovna all lived on the ground floor, in a part of the house to which they had been moved at Auntie's own request.

Since our family was growing so, the old lady had insisted on moving downstairs and leaving her former room free for the children. Here is how my father recounts the incident: 'One day, some time after my marriage when she was beginning to decline in health, I was in her room with her. She turned her head away and said to me (I could see that she was on the brink of tears): "Well now, my dears, this room couldn't be nicer, and you're going to be needing it. If I were to die in this room," she went on in a tremulous voice, "that would give you an unpleasant memory of it. So you move me somewhere else, just to make sure I don't die here." '

Papa was deeply touched by this fresh instance of her self-abnegation, and accepted her decision. From that time on, until the end of her life, Tatyana Alexandrovna lived in a small north-west facing room with windows that looked out on the courtyard.

She lived quite independently from the rest of the household. In one corner of her bedroom there was a great big ikon of the Saviour with a burnished silver frame. The face was so darkened with age that it was difficult even making out the features. There was also a stained glass ikon window. The room smelled of lamp oil and cypress. Tatyana Alexandrovna was short and slight. When we went in to see her she would open a drawer with her delicate white hands and offer us each a piece of gingerbread.

That gingerbread is linked in my mind with a memory that still fills me with confusion. I went one day with my brothers to pay a visit on Auntie. We were all in a particularly mischievous mood. Normally, Tatyana Alexandrovna's room inspired us with a certain awe, and we tended to lower our voices when we went in there, even though we were probably not conscious of the fact. But this day it was different. As soon as she had pulled open her drawer, Ilya and I rushed forward and began snatching pieces of gingerbread, stuffing them into our mouths and filling our pockets. Tatyana Alexandrovna tried to reason with us, to stop us behaving like that. But it was no good: in our excitement we were beyond reason. Seeing as much, she moved away from the chest of drawers and sat down, fright and bewilderment in her eyes. I shall never forget that look.

Suddenly I was so ashamed that I dropped the pieces of gingerbread back, giving a little forced laugh that was meant to convey that it had all been just a friendly game. Then I fled from the room. But my shame stayed with me, and I have never forgiven myself that outburst of bad manners inflicted on so refined and so well-bred an old lady, whom papa always addressed with such marked courtesy.

16

Someone else I remember very well in my childhood is my cousin Varya, the daughter of my aunt the Countess Marya Nicolayevna Tolstoy (23).

Varya often came to stay at Yasnaya Polyana. I remember her when she was still just a girl. Her mother had sent her to Yasnaya Polyana to forget a man she was in love with and wanted to marry. I saw her weeping on more than one occasion, and I remember as though it were yesterday the feeling of love and compassion I experienced as I sat on her lap and leaned my head against her breast.

She was a wonderful storyteller. I have never heard droller stories than the ones she told us in the evenings then, sitting in the half-dark on the big divan.

Our Hannah sometimes used to go on visits to her sister, or spend a little while in Tula with some English people papa had unearthed to provide a change for her. It was on such occasions that Varya used to come down and sleep with us in the vaulted room. Before leaving, Hannah would give Varya instructions about how to deal with us, about what was allowed and what wasn't.

Every night, when she tucked us into bed, it was Hannah's custom to give us each a little piece of licorice, which we loved. Varya was therefore issued with a large, round stick of licorice from which she was to slice us off a tiny roundel each every evening. To my great shame I must admit to such greediness that even today, more than fifty years later, I can still recall the pleasure with which I received from Varya a lump of licorice so large that Hannah would have made it last five or six evenings at the least. But my pleasure was shortlived: I simply couldn't manage to finish this oversized treat, which eventually began to make me feel sick. And I was so sleepy by then that I simply took it out of my mouth and surreptitiously dropped it on the floor, behind my bed.

Varya was very vague and absent-minded, and all sorts of stories circulated in the family on the subject of this failing. We all loved recounting them. And while they were being told Varya would sit with a shamefaced smile on her face, blinking her eyes and shaking her head as she said: 'I mean, can you imagine, it's true, that's just what happened.' Or else, on other occasions: 'No, now that really is a fib, honestly.'

When she got married papa presented her with a ten thousand ruble note. It was part of the money earned from *War and Peace,* which he had arranged to share with his sister's children. Varya thanked her uncle very much and laid the note down on a table. Late that evening, since one of her bedroom windowpanes was broken and the night was bitterly cold, she decided she'd better do some temporary repairs. So she snatched up a sheet of paper, neatly stuck it over the hole with some gum arabic that chance to be at hand, then jumped back into bed feeling very pleased with herself.

Next day, in conversation, the subject of the money Varya had been given happened to come up. She herself had already forgotten about it, since she always had great difficulty attaching much importance to material possessions. All the same she began looking about for the banknote: it had vanished. She continued searching, several helpers joined in, but still no banknote. At last someone happened to glance at the window and saw the ten thousand ruble note stuck on the windowpane. Varya darted her eyes this way and that in her confusion, then cried out, absolutely horrified: 'How could I ever have done such a scatterbrained thing?' But even that didn't cure her of her vagueness. And a very good thing too: she never did succeed in attaching any great value to material possessions.

Varya's husband also used to tell us various stories about his wife's scatterbrained behaviour, though always in the nicest, most indulgent way.

'Do you know, a few days ago I went out hunting with some friends and asked Varya to have dinner ready for us all. We arrived home, ravenous as wolves, and I asked: "Varya, is dinner ready?" Varya looked shamefaced: "Oh, Kolya, do you know, I've been racking my brains all day long over what I could cook for you, and I just couldn't make up my mind." So we went out to a restaurant,' he added with an indulgent smile.

On another occasion, Varya and her husband took a box at a theatre with some friends and relatives. During the first interval they took a turn in the foyer. When they had all returned to the box it was noticed that Varya was missing. They sat through the next act of the play, but still no Varya. Her husband began to get worried. At last he had the idea of going down into the pit and casting his eyes round all the boxes from below. There in the box directly above theirs, in an otherwise empty tier, he caught sight of Varya. She was visibly very worried, peering anxiously about her, wearing that familiar shamefaced expression, and blinking her eyes faster than ever.

'I mean, can you imagine,' she began as always, 'I did think it so odd the way you'd all vanished like that, I mean in a flash . . .'

One Sunday she went to mass with Bolya, her eldest son. On the way a mother-of-pearl button came loose on the little boy's coat, so Varya carefully removed it and tucked it safely into her pocket, where there was already a twenty kopek piece for the collection. When the collection plates came round Varya took out what she supposed was her coin, laid it in the first plate, and took out ten kopeks change for the second plate. Then almost immediately she realized with horror that she'd put in the button instead of the twenty kopeks. And it was too late to repair her blunder because the verger was already moving on. In her confusion Varya also forgot to put the ill-gotten ten kopeks into the second plate. So not only had she not added to the church's wealth, she had actually robbed it!

I must also add here that Varya did eventually marry the man she loved, N. N. Nargorny, despite her relatives' wish to prevent it. Moreover he proved an excellent husband and she never regretted her choice.

17

Our family was still growing. When Ilya was three, mamma gave birth to another boy, Lev. I was very disappointed at having yet another brother. I'd had enough of boys and longed passionately for a sister. I envisaged myself playing dolls with her, and I told myself that with a sister, instead of just all these brothers, my life would become quite different. Without prompting from anyone, I took to inserting an additional request into my morning and evening prayers, in English: 'Please God, send me a little sister.'

On February 12th 1870, mamma was delivered of a daughter. I was convinced that this event was due entirely to my prayers and could hardly wait for my first glimpse of the baby. At last we were told we could go to mamma's bedroom. There in the dim light of the shaded room I saw my mother lying very quiet in her bed. She looked pretty but was still weak. Beside her she had a tiny, red, wrinkled creature that smelled of damp flannel and talcum powder. This tiny creature was wriggling very feebly and emitting pitiful mewing noises. 'Is that the playfellow I have waited so long for,' I asked myself, 'the confidante of my innermost thoughts, of all the feminine feelings the boys just don't understand? It's going to be a long time before this defenceless little thing turns into a proper little girl!'

We weren't allowed to stay long. I leaned very cautiously over my little sister to kiss her; it was a maternal feeling of pity and tenderness I felt for her, not that of a sister. Then I gave mamma a kiss too and left the room, moved but decidedly dissatisfied.

Not long after that we were told that mamma was seriously ill and that the baby was very sickly.

The next few days were long and sad. We didn't go in to see mamma. Papa sometimes came in to say hello to us, but he always seemed very anxious and in a hurry. When I went to see Masha—the name of my little sister—Marya Afanassyevna who was looking after her always seemed very grumpy: Masha cried almost the whole time, Marya Afanassyevna was perpetually either rocking her in her arms or changing her, so I just felt in the way and got no pleasure from my visits at all.

At last, after a very long and painful illness, mamma got better. Masha, on the other hand, remained as sickly as ever. Among other complaints she suffered from scrofula. I can remember her scalp covered with oozing scabs. Marya Afanassyevna treated the disease as best she could, which involved smearing the infant's head with fresh cream. The cream would then go off, so that Masha smelled of sour milk the whole time.

Having yearned so long and ardently for a new playfellow, I for my part felt very let down, and returned to the company of my brothers and Hannah.

Masha's scabs did go away in the end, but she remained sickly and weak, not only as a child but for the rest of her life.

18

As children, we three older ones lived quite separately from the later arrivals. I used to enjoy going up to the nursery to play with the babies, but my life was really lived with Seryozha and Ilya. My two brothers felt much as I did.

'Our infant horde was divided into two distinct groups,' Ilya writes in his *Reminiscences*, 'the "big ones" and the "little ones". The big ones were Seryozha, Tanya, and me. The little ones were my brother Lev and my sister Little-Masha.

'Because of the little ones we always had to get home earlier, in case they caught chills. We weren't allowed to make any noise when they were having their nap. When one of the little ones started crying and went to mamma to complain about us, then it was always the big ones who were in the wrong, and we were always being scolded and punished on their account.

'For reasons of age and temperament it was with my sister Tanya I always got on best. She was eighteen months older than me, with dark eyes, and was very quick-witted and inventive. With her about one was never in want of amusements, and we understood one another as if by instinct.

'We knew things that no one else except us could understand.

'We loved having chases round the dining-room table. I would tap her on the shoulder then turn and speed away as fast as my legs would carry me in the opposite direction.

' "You're the cat, you're the cat," I would cry.

'Then she'd catch me up, touch me in her turn, and speed away:

' "You're the cat, you're the cat."

'Once I was just reaching out my arm to touch her when she whirled round, began jumping up and down on the spot, waving her little hands in front of her face, and saying:

' "I'm the owl, I'm the owl."

'I grasped at once that if she was an owl then that meant I wasn't allowed to touch her, and from that day on it became an accepted rule. When one of us cried: "I'm the owl", that meant "pax".

'Seryozha would never have been able to fathom a game like that. For a start he would have insisted on you explaining the reason why you couldn't touch an owl, and then he would have informed you that it wasn't in the least amusing; whereas I understood right away how ingenious it was. And Tanya knew in advance that I would know just what she meant.'

Summer and winter alike, we lived at Yasnaya Polyana without ever getting bored.

My father knew the charm and the benefits 'of a quiet and solitary life' because he had absorbed that knowledge from his aunt Tatyana Alexandrovna, and he wanted a similar life for his family. I have always been grateful to him for it. Brought up as we were in the country, our powers of appreciation were never blunted by artificial pleasures. We learned to love and value our life in the heart of the countryside, and we acquired the habit of seeking our pastimes in ourselves and in nature.

I don't think any city child could ever appreciate the delight I felt when at the end of a long hard winter I discovered the first tufts of sweet-smelling grass in the circle of black, spongy earth around the foot of a birch tree. And all these joys were shared with Hannah, who taught me the English names of all the plants.

Since we were given very few toys we made many of our playthings ourselves. One of our favourite games was acting out stories we had read with the aid of little paper figures we cut out and coloured ourselves. We would lie on the floor for ages, flat on our stomachs, moving our paper characters about, speaking their words for them, and identifying with them totally.

When spring came we had larks baked out of rye-flour paste to play with. These were made for us every ninth of March by the cook's son, Senya Rumyantsev, who is now cook himself at Yasnaya Polyana.

There was a whole family of these larks. The biggest, the mother, had a big flat back with a whole nestful of little ones clustered on top of it. Sometimes there was also a nest with eggs in it. I would tie a different coloured woollen thread round the neck of each baby bird, and for the mother I always tried to find a pretty ribbon. When we went out for a walk I took my lark with me, attached to a length of string so that I could pull her behind me over the thawing snow.

When the lark began to get soft and fall apart there was nothing to be done but eat up my toy. It smelled rather of melted snow and horse dung, but that didn't stop me finding it very palatable.

My most beautiful dolls were given me by my godfather Dmitri Alexeyevich Dyakov. I loved him tremendously, and I thought he and papa were the two best looking men in the world. Though heaven knows, great qualities though they both undoubtedly possessed, personal beauty was hardly among them. Dmitri Alexeyevich especially was far from the most handsome of men: he had a ginger beard, a big paunch, and tiny grey eyes surrounded by bulges of fat.

Never mind, those eyes were also kindly, mischievous, and merry. And when my godfather came to see us we all found him so entertaining that we would laugh like lunatics even during mealtimes. Sometimes our servant Egor couldn't go on serving the meal. And on one occasion he even began to laugh so noisily himself that he was forced

a Tolstoy and her children Seryozha
Tatyana (1867)

*are terribly happy in our relations with
another, in our children, and in our life.'*
ia Tolstoy 1866)

stoy's four eldest children: Ilya, Lev,
yana and Seryozha (hitherto unpub-
ed)

*a almost never punishes us. But if he
s me right in the eyes he knows everything
thinking and I feel uncomfortable. I can
ibs to mamma, but not to papa. He knows
ur secrets.'* (Ilya Tolstoy)

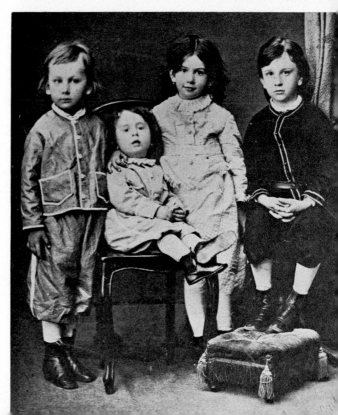

Tatyana Tolstoy at the age of ten
'*A few days ago I took her to Tula to be photographed. She asked me to buy a penknife for Seryozha . . . She knows exactly what will give everyone most pleasure. She didn't think of herself for an instant.*' (Tolstoy)

to drop his tray on the sideboard and dash back to the pantry overcome with embarrassment.

Almost every year my godfather gave me a doll. She was always called Masha, in honour of his daughter, and she was so beautiful that I hardly dared to touch her. All these dolls had real blonde hair, their eyes opened and closed, and they could say 'papa' and 'mamma' in a little squeaky voice when you pulled one of the two strings at the back, one with a blue bead on the end and the other with a green one.

The head and arms were made of china, with pink dimples at the knuckles and elbows. It didn't matter how careful I was with these Mashas, one by one their fingers broke off, their hair grew thinner, and eventually their heads got smashed.

One day when I was playing dolls with Ilya we managed to drop a Masha on to the floor, and her pretty head shattered into fragments. Ilya and I just stared into one another's eyes, quite speechless, then we burst into loud sobs and went on weeping like that for ages, lying flat on our stomachs on the floor. Eventually Hannah came in and consoled us, but it was a long while before we resigned ourselves to the loss of our little friend.

I also had seven tiny china dolls I could give baths to. This is how I acquired them:

I was ill and confined to bed. Papa was away on a trip somewhere. When he got back he came in to see me. And when papa came to my bedroom, even up till the very end of his life, it was always an event that filled me with joy and left me in a particular state of mind, happy, soothed, and contented.

He came in and sat down on the bed. As always when I was ill he began by asking me:

'Well, are you going to stop all this pretending to be ill soon?'

Then he started suddenly, and put a hand up to his neck as though something had stung him.

'Look, Tanya, look and see what it is stinging me. Round there, down my neck.'

I slid my hand under his collar and pulled out a tiny porcelain doll. I still hadn't recovered from my astonishment when papa pretended he'd been stung on the wrist. I looked inside the sleeve of his smock and there was another doll scarcely any bigger than the first. Then a third doll, very slightly larger, stung him inside one of his socks, and so on. By the end I had found seven dolls in various places, the seventh being the largest of all. And last of all there came a little

C

bathtub just the right size to fit them. These dolls were the only toy my father ever gave me. I was very fond of them and kept them a long while.

I was often ill as a child. Sometimes I used to wake up in the early morning with a headache, and then I would make my way, still half asleep, into the room next to my parents' bedroom where there was a big black bearskin I could lie down on with my head resting against the bear's.

It was a very special bear. It looked just as though it was alive. Its chestnut-coloured glass eyes looked real, it had real teeth, and it even had a tongue. But above all it was special because we knew it was the very bear that had bitten papa and given him the curved scar on his forehead.

We often told this story to other children and there were times when papa was quite puzzled to see them staring at him so hard. But when he realized why, he was perfectly happy to let them examine his scar. And often he would even tell them about how it happened. One day, a long while before, in the Smolensk district, he had shot at a bear and wounded it. The bear, maddened by the bullet, had hurled itself upon him, knocked him down, and begun tearing at him with its teeth. Papa said that he had felt the beast's burning breath on his face. His hunting companion, a mujik, had rescued him by driving the animal off with a stake.

Lying on its rough fur, I ran my fingers over the bear's teeth thinking of the danger papa had run, and eventually I would drop off to sleep again until papa, in his dressing-gown with his hair sticking up on end and his beard all sideways, emerged from his bedroom to get dressed, woke me up, and packed me back off to my bed.

19

Our childish ailments always came on without any apparent cause. Whenever we did silly things that might have been expected to produce unfortunate consequences nothing ever seemed to come of it. For example, one day when it was pouring with rain I imitated the heroine of *Les Malheurs de Sophie* and stood under a gutter-spout. On another occasion, as a result of a snowball fight with my brothers, I got so wet that I was covered in ice from head to foot.

I remember another occasion too, one spring, when the snow was beginning to melt and we went out for a walk with Hannah after breakfast. It was one of those heady March days with the sun at its most dazzling and the larks singing as they rise higher and higher through the luminous blue overhead; the snow, already half thawed, was porous and crumbly; the earth, visible here and there through the snow and warmed by the sun, was softening and giving off a strong and wholesome odour; the tender young blades of grass seemed to be growing before our eyes, and on south-facing banks the first downy yellow flowers were opening. On such days the cries of human voices, the barking of dogs, the song of the birds, and the sound of rushing water all carry so clearly in the springtime air.

Both Ilya and I possessed an abundance of that vital energy the English call animal spirits, and sometimes it took us over so completely that we became almost drunk with it and lost all control of ourselves. That is what happened on this springtime day. Ignoring Hannah's calls, we ran on and on like runaway horses, plunging straight ahead without the slightest regard for the sodden condition of the ground.

At last we reached the Yasenka. This was a little river, or rather a brook, which runs along the bottom of the garden and in summer dries up almost completely. But at that time of year the Yasenka was swollen with the thaw. It was a veritable torrent swirling lumps of ice along in its yellow, muddy tide.

I ran and ran with Ilya through the snow, with the water-sodden earth making sucking noises as we withdrew our feet. As we reached the stream we paused, just for a tiny moment, then without exchanging a single word we both waded boldly out into the water. We were wearing high dubbined boots, but they were soon full. Completely unconcerned, we began walking upstream against the current.

I still remember the pleasure I felt. When one of my feet went into a hole the water would come almost up to my chin; but I kept going, torso bent forward to counter the tremendous pressure of the current. The lumps of ice banged into my chest, but I felt neither pain nor fatigue as I continued on my triumphal way!

As I emerged from the water I became aware of the weight of my icy clothes. The water swooshed in my boots and splashed out at every step. How was I to face Hannah and my parents after such a terrible misdeed? What shame and apprehension I felt! And yet my pleasure had been so great that I could not find it in me to repent having disobeyed my dearest Hannah.

We neither of us caught cold, and patiently endured the punishment our bad behaviour had brought upon us. We were deprived of walks for three days. So we stayed inside, but our minds still dwelt with lasting pleasure on our thrilling escapade.

20

During the winter of 1870–71 papa immersed himself totally in the study of Greek. He read and translated the classics from morning till night. As was customary with him, he was only too eager to talk about his new passion, and was constantly sharing his admiration for the Greek language with us all. Whenever one of papa's friends came on a visit he was obliged to set papa translation tests both into and from the Greek. I can still see him, hunched over a book, face all concentration, his eyebrows shooting heavenwards whenever he stumbled over the meaning of a word.

On December 8th 1870 he wrote to Fet telling him that he was working at his Greek from morning till night. 'I'm not writing a thing any more, just studying.' Fet didn't believe papa could possibly succeed in mastering so difficult a language all on his own, and told his friends that if ever Tolstoy did succeed in learning Greek he would donate his own skin to make the parchment for his diploma.

'That skin of yours you promised for my diploma is in danger now,' my father wrote to Fet. 'It's unbelievable and staggering, but I have got through Xenophon now and can read him without a crib . . . How happy I am to have got this craze into my head. Primo, it gives me pleasure. Secundo, I have now realized that I was completely ignorant of the most authentic and austerely beautiful products of human language, like everyone else be it added; and those who know them don't understand them. Tertio, I am no longer writing rubbish, never will again . . . For the love of heaven, explain to me why no one knows the fables of Aesop, or even the charming Xenophon, not to mention Plato, Homer . . .'

This 'craze' cost my father dear. He worked himself too hard and ended up making himself ill, even though the exact nature of the illness remained indefinable. Mamma, extremely worried, urged him to consult a doctor in Moscow. Papa took notice of what she said and went to see a good friend of his, Doctor Zakharin, who was a very famous medical practitioner of the day.

'If it's been so long since I wrote to you and visited you,' he wrote to Fet in June 1871, 'it is because I have been and still am ill. With what? I myself haven't the faintest idea, but I have the feeling it's going to turn out badly, or well, depending on what name one gives to our end. I am utterly empty, I need and want nothing, except peace, and that is exactly what I lack . . .'

Zakharin took a very serious view of my father's trouble and advised him to spend several weeks in the steppes of Samara, where he was to rest totally and take the kumiss [fermented mare's milk] cure. Papa decided to follow this advice and set off for Samara accompanied by his brother-in-law Stepan Behrs.

During the summer of 1871, Turgenyev wrote to Fet on the subject of papa: '. . . I am very afraid for him: after all, two of his brothers have already died of tuberculosis. I'm very glad to hear he's going to take the kumiss cure, since I believe it to be very effective and beneficial. Tolstoy, the one hope of our orphaned literature, cannot and must not vanish from the face of the earth as prematurely as his predecessors, Pushkin, Lermontov, Gogol. But why this sudden passion for Greek?'

Papa spent six weeks in the steppes. His condition improved steadily day by day.

His fellow-writers were very concerned about his health. Fet kept Turgenyev posted on his progress. 'Thank you for the news you send,' Turgenyev wrote to Fet on August 6th 1871. 'I am delighted that Tolstoy is feeling better, and that he has acquired such mastery of the Greek language; it does him great credit and will stand him in good stead.' In another letter he wrote: 'The news you passed on regarding Tolstoy gave me great pleasure. I am truly delighted that he has recovered and is working again. Whatever he produces it will be good . . .'

For us children that summer began dismally. Papa was away, mamma was missing him and fretting about him. Hannah too was unwell, which alarmed and upset my parents. Mamma wrote about her condition to my father, and he replied:

'I wish I could have brought you with me, you, Seryozha, and

Hannah. The state of her health does prey so on my mind. I only hope she doesn't fall seriously ill . . .'

During this period Lyubov Behrs, my grandmother—and also my godmother—was staying in the house with us to help mamma. She supervised our schoolwork and often took us for walks instead of Hannah. Mamma was busy all day with the babies, especially Masha, who was still sickly. She wrote to papa that she had become 'so painfully attached to my little Masha. I can't hear her pitiful cries and see her tiny, sickly body without sadness. I am constantly fussing over her, I would so much like her to be bonnier.'

We too wrote to papa. In June I received the following letter from him: 'Tanya, there is a little boy here, four years old, called Aziz. He is fat and round just like a ball, drinks kumiss, and laughs the whole time. Stepan is very fond of him and gives him sweets. Aziz walks about without any clothes on. We live with a gentleman who is very hungry because there's nothing here to eat except mutton. And this gentleman says: "I'd love to gobble Aziz up, he's so nice and plump." Send me your conduct marks. Here's a big kiss for you.'

I wrote to papa all on my own, but Ilya was still too little for that. Mamma wrote to my father: 'I shall read the children your letters to them tomorrow . . . They will certainly write answers straight away. Ilya asked me yesterday if I would write for him, explaining that he couldn't write properly yet, all in such a heart-wrenching little voice I was quite amazed.'

In about July our life became slightly more eventful. Before leaving for Samara papa had bought a giant's-stride for us in Moscow and sent detailed instruction on how to set it up. It arrived, the carpenters were sent for, we selected a site on the front lawn, had a nice straight oak post cut, and several days later we all began having goes on it.

'Yesterday, for the first time,' mamma wrote, 'we were all of us outside, big ones and little ones alike, playing like lunatics on the giant's-stride . . . The children are quite thrilled with it, enjoyed it enormously, and didn't want to go to bed or have their tea. All they could think of was getting back out on to the lawn.'

Before long Seryozha and I were striding out without difficulty, but fat little Ilya kept falling down all the time. He wouldn't let go of the ring and just kept going round till he found himself dumped down again on his behind.

By the end of the summer Hannah was much better, as my mother delightedly informed my father. 'Hannah is very well and in high spirits, I still get on with her as well as ever. She really is a friend and a priceless help to me.'

Then papa came home and we were totally happy again. When he wasn't there we had the feeling that life was incomplete, that there was some essential element missing from our existence. It was as though life couldn't really begin again properly until he was back. As soon as he came home we initiated him into our big craze of the moment, the giant's-stride. He learned how to use it very quickly, and often came out to play on it with us.

One day during dinner, Ilya, then aged five, began explaining to papa a scheme he'd thought up for making the giant's-stride even more interesting.

'You know what idea I've had, papa?' he began. 'It'll be ever such fun . . . You need a stick, then on the stick a little board . . .'

Seryozha and I burst out laughing.

'And on the stick a board, and on the board a stick.' Seryozha added to tease Ilya.

I joined in:

'And on the stick a board, and on the board a stick . . . Ha! ha! ha! . . . And on the stick a board . . . Is that it, Ilya?'

Finding our teasing too much to bear, Ilya burst into noisy sobs. 'Come on now, don't cry,' papa said, knowing that his second son did in fact possess a definite talent for inventing things, and thinking that there must certainly be something sensible in his idea. 'You explain your plan to me, and then we'll see if we can't arrange it.'

When Ilya had been comforted and was in a state to explain his plan it turned out not to be so silly after all, and the Yasnaya Polyana carpenter was assigned the task of putting it into effect. At one point on the periphery of the giant's-stride a stake was driven into the earth, then a little board was made with a handle at one end and a hole in the other. The person whose turn it was had to slip the board over the stake as he or she went past. And the stake also had a little peg sticking out near the top to stop the board sliding right down to the ground.

Ilya was enchanted: his idea of 'a board on a stick and a stick on a board' was not only not silly, but papa had actually arranged for it to be made a reality, and even joined in playing it with us sometimes.

21

Papa came back from Samara cured and in top form; and our life resumed its former happy flow. We were all very busy: the children had their lessons and papa, with mamma's help, had begun compiling his *Russian Readers* and his *ABC*. I too contributed to this scheme by providing drawings to illustrate the letters of the alphabet. I diligently drew nice big pumpkins for the letter P and tubs for the letter T.

There was always some member of the family staying at Yasnaya Polyana. That autumn it was one of mamma's brothers, Volodya. And later we had her uncle, Islavin—uncle Kostya as he was called by everyone, even the servants—who came to spend the winter with us. They too did their share in the assembly of the reading primers.

During these months mamma wrote many letters to her sister Tatyana Kuzminsky, who was by then living at Kutais in the Caucasus, keeping her up to date with all the goings on at Yasnaya Polyana. 'We are once again all immersed in the reading primers and the ABC,' she wrote on September 20th 1871. 'Lyovochka writes, Volodya and I copy, and it's all going very well. If it turns out they can be published quite soon I shall send the first copy to Dasha. I shall send one in any case. When you come to teaching your children to read you'll be very glad we devised these books.'

In those days there weren't as many children's books as there are today, and those that did exist were either very uninteresting or else incomprehensible, especially for the little peasant children papa was thinking of when he thought up his scheme. And being incapable of skimping any task whatever, he devoted an enormous amount of his time and energy to producing these four *Russian Readers* and his *ABC*.

In order to find subjects that would be really interesting as well as educational he read textbooks on astronomy and physics, collections of proverbs, Aesop's fables, and many books for children by American and British authors. Like a bee plundering flowers to provide honey for its hive, he took the best wherever he found it to enrich his own books.

When he wanted to write a number of pieces about astronomy, not only did he read everything on the subject he could lay hands on, he even spent nights observing the stars and consulting celestial charts. 'I am so busy helping Lyovochka with his primers,' mamma wrote to her sister on May 28th 1871, 'that it's all I can do to get through all that has to be done in the day. And even so the books are still not going to be ready for a while yet. You know how Lyovochka loves to fuss and fiddle with everything, right down to the tiniest details . . .'

Just before Christmas in the same year, on December 22nd, she wrote again to her sister: 'We've been spending our time, uncle Kostya and I, copying and recopying those *Readers* I told you about so that they'd be over and done with before the holidays are upon us. And we've succeeded too. Lyovochka has gone off to Moscow taking the first batch with him.'

On January 12th, my father wrote to his friend and relative Countess Alexandra Andreyevna Tolstoy: 'These last few years I've been working on an *ABC* I'm going to publish. To explain what this very long-term labour means to me is very difficult. Here is my proud dream for this book: it is from this *ABC* that two generations of Russian children, *all of them,* from those of the Tsar to those of our peasants, will learn to read and receive their first poetic impressions. After writing this *ABC* I shall be able to die in peace.'

As my father took his *ABC* to the printer so he went on revising it and adding to it. 'My *ABC* is being printed at one end while it is still being written and extended at the other,' he explained to the same Alexandra Andreyevna. 'This *ABC* alone could provide me with work for a hundred years. It necessitates a knowledge of Greek, Indian, and Arab literature, of the natural sciences, of astronomy and physics, and besides that the actual wording involves such tremendous work. It is essential that everything should be exactly right, beautiful, simple, and above all clear.'

22

Since the house was now getting too small for our growing family, papa sent for an architect from Tula and asked him to add another large room to the main body of the house. It was to be ready for Christmas 1871. I remember the ceremony to mark the start of the actual building work. When the footings had been dug out, papa handed me a silver ruble and told me to throw it in. Everyone stood around in a circle, we crossed ourselves, and work began. The masons, joiners, carpenters, and plasterers worked flat out right up to the last moment.

A few days before Christmas, with papa still not back from Moscow, mamma and uncle Kostya busily set about getting the new room ready. Uncle Kostya had a great fondness for beautiful furnishings, so he took on the job of hanging the pictures, looking-glasses, chandeliers, and curtains. Mamma and the workmen rummaged in a storeroom and brought out mattresses, cushions, candelabras, dishes, and all sorts of furniture and other things.

There never were such preparations for Christmas as we had that year. We were expecting a lot of guests, and to make sure they weren't bored all sorts of entertainments were to be provided—a Christmas tree, fancy-dresses, tobogganing, skating, and I don't know what else. Several days beforehand daily women came in, tucked up their skirts, and poured torrents of water over the floors. Others clambered bare-footed up on to the windowsills and washed the windows, while the porter polished all the brass door fittings and the heating grilles with ground pumice.

Under Hannah's supervision, we children mixed an enormous plum pudding and made decorations for the Christmas tree. Every evening we all took our places around a big circular table with a lamp over it and set to work. After weeks of concentrated schoolwork any new occupation was as good as a rest to us. And also we had just spent months and months without seeing anyone, so that the arrival of guests was for us a promise of pleasure and excitement.

Mamma brought us in a big bag of walnuts and pots of the cherry-tree gum that we'd helped collect some while before from the old cherry trees out in the greenhouses. Then she handed us each a brush, together with sheets of gold and silver paper so thin that they quivered at the slightest breath of air. Using our brushes, we coated a nut with gum, then laid it down on a piece of the paper and very carefully, scarcely touching it, moulded the gold or silver covering around the nut. Once they'd been given their gold or silver coating the nuts were placed in a dish. Then, when they were dry, we fixed a pink ribbon on to each one with a pin, so that it could be hung on the Christmas tree. That was the really tricky part: in order to drive your pin all the way home you had to find a place in the shell where it would go in easily, otherwise, as often happened, the pin bent, you pricked your finger, and because the ribbon wasn't firm it unravelled under the weight of the nut and came loose.

When we'd done all the nuts we went on to making paper chains by folding coloured or gold and silver paper strips. We also had silver tinsel and stars to decorate the boxes we'd made. Everyone tried to make something original and pretty. We made baskets, goblets, saucepans, barrels, and little chests decorated with all sorts of designs.

After that it was time to make the clothes for the 'skeletons'. It's many years now since this kind of doll disappeared from the scene, but in my childhood it wouldn't have been Christmas without 'skeletons'. They were wooden dolls, without clothes, jointed only at the waist, with black hair painted on their heads and bright pink cheeks. The head and torso were all in one piece, and the feet were fixed on to a little board so that the doll would stand upright.

Mamma bought these 'skeletons' in boxes of a hundred. They cost five kopeks, and when we had put clothes on them we gave them as presents to the children who were invited up to our Christmas tree party. At the same time as the box of skeletons mamma also brought in a big bundle stuffed with remnants of material in every imaginable colour. Once we had been provided with needles, thread, and scissors, we set about providing our skeletons with garments. We dressed them as girls, as boys, as angels, as kings, as queens; there were also Russian peasant women, Scotsmen in kilts, Italians of both sexes, and heaven knows what else we didn't think up, with mamma's and Hannah's help!

Everything was ready in time.

'Sergei,' my father ordered, 'harness three sleighs for this evening.'

We pricked up our ears.

'Papa, where are you going?'

'To the station. To collect our guests.'

'Can we come?' I asked.

'Heavens no. We shan't get back till terribly late. Mamma isn't coming either.'

That placated us. We were sent off to bed; but before we went to sleep we slipped in to have one last look at the new room, which had been finished just in time for our festivities. It was splendid: the waxed floor shone like a mirror, hanging on the walls there were portraits of our ancestors, looking-glasses, and opposite them two big paraffin chandeliers. In the middle of the room stood a long table. It was covered with a white cloth and laden with china and food ready for the expected guests. In the bedrooms, beds had been made and aired for them. We counted: seven beds. So there were seven guests coming. Then we went off to bed, very excited, our heads full of the joys and pleasures awaiting us in the days ahead.

Next morning we were all up early, and every minute seemed to drag on for ever because we were so looking forward to seeing our guests. After their tiring journey and such a late supper they slept in much longer than was usual. But at long last they appeared: first Dmitri Alexeyevich Dyakov, my dear godfather, portly and benevolent, whom we called Miklikseyich because it took far too long to say all of his name, and whom we all treated very familiarly, even though he was older even than papa. He was always in a good humour and ready for a joke, so we were all already laughing as we rushed to throw our arms around his neck.

'Now then, Tanya, let me have a look at you,' he said. 'What's this? Why have you still got a figure like an egg? Bigger round the middle than you are at the bottom and the top?'

I laughed, but I was really a little bit put out, and lost no time in giving my godfather a sly dig in return.

'Do you know, Miklikseyich, I had a whitlow on my thumb. I had a plaster on to draw it out, and then a bandage on top of that. It was so fat, my thumb, that we called it Miklikseyich.'

Then came Dmitri Alexeyevich's daughter, pretty Masha, tall and blonde. She was slender and supple with such delicate bones. I was very fond of her, and above all I admired her. She was with her companion Sofesha, a stocky, goodhearted girl. The Dyakovs had also brought our charming cousin Varya with them, vague and head-in-the-clouds as ever.

During the day another cousin arrived from Tula. This was Lisa, who came with her husband Leonid Obolenski and her brother Nikolenka Tolstoy. These last two were also well loved at Yasnaya Polyana. Leonid was merry and goodnatured, and what was more extremely accommodating, so that he always gave way to all my demands.

'Leonid,' we cried, 'let's go skating!'

'Don't be silly! You can't be serious! I should only fall straight on my bottom, and then I'd break the ice for you all,' portly Leonid answered.

But we gave him no peace.

'Never mind, let's go. Lisa's coming, and so are Masha and Sofesha, and Nikolenka . . .'

Eventually Leonid gave way, and we all flocked out to the pond, where a skating rink had been cleared for us. And there was also a big toboggan for us to whizz down the hill on. Merry falls, clumsy flailings and comical capers, tumbles in the snow. We children all vied with one another in our attempts to dazzle the grown-ups with our virtuosity on the ice.

Laughing, pink with the cold and exercise, we scampered back to the house. We weren't allowed into the big drawing-room. Mamma and the guests had begun decorating the Christmas tree and arranging all the presents on tables. There was a pleasant piney smell floating in the air.

We had Christmas dinner in papa's new study downstairs. During the meal we heard the sound of lots of voices out in the hall. It was the village children and the servants' children arriving. They stamped their feet, whispered, bumped and pushed one another, and from all these tell-tale sounds we knew they were burning with the same impatience as ourselves.

The meal seemed to go on for ever. When we had had our fill of roast turkey the servant brought in the plum pudding, which was sprinkled with rum and set ablaze. The servant held his head well back so as not to get his face scorched. I stared at the flickering flame, hoping and hoping it wouldn't go out before it was my turn to be served. We were all very proud because the pudding had been our handiwork. The day before, under Hannah's supervision, we had seeded the raisins and blanched and pounded the almonds.

The meal came to an end at last and we went upstairs. As we passed the doorway into the hall we exchanged conspiratorial glances with the children out there we knew. We glimpsed the cook's sons, Egor and our friend Senya, who cooked us such amazing larks every ninth of March, the laundress's pretty daughter Natasha with her dark eyes and ringlets, her sisters Varya and Masha, and lots of other children. They gave off a smell of cold and sheepskin. Upstairs we were shut in the small drawing-room while mamma and the guests went in to light the tree in the big drawing-room.

It was absolutely impossible for us to keep still; we ran from one door to another trying to peer through the chinks, or else we strained our ears to catch what they were saying through in the big room. Then we heard a great galloping on the stairs. It was so loud it might have been a whole herd of horses. Our excitement reached its peak. We knew that the little peasant children had been let in, and that someone would come now to let us out. And so they did. As the noise of charging feet subsided slightly we could make out mamma's footsteps coming nearer. The double doors swung wide, and we were allowed in.

At first we just stood rigid with amazement at the sight of the huge tree. It reached almost up to the ceiling, shimmering with its vast array of candles, glittering with an infinity of shining baubles. Around the tree were the Dyakovs, Varya, Lisa, Leonid, and Hannah. Mamma beckoned us closer so that we could look at our presents, which were laid out on tables near the tree.

Dazed with wonder I soaked it all in. I examined my own presents, then my brothers'. After that I walked around the tree gazing up at all the toys and treats hanging from its boughs. I searched first of all for the 'skeletons' I had dressed and the decorations I had made. But there was so much else besides. Here, gingerbreads shaped like lions, like fishes, like cats. There, arranged in filmy muslin nests, candies wrapped in glittering paper decorated with silhouettes of swans, butterflies, and other creatures. Elsewhere, simply gorgeous little bottles in the shape of baby goats, piglets, and geese, all filled with red, yellow, or green scent. The piglets and the kids had stoppers in their mouths, the geese had them in their tails.

The village children stared from a distance at all the things hanging on the tree and pointed their fingers at whatever had caught their fancy most . . .

And papa? Where was papa? I cast my eyes about for him, for I could never be really completely happy if he wasn't sharing my joy. And yet my seven year old's heart sensed instinctively, obscurely, that this delight I was experiencing would find no strong echo in his. All the same I looked round for him. There he was, standing apart in his everlasting grey smock, hands tucked inside his belt. I looked across at him with a smile. He smiled back, a kind, indulgent smile in which I could sense the unspoken message: 'I'd rather you didn't delight so in such idiocies, and that they didn't tempt you with such things. But what can I do? I'm just not strong enough on my own to fight them all. But never mind, I'm glad you're enjoying yourself, because I love you . . .'

I seized hold of his big hand, which I loved so, and even though he disapproved of it all I led him over to my table and showed him my presents. There was a gold medallion in a case from Lisa. And the Dyakovs, having decided that I was too big for a doll that year, instead of the usual Masha had given me a real cooking set made of copper. They'd also given me a sewing kit with everything in it I could possibly need: ribbons, pieces of cloth, needles, thread, hanks of yarn, hooks and eyes, pins, scissors, a thimble, and I forget what else. I was absolutely thrilled with this new acquisition and always took great care of it. I still have it to this day, even though Dmitri Alexeyevich, Masha, and Sofesha, are all now departed from this world.

When we had thoroughly admired the Christmas tree and the presents, it was time for mamma to go round, helped by Hannah and the guests, handing out the 'skeletons', gingerbread, apples, sweets, and the gold- and silver-wrapped nuts to the other children. Then everyone went home, laden down with presents and treats.

We all bore our gifts off to our room and put them away in our lockers. Among his other presents Ilya had been given a cup that had particularly caught his fancy. He paraded round from guest to guest, holding his treasure up to them with the utmost precaution so that they could admire it. Then, eyes still riveted on the new gift, he set off back to our room. But between the big new room and the little drawing-room there was a step he still hadn't got used to. He tripped and fell absolutely flat. The pretty porcelain cup was in fragments! Ilya burst into tears.

'It's . . . it's . . .' he stammered between his sobs, '. . . not my fault . . . It was . . . the architect's fault.'

He had heard the grown-ups criticizing the architect for this awkward step, and it seemed to him that it would be better somehow if he accused someone else of his misfortune. Mamma picked him up and set about trying to comfort him. She told him that it wasn't the architect who was responsible for his accident but himself, because he should have looked where he was going. Papa, who had as usual been observing the scene attentively, noted this wish of Ilya's to make someone else responsible for his own clumsiness and poked gentle fun at him. This made Ilya more upset than ever, and he went off to bed with a very heavy heart and still in floods of tears.

Ever since that day the phrase 'it's the architect's fault' became part of the family vocabulary. Whenever one of us blamed chance or some other person for our own errors, someone else would unfailingly remark with a sly smile that it must undoubtedly have been 'the architect's fault'.

23

The big item on the next day's agenda was a fancy-dress party.

The costumes were all ready, and immediately after lunch we all went to our own rooms to put them on. We all made great haste because we didn't want to be late. Mamma ran from room to room helping us all. Then at the last moment she quickly changed her own frock and dressed up as a peasant woman.

After that she went looking for uncle Kostya and asked him to sit at the piano and play a march. We all assembled outside the doors into the big new room and waited to be told when it was time to make our entrance. Mamma sorted us out into couples. The first chords of the march rang out and we advanced into the room two by two.

At the head of the procession came Ilya and Kitty, who was a little English girl invited specially for the occasion. Ilya was a little girl with a red skirt, Kitty was a clown. Seryozha and I came next. I was dressed as a French marquis: blue jacket and breeches, white stockings with court shoes, and my hair powdered white. My escort, Seryozha, was dressed as my marquise. Lisa had come as a mujik, Masha Dyakova as a peasant woman. Varya was a clown, and mamma another peasant woman. Bringing up the rear came a little old hunchbacked man in a mask. He had a simply huge hump on his back, long white hair, a beard, a stick in one hand, and his tiny little feet were encased in ladies high-heeled shoes: it was Sofesha.

We peered at one another trying to guess who was there behind the masks, then everyone began to dance. We didn't actually know any particular dances, so we just hopped about wildly in all directions doing as best we could. But we enjoyed ourselves thoroughly, perhaps even more than if we'd been executing some correct step. And all those who could play the piano took turns providing us with music.

Suddenly it seemed to me that the general air of merriment had slackened a little. I looked around: neither papa nor Miklikseyich was to be seen. Nor uncle Kostya. And where was Nikolenka? We were already beginning to be just a little bored . . . But what was all that commotion over by the doorway? I turned. A bear-trainer was making his way through the crowd of domestics clustered at the door accompanied by his two bears and a nanny-goat. (In those days it was still customary for performing bears to be taken round the villages and big houses. Later on such exhibitions were banned because some of the bear-trainers maltreated their animals.)

I could see right away that they weren't real bears, but people with their big winter coats on furry side out. But I was frightened all the same, and when they came near me I ran away shrieking. The two bears growled a little, but their trainer calmed them down. The nanny-goat was very funny. Her body looked like a big bundle stuffed inside a sort of big bag, her neck was a stick, and on top of it she had not a head but just two flat pieces of wood. These two little boards were supposed to be her mouth, and they opened and closed when whoever was inside pulled strings. No one could have said exactly why it was called a nanny-goat, but in my young day all the children just knew somehow, without being told, that that's what it was. And very impressive she was too, especially when she opened and closed her 'lips'.

The trainer made his bears do all sorts of amusing tricks. They imitated children stealing peas, then a beautiful lady admiring herself in a mirror, then an old peasant woman hobbling off very grumpily to do some nasty job or other. And meanwhile the trainer kept up a running commentary spiced with all sorts of jokes that had the audience in fits of laughter.

The music began again, even merrier and more irresistible, and the nanny-goat, the bears, and the trainer all began to dance. The nanny-goat was very funny with her wooden lips going clickety-clack. We children didn't dance, we were quite content just looking on and trying to guess who was underneath the disguises. With the trainer it wasn't difficult. Who else could have such a big paunch or say such funny things but Miklikseyich?

'Miklikseyich!' we all yelled, 'it's Miklikseyich!'

'And that's papa,' we said, edging a little nearer to the nanny-goat. Yes, it was papa who was dancing so comically and clicking the little boards. And then we saw that the two bears were uncle Kostya and Nikolenka.

In the end they got so hot that they had to go away and come back in their ordinary clothes, all except for Nikolenka, who had got so caught up in the party spirit that he dressed up next as an old woman. He made himself a hump, pulled on a dress, put on a bonnet, then a terrifying yet somehow comic mask with a great hooked nose and one enormous tooth sticking out. He burst into the room in this get-up and asked Sofesha to dance the trepak with him. Sofesha, still dressed as a little old man, accepted the invitation, and they were so comic dancing together that we all laughed till we cried.

But for the children it was time for bed. We were dripping with sweat and quite worn out—and yet we didn't want to go to bed in the slightest . . . Surely we didn't want to carry on dancing and hopping about? Oh yes we did . . . Besides, we'd heard that after dinner 'the big ones' might be going in a troika to the station with the Dyakovs. They were leaving that evening. I gazed out of the window. It was a beautiful clear night with a full moon. The old birches in the garden were absolutely still beneath their sparkling covering of frost. Ah, when would I be grown up and able to do just as I liked?

But Hannah was adamant, and we had to say goodbye to our guests. I kissed Masha Dyakov with particular tenderness. She took me on her lap and petted me. I would see her again. All the same, I would have liked to stay with her longer . . . The tears were all ready to flow, but Miklikseyich diverted my thoughts in time with one of his jokes. With Hannah as escort, Seryozha, Ilya, and I trooped off to our vaulted room, to our iron rings hanging from the ceiling . . . I wanted to laugh and cry all at the same time.

Next day the Obolenskis left, then a few days later our cousins Varya and Nikolenka.

24

After all the excitement of Christmas it was time to get back to our studies.

One morning when she came in to say good morning to us, mamma noticed there were spots on my face. Worried, she pressed her lips against my forehead to see if I had a temperature, then asked me if my head ached and made me put out my tongue. Since I did have a slight headache she sent me back to bed, even though she wasn't at all convinced that I was feverish.

Before long the same sort of spots appeared on my brothers' faces and hands. We were all kept in bed. Hannah and mamma fussed over us, but we didn't seem to be really ill. My headache had vanished, and although the spots had now spread all over our hands none of us felt at all unwell.

It was very nice being able to drink tea with rapsberry jam instead of the usual old milk, and being let off private study and lessons. But staying in bed, when we wanted to be out running and skating, was very hard. We kicked up such a row playing about on our beds that Hannah sometimes lost patience with us.

'What sort of patients do you call these?' she said to mamma. 'They're all as healthy as the day is long.'

'But they do have that rash,' my mother rejoined. 'There's quite an epidemic of measles down in the village. I'm sure ours must have caught it playing with the peasant children.'

'But they'd have temperatures with measles,' Hannah objected.

'Oh Hannah, you know it's possible to have measles only very slightly. I think this must be a very mild form that's all.'

To settle the matter one way or the other they sent over to Tula for dear Nicolai Andreyevich Knerzer, our old family doctor. He duly appeared, wished us all good day, and pulled up a chair beside my bed. He examined the spots on my face and hands, looked to see if there were any others on the rest of my body, felt my forehead, took my pulse, and made me put out my tongue. He gazed at me thoughtfully through his spectacles, then over the top of his spectacles, and I thought I caught a glint of mischief in his eyes.

Knerzer then went through the same procedure with my brothers.

'Well?' my mother asked.

'The children don't have measles,' he said finally. 'They have no fever, and the rash is confined solely to their faces and hands. Have they perhaps been in contact with some substance that might produce a rash of this sort?'

'I don't know,' mamma said. Then turning to us: 'You haven't been rubbing anything on your faces and hands, have you?'

A thought flashed into my mind: it was the scent in glass piglets and kids and geese that we'd been sprinkling on our hands and faces. I wriggled over on to my stomach and buried my face in my pillow, giggling helplessly and kicking my feet under the bedclothes.

'What's the matter with you?' my mother asked.

'It's the geese!' I cried. 'And the kids and the piglets!'

The boys realized what I meant and repeated in chorus:

'It's the geese! And the piglets! The chickens! The kids!'

Knerzer looked from one to another of us in bewilderment, obviously thinking we'd taken leave of our senses. Then after we'd explained to him what it was all about he told us to empty all the little bottles into the slop-pail. We were told to get up and dress. And since we'd all had quite enough of staying in bed we were only too glad to obey. We emptied the piglets and the kids through their mouths, the geese through their tails, then donned our clothes without regret and life resumed its normal course.

25

That January our daily lessons were supplemented with a new and fascinating occupation.

Before his marriage my father had already taken an active part in educating the peasant children. He had turned part of the house into a school, brought in schoolteachers, and begun publishing an educational magazine called *Yasnaya Polyana*. In May 1865 he wrote to Fet: 'I hope to make a book out of it all, with my conclusions on these three years of fascinating work.'

Having completed his four *Readers* and his *ABC*, papa decided he really ought to try them out for himself, so he resumed what had previously been a favourite pursuit of his, that of teaching the local peasant children.

Seryozha and I could already read and write quite passably. Ilya, then about six, could only just read and was very bad at writing; nevertheless he announced that he was going to teach the youngest class. Papa agreed and the lessons began.

They lasted for slightly over two hours every day, beginning after our dinner, which was served between five and six, and continuing till it was time for us to go to bed. Papa took the boys' class in his study. The girls were mamma's responsibility, and she taught them separately in another room. We three children taught the absolute beginners their ABC. Our classroom was the hall, where we had a big cardboard placard hung on the wall, and fat Ilya, a big pointer clutched in one hand, would try to teach the alphabet to rows of stolid little children much the same size as himself.

He was very stern with them. One day I overheard the following dialogue as he indicated the letter A with his pointer and addressed a little boy.

'What letter is this?'

'I don't know.'

'You don't know? Outside with you then!'

Then it was the next child's turn.

'What letter is this?'

'I don't know.'

'So you don't know either! Outside with you!'

He put all the beginners through this kind of examination, and concluded from the results that he had been allotted all the stupidest pupils.

Gradually a class of 'nomads' came into being. This was how we referred to all those who either wouldn't or couldn't do the lessons properly. They were allowed to sit in on any class they chose and just listen, on condition they didn't disturb anyone. And oddly enough, as it turned out, these 'nomads' took no longer to assimilate their alphabet than the others who stayed in the same place.

We became great friends with the visiting schoolchildren. They brought us simple playthings, biscuits, and treats. Also we enjoyed teaching our little ones enormously, because they learned so quickly and with such pleasure.

On February 2nd 1872, mamma wrote to her sister: 'After the holidays we had the idea of starting a school, and now we have thirty-five children coming up to the house every day. Everyone is giving a hand, Seryozha, Tanya, uncle Kostya, Lyovochka, and myself. It's very hard supervising ten pupils all at once, but on the other hand it's quite enjoyable and pleasant. We have shared the work out between us: I took eight girls and two boys. Tanya and Seryozha make quite passable dominies. In only one week the children have all learned their alphabet and the rudiments of spelling . . . What really spurred us on to teach them to read was simply the crying need for it, and the fact that they all work away with such enjoyment and enthusiasm.'

'The school is still going ahead,' she wrote in March. 'It's working well . . . Every day we have a mob of children, a great racket, reading aloud, and telling them stories, sometimes my head quite spins with it all.' In another letter, also written in March: 'We keep on with the school. It's going well still. Our pupils bring the children little rustic offerings: bits of carved wood, rye-paste larks. After class they carry Tanya around in their arms, and sometimes they get rather rowdy, but they've almost all learned to read now, and not at all badly either.'

At much the same time, on February 20th 1872, papa was writing to Fet: 'All this winter we've been using the new room. And another novelty: I've opened a school again. My wife, the children, all of us take classes and are pleased with our results . . .'

Towards the end of winter, in April, probably rather tired of the school by now, mamma wrote to her sister: 'Every morning I have the children's lessons to supervise, and every afternoon there's the school. It's hard, but it would be a pity to give up now. It's going so well. They can all read and write, not with perfect fluency, but correctly. Only a little while longer and they will have it for the rest of their lives.'

When summer came the school was closed, and the next year it didn't reopen.

26

That winter our dear Hannah was unwell again, which worried and upset my parents no end. In addition, she kept receiving letter after letter full of bad news from England. During the summer she had heard of the death of her eldest sister, who had left a husband and two little girls. Then, in early winter, she received news that her father was very ill. Hannah had begun to think of going back to England, but she was still wavering, waiting for further news first.

Mamma mentions all this in several of her letters to her sister. 'Hannah is intending to leave us. She is ill, losing weight, and depressed . . . Seryozha has burst into tears on three occasions; I'm afraid the children will grieve terribly if she goes. I'm very upset myself, I shall be losing not only an excellent governess but a friend too if she does leave.'

Shortly after, the news reached us that Hannah's father had died. Hannah cried a lot, her grief was intense, and we shared it, weeping with her for the old gardener in Windsor whom we had never seen, but whom we had loved all the same through his daughter.

Then letters began to arrive from England that left us perplexed and indignant. The husband of Hannah's dead sister wrote asking her to marry him. And Hannah's relatives pressed her to accept, so that the two little orphans would have a new mother to look after them.

Hannah wavered. Loving her as I did with all my heart, and sensing the battle that was going on inside her, I divined her hesitations, which filled me with despair. Was it possible she would abandon us? That she would inflict such grief on us? On us who loved her so much we couldn't imagine life without her. Did our love give us no rights over her? Could she who was so dear to us, whom we needed so much, really break the bonds of affection that bound her to us just like that, with impunity? Was she capable of doing such a thing, she who not only said but proved by her every action how much she loved us?

All this I felt rather than thought. 'Will she do such a thing, will she do it?' I asked myself night and day. In the end she didn't. She felt, as we did, that our attachment to her had created obligations that bound her to us till death.

She stayed. But the inner struggle she had endured left her depleted. Her health had been undermined.

27

There had been hopes that we would all be spending the summer on our property near Samara, out in the steppe, so that papa and Hannah could take the kumiss cure and recover their strength. But the plan had to be abandoned, for a variety of reasons. One of the main ones was that the house there was simply not equipped for a family as large as ours. So it was decided to postpone the visit by the whole family until the following year: papa would go alone toward the end of the summer.

Mamma wrote to her sister Tatyana asking her to come and spend the summer with us at Yasnaya Polyana. She accepted, undaunted by the prospect of the long hard journey—accompanied by three very young children—from the Caucasus all the way to Tula, part of which, from Tiflis to Vladikavlas, would have to be made in horse-drawn vehicles. Aunt Tanya was young, bursting with energy, and above all extremely fond of Yasnaya Polyana and all of us living there. So she wasn't to be put off by the length and difficulty of the journey.

Aunt Tanya was my mother's younger sister. They were very close, and my aunt always came to stay with us whenever she could. As a girl she had been a frequent visitor, and even after her marriage to her cousin Kuzminski she still continued to come with her husband and children and spend the summers at Yasnaya Polyana.

During the early years of her marriage this had presented no difficulty, since my aunt was living at Tula, where her husband had official duties. This meant that as soon as the good weather came she was able to move out very easily to Yasnaya Polyana and settle in with her family and a servant.

But in 1869 my uncle was appointed to a post in Tiflis, and the Kuziminskis, apprehensive of the effect so tiring a journey might have on their children, had spent the summer in the Caucasus. It had been a terrible disappointment to my mother as well as to us children.

In 1871, however, aunt Tanya did come to Yasnaya Polyana for the holidays. Since her children were by now a little older she was less worried about the journey on their account, and in addition she knew she would be giving all of us enormous pleasure. We awaited her arrival bursting with joyful impatience. In our minds the appearance of the Kuzminskis had come to represent the starting signal for a summer of non-stop festivity.

During the winter our lesson-filled life was no burden to us. But as soon as the first fine days came we began to find it wearisome. When the sun was rising earlier, brightening the young green blades of grass sprouting all over the lawn, when the first flowers were opening and the birds chirping so merrily, then it was hard to be good, hard to sit conjugating French verbs or practising our scales at the piano. We could hear the woods of Yasnaya Polyana calling. Our healthy children's bodies longed to expend their pent-up energies, our lungs craved fresh air.

Doctor Zakharin, a famous physician of the day who happened to be a good friend of papa's, had advised our parents to let us off all schoolwork during the summer, even if only for a brief period. So we were granted at least six weeks of total respite.

During those six weeks we didn't open a single book, and spent most of our time outside, gathering mushrooms and wild berries, swimming in the Voronka, our little crystal clear river, riding, or going for outings in the carriage, observing the birds, the butterflies, the may-bugs, and all the rest of God's creatures.

I think we learned just as much during those weeks of freedom as we did studying our books.

As soon as May came round my mother began getting ready 'the Kuzminskis' house', as we all called the little building that was always kept for them.

That year we awaited the Kuzminskis' arrival with extra-special anticipation. The day they were due, a carriage-and-four was sent off to Tula accompanied by several carts. Hearts thumping, unable to stay in one place for a single moment, we ran from one window to the next, straining our ears to pick up the slightest sound from outside. At last the muffled sound of a sprung carriage could be heard in the distance. We rushed to the window looking out along the birch drive.

Yes! There they were! The carriage turned into the drive, and already, inside it, we could make out a number of childish and grown-up faces. We hurtled down the stairs and rushed out to the little house where mamma was already waiting.

Yes, it was really them. There was aunt Tanya, pretty, dazzling, smiling and loving. Here was her eldest daughter Dasha, throwing herself on my neck. We hugged one another cheek to cheek. But then little Masha, toddling after her, was hoisting herself up on tiptoe and pushing us apart, wanting to kiss me too. Then Vera the baby was handed out of the carriage. And the last to climb down was Trifonovna, the Kuzminkis' old cook, very stout and dressed as usual all in white.

Everyone talked at once, the children were pulling off their coats, and we all went in together to unpack the luggage. I helped Dasha and was shown all her things.

The day of their arrival the Kuzminskis ate with us. But next day the little house's kitchen was soon humming with Trifonovna's activities. We all loved eating with our cousins, and our parents arranged a system of exchanges so that all the children should never all be at the same table: if Dasha ate with us, then one of us would go and take her place at the Kuzminskis' table. On Sundays, however, all the Kuzminskis came and ate lunch at the 'big' house.

That summer I became deeply attached to Dasha, my charming dark-eyed cousin. The fact that there was a difference of two or three years in our ages didn't stop us becoming fast friends.

Life became more entertaining. Hannah was feeling a little better and recovering some of her gaiety. Gathering mushrooms or wild fruit, swimming, everything was more fun with the Kuzminskis. Sometimes we had our big lineika [an open carriage with a single seat running from front to back] harnessed up and all went swimming in the clear, cold water of the Voronka. We had a special bathing place on the bank, with one part of it set aside for us children. Trifonovna, whom we all loved dearly, often used to come with us. She looked so fresh and clean in her white cap and apron.

'Come on, Trifonovna,' we all shouted to her, 'you get in first to warm it up!'

We felt that her big white body, always warm from her stoves, would warm the cold water up for us.

In June our family was increased still further by the arrival of a big, robust baby boy who was christened Piotr [1872–3]. A month later my father set off for Samara. He did not return until August, and by then it was the Kuzminskis' turn to start thinking about leaving.

In late summer Hannah's health once again gave cause for great anxiety. My parents didn't know what to do. In the end it was decided that Hannah should go and spend the winter with the Kuzminskis at Kutais, where the excellent climate would help her to get better. Hannah had a horror of idleness and said she was quite healthy enough to work; so she determined to take charge of Dasha and Masha Kuzminski's education.

We children weren't asked what we thought. I don't know what I would have answered if the grown-ups had in fact asked me. However intolerable I found the idea of being separated from Hannah, I realized that it was for her good that she should leave, and possibly I would not have wished to stop her. Besides, I also found consolation in the knowledge that we would be seeing her again in Samara, where it had been agreed that we were all to meet the following summer.

How I said goodbye to Hannah, what our actual parting was like, has not remained in my memory. All I remember is that it marked for me the beginning of a period of glum despair. I no longer showed any interest in anything. Everything seemed just stupid and tiresome. The house itself became empty and deserted. At night I went to bed in tears. In the morning I didn't want to get up. What for? Nothing had any meaning any longer, all joy had gone . . .

We were forbidden to go in and disturb papa while he was writing. And at mealtimes he remained silent and solemn. That winter he was particularly gloomy. I had heard the grown-ups saying he'd begun a novel set in the time of Peter the Great, but that it wasn't going well. [This book was never finished.] He was still involved with the problem of popular education as well, and often spoke about that (24). But now it left me cold. All I wanted was to talk to Hannah.

If I went in to see mamma I always found her feeding little Petya; and as soon as I mentioned Hannah or the Kuzminskis her eyes brimmed with tears. So it was better to say nothing. Then I would pay Auntie a visit. Her room was full of darkness and silence. Natalya Petrovna, her companion, whispered: 'Sssh . . . Sssh . . . Tatyana Alexandrovna is sleeping . . .'

I had already noticed that for some time now Auntie was tending to doze off extremely often. When she was awake she was still as kind and sweet as ever, but one had the feeling that she was less and less interested in the outside world, and that she was losing her memory a little. So I left Auntie sleeping and went through into the big drawing-room. I looked out of the window at the fine autumn rain. What could I do to fill the long, dismal day?

My grandmother, Lyubov Alexandrovna Behrs, who was living in St Petersburg by this time, sensed our sadness, was distressed by it, and one fine day simply appeared out of the blue. Her presence was a tremendous comfort both to mamma and myself. The whole of the while my grandmother remained at Yasnaya Polyana I never left her side. I slept in her room, did my lessons with her, and went for walks only with her.

Nature took pity on us too. The end of October brought us a succession of days so fine that even the flowers were taken in, and thinking it was a second summer bloomed again. On October 28th my mother wrote to aunt Tanya:

'We are having such splendid weather: yesterday we picked a great bunch of wild flowers only just opening, vetches, meadow-sweet, cornflowers. No one here can remember such a wonderful St Martin's summer . . .'

My grandmother did not stay very long at Yasnaya Polyana, but she had helped mamma get through the worst days of that sad time.

Hannah's departure brought my happy childhood to a close. That period of utter freedom from care, of trust in adults, of perfect love for all the creatures and people around me, had slid irrevocably into the past. I was almost nine, I had left my early childhood behind.

I have often experienced moments of great happiness since then, but that state of moral and emotional tranquillity I knew when I lived with Hannah in our vaulted room is something I have never found again.

Adolescence

I

In 1873 there were six of us children. Seryozha the eldest was ten, I was almost nine, and Petya the youngest was only a few months. Here is a description of us that papa wrote for a relative, Countess Alexandra Andreyevna Tolstoy:

'The eldest is Seryozha, blonde, really quite a good-looking boy; there is something weak, patient, and very gentle about the expression of his face. When he laughs his gaiety is not infectious, but when he weeps I find it hard to restrain my own tears. Everyone says that he looks terribly like my eldest brother. I don't dare to believe it myself. It would be too wonderful. The principal trait in my brother's character was neither egoism nor self-sacrifice, but a just mean between the two: he was not given to self-abnegation on others' behalf, but nor did he ever do harm or cause embarrassment to anyone. He was happy or unhappy alone, inside himself. Seryozha is intelligent—he has a mathematical mind—and does not lack artistic sensibility. He is a very good pupil, very good at jumping and gymnastics, but he has a tendency to vagueness.

'Ilya, the third oldest, is never ill; very well put together, blonde, with a high colour and a beaming face; he's not a hard worker. His mind is always on something other than what you are asking him. He invents all his games himself. Impulsive, violent, always ready for a fight, yet with an affectionate, sensitive nature . . . He likes eating and being left in peace . . . Original in everything. When he cries he flies into a rage at the same time, and that's unappealing; when he laughs we all laugh . . . This summer we went swimming together sometimes; Seryozha had his own horse and I took Ilya up with me. One morning I came out of the house and they were both there waiting for me, Ilya with his hat and towel, very neat, beaming; Seryozha just that moment arrived, panting, without a hat.

' "Find your hat, otherwise I shan't take you."

'He rushed hither and thither, but no hat.

' "It's no good. Without a hat you can't come . . . Let this be a lesson to you, you're always losing things."

'He was on the verge of tears. I set off with Ilya, wondering whether he was going to express any compassion for his brother's plight. Not at all. He was all exuberance, chattering on about horses.

'My wife found Seryozha in tears. She searched in vain for the hat. Then she began to suspect that her brother, Lev, had put on Seryozha's hat when he went out fishing earlier that morning. She wrote me a note telling me that the bearer was probably not responsible for the loss of his hat and that she was sending him after us in his cap. Her suspicions later proved correct. I heard the sound of running feet on the landing-stage. It was Seryozha. He had lost the note on the way and began sobbing. Ilya too, and even me a little.

'Tanya is eight. Everyone says she looks like Sonya. I believe that because it is self-evident. If she had been Adam's eldest daughter and there hadn't been any children younger than herself she would have been miserable: her greatest pleasure is helping with the babies. There is no doubt whatever that she derives a physical happiness from holding, from touching their little bodies. Her dream—a conscious one now—is to have children. Recently we went over to Tula to have her photograph taken. She asked me to buy a penknife for Seryozha, then various other things for this one and that one. She knows exactly what will give everyone most pleasure. I didn't offer to buy anything for her, and she didn't think of herself for a moment. On our way home:

' "Tanya, are you asleep?"

' "No."

' "What are you thinking about?"

' "About when we get back home. I shall ask mamma if Lyova has been good, then I shall give him his present. Seryozha will pretend he isn't all that pleased with his, but he will be really."

'Fourth comes Lev. Sweet, bright, a lively mind, a winning manner. Everything he wears seems to have been made to measure for him. He imitates everything you do, and very well, very skilfully.

'Fifth is Masha. Two years old. A sickly, puny child. Body white as milk, hair curly and very blonde, big blue eyes, with a strangely serious and profound look in them. Very intelligent and completely without beauty. She will suffer, she will search, but in vain, perpetually in quest of the inaccessible, and will remain an enigma.

'The sixth is Petya. A colossus, a big faf baby, adorable in his bonnet. Always wriggling to get out of his swaddling-clothes.'

2

In the autumn of 1872 a German tutor named Fedor Fedorovich Kaufman was engaged for Seryozha and Ilya. Our friend Fet had recommended him because he'd been tutor to his nephew and the boy's parents had been very pleased with him.

Kaufman made a preliminary visit to present himself and make our acquaintance. Both parties were pleased with what they saw and he committed himself to taking up his duties at Yasnaya Polyana in mid-October. 'I thank you heartily for Fedor Fedorovich,' papa wrote to Fet. 'He has been over and has promised to start here on the sixteenth. I like him a great deal.'

We children awaited our new tutor with great impatience. He was to teach me German, and the three boys were going to be living with him in the vaulted room so dear to my heart.

This meant that little Lyova, who was still not quite four, had to leave the nursery he had been sharing with Masha and move downstairs with his brothers and Fedor Fedorovich. I can still see him, so sweet with his curly blonde hair, standing at the top of the stairs and clinging to the bannisters because he didn't want to go down. Fedor Fedorovich, already several steps lower down, turned and looked up with a smile, urging Lyova to follow him. The little figure hesitated:

'I don't really want to go down . . . I shall start being bad down there . . .'

Mamma was upset at having to make him go, but it had to be done. She would have to scrap all her careful domestic rearrangements and start all over again if he didn't go downstairs and live with the boys. I too felt sorry for him. I fathomed in some obscure way that he wanted to keep his soul pure and tender for as long as possible, that he didn't feel ready to leave his nursery, where everything was sweetness, warmth, and innocence. But the wheel of life cannot be halted to ease the heart of one small child. He was made to move in with the big boys, down there where he was afraid of 'becoming bad'.

I too was obliged to move. Out of the room where I had spent my whole childhood with Seryozha, Ilya, and Hannah my adored governess.

And for a while I remained without companions; I slept upstairs with Dunyasha the housemaid. She was always up in the morning long before me, because she had her housework to do, so I would have to get up and dress on my own. Those merry mornings with Hannah and my brothers were a thing of the past. I was destined to total solitude.

At this time I felt abandoned and unhappy. The boys had moved away from me. I saw them only rarely. They lived downstairs with Fedor Fedorovich, whom they soon began calling Fo-Fo and with whom they had long conversations about hunting, guns, dogs, and horses. I was excluded from these conversations. I saw just as little of my mother, who was perpetually feeding her many children, sewing on her machine, or copying out papa's manuscripts.

As for papa himself, any companionship with him seemed out of the question. He spent all his time 'working'. And when he wasn't actually 'working' he was tired. He seemed to be not really there, and unaware of our presence. We understood that his 'work' was very important, and I realized that all my unhappiness was as nothing beside that work. Consequently I never plucked up sufficient courage to tell him about it. If I had done so, and if I had been able to make him understand my state of mind, perhaps he would have found the words to reassure me and comfort me. But I had turned too far in upon myself, I kept everything jealously to myself and wasn't able to tell anyone about the distress I was going through.

I had got so into the habit of concealing my thoughts and feelings that the results verged on absurdity. When asked something, my first reaction was always not to tell the truth, to invent something, anything, simply so that no one should see what was going on in my heart.

Here is an example. One day mamma was giving us French dictation. Ilya was a slow writer, so I had a lot of time to spare. For something to do, after every phrase of dictation I closed the top of my inkwell so that I could calculate how many lines it was possible to write with one dip of ink.

While we were writing papa came in. He leaned over me to look at my dictation. Noticing that I was closing my inkwell every time I dipped my pen in it, he asked me why I was doing it.

'The ink evaporates,' I said.

'Evaporates?' papa repeated in astonishment.

'Yes,' I insisted stubbornly. 'I close the inkwell so the ink won't evaporate and get wasted.'

Papa said nothing. But next time I offered him an equally absurd and untrue explanation of my behaviour he murmured:

'Yes, the ink evaporates . . .'

Why didn't I tell him the truth? That I was simply engaging in a perfectly innocent experiment? I think it was because I didn't want anyone—even the being nearest and dearest to me—penetrating my inner world. I had locked myself away in my own solitude and I didn't want to share my thoughts and feelings, however insignificant, with anyone at all.

3

One day that autumn I suddenly got it into my head that I'd gone mad. I made great efforts to control the train of my thoughts, and did my best to concentrate on some specific object so as to prevent my mind running away with me. But it didn't matter how hard I tried, whatever I set my thoughts on gradually faded away giving place to other thoughts. In the evening especially, in bed before going off to sleep, I found myself mouthing totally meaningless phrases. I would get up again, seized with panic, trembling and soaked in sweat.

'Is it possible that all people's minds are so muddled up inside? Or is it a sign of madness?' I asked myself. I was afraid to talk about it in case I was told that it happened only to me. 'How queer it is,' I thought, 'that I have absolutely no way of knowing what's going on in other people's heads, that I can't fathom other people's thoughts . . .'

I became sullen, irritable, and unsociable. My parents, presumably realizing that I was going through a crisis of some sort, treated me with tact and kindness. That only strengthened my conviction that I was mad. 'They feel sorry for me. They talk to me like someone who's ill. They must certainly notice I say crazy things, but they don't want me to know I'm doing it . . .'

I began keeping a close watch on everything I said, and spoke as little as possible. I often compared my own words and actions with those of my brothers, fearful of appearing too different from them. I became more and more gloomy and closed in on myself.

As a distraction from my solitude I had invented a 'friend' for myself. This 'friend' existed only in my imagination. He was invisible and lived in an old lilac opposite the house. I used to climb up into the lilac, settle myself on one of its branches, and tell this 'friend' all

Top: The house at Yasnaya Polyana (*Popperfoto*)

Above: Entrance to the estate (hitherto unpublished drawing by Tatyana Tolstoy)

Below: Tolstoy's bedroom at Yasnaya Polyana (*Novosti*)

Leo Tolstoy (1910. Hitherto unpublished drawing by Tatyana Tolstoy)

Left: Tolstoy (1897. Hitherto unpublished)
'*And suddenly under the mujik's beard, beneath the democratic, threadbare smock, there appeared the aging Russian nobleman, the magnificent aristocrat.*' (M. Gorki)

Right: Tolstoy on horseback (1910. Hitherto unpublished)
'*Lev Nicholayevich, up on Delire, urged his horse deliberately into the thickest of the snow, then gave great cries of triumph as his mount floundered victoriously through.*' (V. V. Chertkov).

my secrets, my dreams, my sorrows. Afterwards I always felt much better.

As time went by I became so accustomed to having this friend, and so fond of him, that I began writing a story in which I described my imaginary companion. But then one day I was seized with panic.

'Is this a symptom of my madness? Who else, apart from me, would understand how my "friend" can live up there in the lilac?'.

I tore up my manuscript and ceased my visits to the lilac.

4

Ah, if only I could have been back with my dear Hannah, even for just an hour! Even though I was ten now I would have clambered up on to her lap, leaned my head against that firm breast, and relieved my tormented heart with torrents of scalding tears. Hannah would have understood me without my having to speak. I could almost hear her voice, saying (in English): 'Don't cry child, things are not so black as they seem to you.' And I would have believed that things were not so black. But she wasn't there. She was so far away, there in the Caucasus.

I transported myself in thought to Kutais. That was where my aunt and the Kuzminski family were that winter. And Hannah was with them. I often envied my cousins Dasha and Masha. 'How happy they must be with Hannah. She is so clever at making life nice and full of things to do . . .'

A lively correspondence had been established between Yasnaya Polyana and Kutais. Mamma wrote to my aunt Tanya Kuzminski: 'I received your letter, and Hannah's. I'm happy you get on so well with her. I was sure things would go well between you. But getting your letters made me feel so alone and sad that I wanted to cry . . . Read her (meaning Hannah) my letter; by which I mean I have no secrets from her. I used to tell her everything, all my sorrows and my joys . . .'

'I'm so glad Hannah is feeling better,' mamma wrote in another letter. 'Tell her to give us more details about her health. We talk about her often and think about her constantly, especially Tanya and I. We've had a photo taken of Tanya for Dasha and Hannah.

'The boys, Seryozha particularly, have taken a great liking to Fedor Fedorovich. He's very good with them; he makes them cardboard

D

boxes, puts all their clothes and things away very neatly, and makes sure they never have any buttons missing. He is bringing on their German very well too. And loves and spoils Lyova so much that he's always tucked away downstairs and we scarcely see him . . .'

'Tanya longs to visit Kutais,' mamma wrote in another letter to aunt Tanya. 'She says her whole happiness is there with Hannah and Dasha . . .'

One joy came to brighten my loneliness: a parcel with my name on it sent from the Caucasus. Hands quivering with excitement, I undid the string, unwrapped the canvas covering, and took out a wonderful white cashmere hood, exactly like Dasha's, then a pair of little Caucasian boots, and a letter! Even before trying on my presents I tore open the letter. It was from Hannah, describing her life in the Caucasus and telling me of her great affection for Dasha and little Masha (1). I felt a little jealous at first, but then Hannah went on to say such nice things about me too that my jealousy was stilled somewhat.

'Tanya is so delighted with Hannah's letter, and with Dasha's hood and your bootees,' my mother confided to her sister, 'that she has spent the whole day jumping up and down and giving little cries of joy, looking up into our faces to see if we are sharing her happiness. We think of our dear Hannah every day, her letters are a great joy to me . . .'

5

My parents probably realized how lonely I was and decided to engage another governess. Papa went to Moscow and brought back a photograph of my future instructress, who was shortly due to arrive at Yasnaya Polyana. I liked the look of her and couldn't wait for her to appear.

'There's only one snag,' papa said, 'Her name is Dora.'

At that time papa had a hunting dog named Dora, and he was worried that the new governess might be put out at having a canine homonym in the household. He wrote to her explaining his concern and received a charming reply. The young Englishwoman informed him that she loved animals, dogs especially, and that she would be delighted to have so engaging a namesake.

This letter disposed me even more in her favour, and I welcomed her warmly. Miss Dora was young and pretty, with long blonde ringlets. I decided she was to be my friend rather than my governess. Mamma wrote to aunt Tanya on November 14th: 'Tanya is delighted at Dora's arrival. She has been so lonely and unhappy recently, missing Hannah and often crying for her at bedtime.' And in another letter: 'For all of them (meaning all of us children), Hannah is still the most important person in the world, and I'm sure they will never love anyone else as much as they do her.' Mamma, with her mother's heart, had divined the truth.

Dora slept in the same room with me, and as long as she didn't ask me to do things our relations were good. She was sweet but completely lacking in authority. In fact I felt it would be easier for me to make her do what I wanted than the other way about. If she gave me an order I just mimicked her or replied with insolence. The slightest deviation from the way things had been done in Hannah's day immediately put my back up, with the result that Dora and I would engage in interminable wrangles.

My relations with her went from bad to worse. In the end mamma decided to let her go and engage yet another governess. 'We still have Dora,' she wrote to her sister shortly before this, 'but Tanya has become very disagreeable, insolent, and ill-mannered . . . The children all criticize Dora and poke fun at her.'

I feel ashamed now when I think back to that time and my attitude to sweetnatured Dora, who was so good and so gentle. How could I have failed to realize that it wasn't love for me that had brought her to Yasnaya Polyana, but sheer necessity? Having to leave her position with us was probably a painful shock for her.

But at that period in my life I was not in a normal state. All my bad instincts seemed to have got the upper hand. Was there something or someone responsible for this, some underlying cause? I myself have no idea. All I know is that it was one of the most sombre periods of my life.

During my whole childhood, by which I mean the time spent with Hannah in the vaulted room, I don't recall a single piece of serious naughtiness or disobedience, a single 'scene'. Hannah never raised her voice. She had only to express a wish for us to execute it forthwith. And in addition—something we appreciated particularly—, she never complained to our parents about us. The unfortunate Dora, on the other hand, had no choice but to seek help and support from mamma.

6

Dora left us. Mamma wrote to the clergyman in England who had found Hannah for us asking him if he could suggest another governess. He wrote back to say that he felt able to recommend a charming young lady named Emily Tabor, who happened to be a distant relative of Hannah's.

'I shall certainly love her,' I told myself. 'She's only the niece of Hannah's brother's wife, but all the same she comes from the same family . . .' I waited impatiently for her to arrive . . . My first impression was not favourable: Emily was plain, taciturn, round-shouldered, walked very slowly and rarely smiled.

After a few weeks of calm the storms began again. I simply couldn't resign myself to obeying anyone other than my parents or Hannah. I had obeyed Hannah gladly, because of the love I felt for her. But I could not and would not submit to this stranger simply because she had been assigned the right to give me orders. There were painful scenes, arguments, and tears, which upset us both.

Mamma wrote to her sister: 'Our English girl is nice enough, but Tanya doesn't get on with her. She stands in scarcely any awe of her, refuses to get fond of her, does everything she can to madden her, and weeps ceaselessly.'

When Emily saw that she was never going to succeed in winning my affection she devoted herself entirely to poor sickly little Masha. Masha in her turn became so enamoured of Emily that she never left her side. And she got on so well with learning English that she even began forgetting her Russian, with the result that whenever some Russian word had slipped her mind she always turned to Emily for assistance.

One day at the meal table she caused us all a great deal of amusement. She wanted an apple, so as usual she turned immediately to Emily and asked, in English:

'Emily, what is iabloko in Russian?'

And it wasn't till we all burst out laughing that Masha realized she had actually spoken the Russian word she had asked Emily to provide.

7

At that time our entire day was taken up with lessons. We got up at eight, and once we'd had our tea, work began. From nine till twelve, with a quarter of an hour's break between each period, we worked first with Fedor Fedorovich, then with our English governess, then at piano practice. At twelve we had lunch, after which we were free till two. From then until five mamma gave us lessons in French, Russian, History, and Geography, arithmetic being papa's province. At five we had dinner, and from seven till nine in the evening we worked on our own at whatever individual tasks we'd been given during the day. Twice weekly a priest came up from the village to teach us our catechism and biblical history. Also twice a week we had a drawing master, a little hunchback named Simonenko who came specially on my account. My parents had decided that I possessed a talent for drawing and that I must be properly taught.

The hardest lessons of all were the arithmetic ones with papa. Outside the schoolroom I was never particularly in awe of him and even played with him sometimes in a way my brothers would never have dared. For example I liked tickling him under the arms to make him laugh, so that I could see into his big mouth with its missing teeth. But during our arithmetic lessons he was a stern, impatient master. I knew that the slightest hesitation on my part would make him start to get angry, raise his voice, and reduce me to a state of total idiocy. At first papa would be quite jolly and everything would go well. My brain was clear, I could understand the sums he gave me and work them out. But the trouble was I got tired rather quickly, and after a while, despite all my efforts, my brain refused to function any more.

I still remember the difficulty I had understanding fractions. And the impatience in papa's voice only made things worse.

'Two fifths and three fifths make what?'

Silence. Papa's voice grew louder.

'Two loaves and three loaves make how many?'

'Five loaves,' I answered in a barely audible whisper.

'Correct. Two fifths and three fifths make what?'

It was no good: I sat in silence with the tears brimming in my eyes. I was afraid to answer that two fifths and three fifths make five fifths, and that five fifths make one. It seemed too easy to be right.

Papa noticed the state I was in and softened.

'All right, have a jump now!'

I was so familiar with his teaching methods by this time that I did as he said without question: I stood up, eyes still filled with tears, and began listlessly jumping up and down on the spot. And in fact my head did immediately begin to clear. When we returned to our problem I was quite certain this time that two fifths and three fifths made five fifths, and that five fifths was the same as one. But why did papa find it necessary to make me wrestle with such outlandish problems?

Fo-Fo taught us German. He made us copy out difficult gothic letters in exercise books he himself had ruled with beautifully straight and regular lines.

The lessons with mamma were uncomplicated: she would dictate a passage to us, then correct any mistakes and make us copy out the words she'd corrected. The history lessons were even simpler still. Mamma would open her Ilovayski (2) and tell us to learn such and such a page.

Emily taught us English. And the easiest lessons of all were those with the priest. He would read us a few lines of the catechism then say: 'Now that we must remember.' And he adopted exactly the same procedure for the liturgy, the various articles used in the services, and so on.

'Now the candlestick with two candles in it, the one the deacon carries during the service, we call that a dvukiryi, don't we?' he would ask.

'Yes, yes, father, dvukiryi,' we all three chorused.

'And the other candlestick, the one with three candles, we call that a trikiryi, don't we?'

'Yes, yes, father, trikiryi,' the three voices agreed.

'Very good. Now that we must remember.'

And having been handed his honorarium our priest went off home.

It was our mother who gave us our first music lessons. But she very quickly realized that she lacked the necessary experience, so she engaged a professional teacher who had to be fetched twice a week from his home near Tula. Of us three older children Seryozha alone possessed any real gift for music. As for Ilya, as the French tutor who was to replace Fo-Fo said: 'When Elie begins playing all the dogs start howling and run away.' As for me, I was so worn out by all the other lessons that I could never summon up the necessary energy and concentration for music lessons as well.

'Why are you staring down at your book with that blank, empty expression?' the teacher would ask me, in despair at ever awakening a love of the piano in me.

8

The winter of 1872-3 was a particularly long and wearisome one for me. I simply couldn't wait for it to end. In the summer I would be seeing Hannah again.

By the spring papa was again not feeling at all well; he was constantly coughing and complained of a pain in his side. The doctors were afraid it was tuberculosis. It was decided that the whole family was to spend the summer in the Samara steppes, where papa had an estate. He was to take the kumiss cure again. And since Hannah wasn't very well either my parents invited her to join us in Samara, so that she could take the cure as well.

Papa wrote to the steward in charge of the estate telling him to make all the necessary preparations for such a large family. Our huge 'sleeper' was sent on ahead to wait for us in Samara, because the property was a hundred and twenty versts outside the city, and that last lap would have to be covered in carriages.

Hannah was sent a letter of invitation plus a detailed itinerary, since the journey from the Caucasus to our estate was a rather complicated one. The date of our departure was set for May 1873. I was so happy at the idea of seeing my dear Hannah again before long that my impatience made me overexcited and I couldn't sleep.

But fate had decreed that I should be allowed no unalloyed joys that year. In May a terrible misfortune occurred. One day papa went into Tula on business and returned in the evening with a letter from Kutais. Aunt Tanya had written to inform us of an appalling piece of news: the death, at the age of six, of her oldest daughter, the adorable Dasha.

Mamma didn't want to tell me there and then. But papa did tell the boys. Seryozha immediately ran in to mamma.

'Dasha is dead!' he said. He couldn't think of anything else to say then, so he just hid behind the window curtain and began sobbing. Then he asked:

'What about aunt Tanya? She must be so unhappy.'

The sad news reached me swiftly enough. I said nothing to anyone.

But I lay in bed weeping hot tears as I thought of my darling cousin, my friend. 'I hadn't told Tanya,' my mother wrote to my aunt. 'I didn't want her to hear just at bedtime. But the boys and Parasha told her. I went in to see her. Her eyes were shining in the dark with her tears. She was huddled under her bedclothes just crying.'

'Tanya, dear friend,' papa wrote separately, 'I cannot convey to you my feelings on hearing of the death of your adorable Dasha, my favourite (as it is now a comfort to recall). I cannot think of her and of you without weeping. I am beset by the selfsame feeling that must certainly be torturing you: forgetting, then remembering, and asking myself in terror: is it true? Will you go on for long waking up every morning with that thought: is it true she's gone? . . . I beg you, read Psalm CXXX, learn it by heart and say it over every day . . . Yes, only prayer can bring comfort. And I am sure that you have grasped the meaning of religion for the first time. In the name of heaven do not forget, do not try to forget, the grief-stricken hours you have gone through, but live with them always.

'Death is a terrifying thing to me, as I remember your saying, yet in the death of someone close, especially that of a being as adorable as a child, above all that child, there is also an amazing consolation, even in despair. Why must a child live and die? It is a terrible enigma. For me there is an explanation: it was better for her. However hackneyed those words may be they are always new and profound if we can understand them. It is better for us too, and we must become better for these griefs. I have trodden that path myself . . . You will find the necessary courage. And above all without protest, but with the thought that we cannot understand who we are and why we exist, and that we must resign ourselves . . .

'May God help you, you and Sasha [Alexander Kuzminski, aunt Tanya's husband] to bear this misfortune that we have not been forced to undergo as yet, though it hangs over us. And above all to bear it without rebellion or too lightly. Ultimately it is not a misfortune strictly speaking, but one of the great stages of life through which all men must pass . . . I arrived back from Tula with the post. Sonya came gaily out to meet me. I said to her: "A great misfortune! A great, great misfortune!" She said: "Hannah is dead?" I answered: "Someone in Kutais, but not Hannah." And without a second's hesitation, as if she had already read the letter, she said: "It's Dasha!" Why? How could she have known? She is in terrible distress, so much so that she is unable to speak. Seryozha was very upset over what you must be feeling, Tanya spent a long while weeping in her bed. Until we meet, my dear friends. May God help you through this grievous moment of your life.'

That summer began sadly for me. I had lost my best friend, my playfellow. We were all grief-stricken. The only consolation we had was the thought of seeing Hannah again soon in Samara.

9

Papa paid a visit to Moscow, where he bought everything we would need for our journey and the first few days of our stay.

On May 11th 1873 he wrote to Fet: 'I have been to Moscow, where I bought forty-three separate items to the value of four hundred and fifty rubles. So our not going this time is out of the question, not after all that.' Papa brought back grey hats and dustcoats for Masha and me, purchased from the very best Moscow shops, plus shoes, suitcases, trunks, picnic equipment, and so on, for everyone.

Each child was issued with a small personal bag for the journey. I had worked out very meticulously exactly what things I would need and set them aside. But when it came to actually packing my bag I soon realized it wasn't going to be big enough. I would have to limit myself to strict necessities: the penknife, for instance, now that really was essential. And the same went for the pencil and little drawing-book I'd made out of one big sheet of paper. If I suddenly felt I wanted to draw or write I certainly couldn't go pestering mamma for such things! Then there were all my sewing things, neatly wrapped in their cloth case: a little worsted book stuck with pins and needles, each with a length of white or black thread carefully wound round it, plus a little box of indispensable buttons and hooks and eyes. Ah, and that length of string! That would be a very sensible thing to take: it would do to make a whip if I played horses with the boys. It would even do for reins . . . Everything that wouldn't fit into my bag I took to mamma and asked her to put it in with the main luggage. She was kneeling in front of a trunk when I found her, neatly packing the piles of linen nurse was handing her. Without even turning her head, mamma listened to my request, took my bundle, and slipped it in between two sheets.

That evening she spread neat blobs of paint round a white plate and set about drawing and colouring a series of pictures to keep us amused during the journey.

My mother made dozens of these picture books during the course of her lifetime, both for her own children and for other people's; they were always a resounding success with her young readers. Which was hardly surprising. The things she managed to cram into those pictures! There were terrifying wolves carrying off little children into dark woods; a scene of mushroom gathering, another of swimming in a river; a fire with figures of children carrying buckets of water; hares stealing cabbages and carrots; a Christmas tree decorated with ginger-bread, apples, and candles; and lots of other things besides. Mamma's drawing displayed scant respect for the rules of perspective, proportion, or verisimilitude . . . The results were naive. But what a wealth of content!

One morning papa gave the order to harness up the carriages that were to take us in to Tula. Before the departure the whole household, family and servants alike, those who were staying as well as those who were leaving, trooped into the big drawing-room, in accordance with tradition, and the doors were then shut. Everyone sat down. Then after a few moments of inner recollection we all stood up again, crossed ourselves, and went down into the hall.

There were several vehicles lined up at the foot of the front steps. We all put on our travelling clothes and were then directed to the appropriate conveyance by papa, some to the barouche, some to the tarantass (3), some to the lineika (4), and some to the telegas (5). There were sixteen of us going: papa, mamma, the six children, Emily, Fo-Fo, and a number of servants. One of mamma's many brothers, the youthful and high-spirited Styopa, was also coming with us.

I had been assigned to the big barouche with mamma. Fearful that his first long journey might result in a chill, she was holding little Petya in her arms and covering him with her coat to protect him from the wind.

For me, everything was new and interesting. I had been to Tula only rarely. A journey of fifteen versts, in an open carriage, along a road that skirted the ancient and beautiful Zassyeka forest, crossed a bridge over the clear waters of the Voronka, then another over the railway, was a most exciting event.

At Tula we caught a train for Nizhni-Novgorod. My brothers and I stayed glued to the windows all the way, except when mamma called us to hand her something, or give us something to eat, or to ask us to look after the babies.

10

The most wonderful part of the journey began at Nizhni-Novgorod, where we had to change on to a boat. To realize what we felt at seeing the vast waters of the Volga stretching before us for the first time, at setting foot on a vast and luxurious paddle-steamer, you need to remember that apart from Yasnaya Polyana, and on rare occasions Tula, we had seen nothing whatever of the world before.

Finding ourselves out in that fresh river air after the tiring railway journey, walking up the gangplank on to the boat swaying with the movement of the water, was a pleasure so acute that I can remember it still. A big cabin had been reserved for us, and mamma settled herself in there with the babies. We three eldest stayed up on deck. The paddle wheels began to turn, the sailors pulled up the gangplank linking us to terra firma, and the Volga carried us gently away from the shore.

It was only the very beginning of summer, so that the river was still swollen with the spring thaw. In places I couldn't even make out the far bank. There was only water, water as far as the eye could see. The air was fresh as air can only be on water. Delighted at the opportunity to stretch our numbed legs we ran here and there all over the boat, eyes wide with wonderment and asking questions about everything we didn't understand. The sailors answered everything we asked them with great good nature. On the third class decks we saw people of all nationalities: Tartars, Bashkirs, Persians. We gazed with great curiosity at their multi-coloured garments, their turbans, their baggy trousers; we listened to their guttural speech and thought it very odd that we couldn't understand them.

By lunchtime we were as ravenous as wolves. We washed our faces and hands and combed our hair in the washroom that opened off our cabin, then we decorously took our places at the table. We were served all sorts of hors d'oeuvres, among them caviare in a goblet on a bed of crushed ice; then a clear sterlet soup, followed by a quantity of dishes each better than the one before. The captain, a very amiable man, suggested we might like second helpings, even after the impressive portions we had already unblushingly caused to be heaped on our plates.

After lunch we went back on deck. We were about to dock at Kazan. Papa told us how he had lived there once with his aunt Pelageya Ilyinishna [P. I. Yushkov (1799–1875), sister of Tolstoy's father] and attended Kazan university [from September 1844 to April 1847].

Since our boat had to take on coal there, the stop at Kazan was expected to be a fairly long one, so papa decided to go ashore with the two boys. Mamma, the babies, and I remained on board.

The refuelling accomplished, the boat sounded a long blast on its siren, people bustled to and fro on the bank and ran up the gangplank, and then we were moving away from the quay. It was just then that mamma noticed the absence of papa and the boys. She set off looking for them but failed to find them anywhere. I too ran all over the boat searching in places I thought they might be, but all in vain!

'Oh heavens!' mamma said. 'What if they've been left behind in Kazan?'

By this time the boat was already so far out into the river that it was no longer possible to make out individual figures on the shore.

Mamma rushed to the captain.

'My husband and sons have been left behind in Kazan,' she blurted out in great distress. 'For the love of heaven, please go back for them. What will happen to them in that place, without money, without papers, without any warm clothes? I'll pay for the extra coal you have to use.'

The captain heard my mother out in silence, then went up on to the bridge and called out crisply: 'Reverse engines!' The boat slowed as the water churned beneath its bows, then slowly swung round and set back for Kazan.

Mamma and I stood on the deck together and gazed anxiously toward the landing-stage. We were both fairly certain that papa and the boys were still back there on the shore, and yet not absolutely certain. Who could tell? Perhaps something terrible had happened to them? I said nothing about my fears to mamma, but all sorts of terrifying scenes flashed through my mind.

'Ilya does such silly things sometimes,' I thought. 'What if he fell in the river? Papa, or Seryozha, or both, would have jumped in to save him . . . The Volga is so deep! And it's hard to swim with your clothes on . . . A boat might have banged into them . . . Who knows what might have happened?'

We said nothing, each keeping our anxious thoughts to ourself, straining to make out the figures on the shore.

'I think that's them there!' I yelled. I could just make out a tall silhouette with a much smaller one on each side of it. Then: 'Yes, I can tell it's the boys from their jackets. I can see papa's beard now!'

Even before the boat had reached the shore we could hear Ilya's loud wails. When he was little and we took him out for walks, you remember, he used to cry when his nurse or Seryozha and I got a few steps ahead, wailing pitifully: 'I'm left behi-i-i-ind!' How much more terrible it was now! A boat had left him behi-i-i-nd!

Papa looked shamefaced. He strode smartly up the gangplank and promptly offered the captain his apologies and thanks, offering to pay for the extra fuel consumed on his account. The captain courteously refused the offer.

Later my brothers described to me how after buying some fruit in the harbour they'd gone off for a wander round the neighbouring district. Even though it was some versts from the landing-stage to Kazan itself, my father had wanted to take a look, even if only from a distance, at the town where he had lived in his youth and been a student. While he was telling the boys all about his life in Kazan the boat had left. And by the time he became aware of the fact our paddle-steamer was already no more than a tiny dot out in the middle of the Volga. Papa got very upset, then made enquiries about the next boat—but there wasn't another going to Samara till next day. Ilya naturally began to cry. What were they to do? Stuck there on the quayside they could see no way out of their situation.

Then it seemed to them that the dot was getting bigger, and before long all doubt vanished: the boat was coming back for its scatter-brained passengers.

After Kazan I saw something very strange: the Volga had grown even wider, and on our left the water was sharply divided into two completely distinct strips of colour, as though someone had unrolled two ribbons side by side, one blue and the other yellow. This was the place where the Kama flows into the Volga, and although there was no physical barrier between the two currents they flowed on for a great distance without mingling, so that you could still distinguish the one from the other by their colour.

After Kazan the right bank of the Volga grows gradually higher and more clifflike, until it finally becomes quite a small chain of mountains.

These little mountains were covered in forests, and whenever the boat went near to the shore we could make out the ancient trees clothing the slopes with their luxuriant foliage. We thought of the brigands who once used to take refuge in those forests, of Stenka Razin (6) who used to lurk there with his companions.

II

In those days, that is in 1873, there was no railway line between Samara and Orenburg. So we had to cover the last hundred and twenty versts across the steppe in various horse-drawn vehicles.

At Samara we spent the night in an hotel. Our huge 'sleeper', sent on ahead from Yasnaya Polyana, was already waiting for us in the courtyard. Next day, its six horses already harnessed up, four between the shafts plus two tracehorses, we found it drawn up outside the hotel entrance. A young lad climbed up on to one of the tracehorses. The 'sleeper' was made up of a landau and a victoria hitched together. The landau, in front, had a coachman's seat, the victoria behind had a collapsible top.

Mamma was in the landau with little Petya, his nurse, and the 'little ones', that is Lyova and Masha. Papa brought up the rear in one of the many pletushkas, light carriages, they sent out from the estate to meet us, each drawn by a pair of lively little steppe horses. The boys, Fo-Fo, Emily, the maids, the menservants, and the cook had been assigned variously to the other pletushkas. I travelled in the victoria with uncle Styopa, who had chosen to ride in the 'sleeper' in case mamma should need help.

It was a tiring journey. At the halfway point we stopped for the night at a country inn. Mamma and the little ones were found rooms inside, while papa and we older children slept outside, on straw in the unharnessed pletushkas. Sleeping in the open air was a totally new experience for me. It took me a long time to get to sleep. I gazed up at the starry sky, I listened to the horses chewing the hay the Bashkirs had given them. I could hear the mice scurrying about in the straw . . .

The dawn was so bright it took away all wish to sleep. The cocks began to crow, the cows and calves were lowing, the sheep bleating. Women got up to milk the cows with a great noise of clanking buckets. Then the big byre doors creaked open and the women drove the cattle out. When everything was quiet again I left my pletushka for the landau, where I sank back into a deep sleep. It was already quite late in the morning when I was woken up to drink my tea before setting off again.

The road ran across desert-like steppes. For verst after verst, as far as the eye could see, there wasn't a single tree, not a hollow, not a pond, not a stream . . . The steppe, always the steppe. The sun beat down mercilessly, there wasn't even a hope of shade anywhere.

'Halt!' the coachman suddenly shouted to our young postillion.

We stopped. Styopa and I got out to see what was happening. One of the tracehorses was lying on its side in the dusty road. The coachman jumped down from his seat and unbuckled the traces. The poor animal had succumbed to the heat and fatigue. It had to be left there on the road. I can still see that big, motionless body with its great curve of belly, the inert legs, the already dulled eye staring upward. The coachman climbed up again and we continued on our way.

We went on for many versts without seeing a living soul or any sign of habitation. Only occasionally did we pass through villages. But when we did the houses looked rather impressive, with wooden roofing strips instead of the thatch we were used to around Tula. Many of these even had an upper storey. The villages were always very extensive, more like small towns. The peasants drove around in light, roomy pletushkas drawn by beautiful horses. The roads were all dusty and flat.

We stopped for a while in the little town of Zemlyanki to rest the horses and take some refreshment ourselves. Zemlyanki was very much a market town. The streets were full of people buying and selling: not only all the things that human labour can produce but even that labour itself.

Papa told us that it was only another twenty versts to our house. That restored our morale and raised our spirits. After watering the horses we set off once again.

'Uncle Styopa,' I asked my travelling companion, 'are there really no woods at all here? And no mushrooms for us to pick?'

'No, there are no woods,' my uncle told me, for he had already visited our estate once before with my father. 'There is a little valley near the house where some birch trees grow. But they are not like the birches at home. They are just bushes no higher than a man.'

'And no ponds or rivers either?'

'No. Your father did have a pond dug, but the water doesn't stay in it. In the summer it just dries up.'

'And rivers?'

'There is one, about fifteen versts from the house, at a place called Karalyk. But it doesn't look at all like our rivers. It isn't one continuous stream but just a string of little ponds, all quite separate from one another.'

'And is it as flat as this everywhere?'

'No, when we're nearly there you'll see some very odd little hills. They are all made of shells and fossils. You'll be able to pick up very curious fossils that they call "devils' fingers", which are really petrified shellfish. They are made of a yellowish grey stone and really do look like fingers, only with the tip more drawn-out and pointed. This whole district we are going though was a vast sea many thousands of years ago, and the fossils we see on the steppes today were once at the bottom of that sea.'

I liked the idea of that, and couldn't wait for the moment when I'd see the little hills.

The last village we went through was Gavriloka. The landscape was still as flat as ever, but then quite suddenly a cone-shaped eminence with a rounded top rose above the horizon.

'Uncle Styopa!' I cried, 'what is that?'

'That's Shishkla [The Hump]. It's between two and three versts from the house.'

All around Shishkla we could now make out other tiny hills, but not so high and less regular in shape. Uncle Styopa explained that they were tumuli, which meant mounds inside which people had buried their dead a long while ago.

At last the house came into view. It was a small, grey, wooden building. The outhouses surrounding it were also made of wood. Beyond it I could see a felt tent, and the local people called it a kibitka.

This was where we were to spend our whole summer.

12

I began by making a tour of this new domain. Seeing over the house didn't take very long: just four small rooms surrounded by a verandah. Papa, mamma, the little ones and I were to live in those. The boys,

Fo-Fo, and Styopa were to sleep in a big barn. Out on the steppe, a few sazhenas [an archaic measure of length equivalent to about two yards] away, stood the kibitka I had seen, which was inhabited by an old Bashkir named Mahomedshah and his family. They prepared the kumiss that people drank as a cure. There were also several other buildings to house the servants, the horses, and the cattle.

Outside the house there wasn't a single tree, a single flower, a single puddle . . . The grass was dry and prickly. The only possible haven from the burning sun was provided by our vast 'sleeper', which stood in the middle of the yard awaiting the day of our eventual departure.

During our first days in the steppe our stomachs were upset by the change of diet and the heat. Mamma was worried. Because of the distance involved there could be no question of sending for a doctor. So we had to do our best with the medicines that mamma in her wisdom had brought with her.

Feeding us presented tremendous problems. For one thing all the water came from a well, and not only did it taste nasty but it was unsafe to drink. There was no white bread, and we had no yeast to make any. So we ate black bread and rusks.

We took our meals out on the verandah, even though the heat and the insects made things difficult. After the sun had set the air became more breathable. In the evenings we would gather out on the verandah again and drink tea. But even then we weren't free of the insects. As soon as the candles were lit, hard, black beetles began descending on the tablecloth. They simply rained down on to the white surface and lay there as if dead, wingcases closed and feet folded in. Then they would gradually wake up from their daze and begin running about all over the table.

After tea I went to bed, but I could never manage to get to sleep because of the heat and the lack of air. I tossed from side to side, I turned my pillow over again and again, constantly searching for some patch of coolness but never finding it. Next morning the inescapable sun rose burning into the sky once again.

I found myself totally without amusements or things to do, and began to think longingly of Yasnaya Polyana. Each day languished on eternally. I was bored. The idea of running away occurred to me. I would get up very early, very quietly, so that no one would hear me, and go back home . . . All my waking thoughts were directed at finding a means of carrying out this plan. But I needed money for the journey, and I didn't have any. What could I do? I pondered ways of obtaining the cash I needed. What about selling the ear-rings my grandmother had given me? They were gold, with real coral . . . But sell them where? And to whom? If I were to ask papa and mamma for money they would want to know why I wanted it. And if I told them they would certainly not give it to me. What about asking Styopa, and confiding my plans to him? But then he couldn't have all that much money to spare, because he was in debt. I'd heard mamma talking to him about it . . .

I decided I would just have to wait till Hannah arrived. Perhaps she would be able to relieve my boredom and make life a little more like the one we had shared at Yasnaya Polyana, in the vaulted room, when she was there looking after us all, Seryozha, Ilya, and me.

Meanwhile I did my best to share in my brothers' activities. They spent their time talking about guns and dogs. Fo-Fo was passionately addicted to shooting. It was his dream to bag at least one bustard, a species of long-legged bird very common in the steppes. They are big birds that look rather like turkeys, but they have very keen hearing, are extremely wary, and never let men get anywhere near them if they can help it.

However, by dint of sheer cunning, moving up on it under cover of a flock of sheep, Fo-Fo did manage to outwit a bustard and kill it. When I got back to the house one day I saw a sort of big board out on the verandah with a beautiful bird nailed to it, wings outstretched. Our German was very proud of his prize and wanted everyone to admire it. He was quite radiant with delight. Mamma had the bird weighed, and it tipped the scales at eighteen pounds. Then it was put to marinate, and little by little we ate our way through Fo-Fo's victim.

Apart from the bustards, which the locals called dudaks, we also saw eagles, sometimes in groups, sometimes alone. One morning, when I came out of the house after breakfast, I saw a score or so of huge black birds on the far side of our dried-up pond. I hurtled back inside to call my brothers. But by the time we came out again the eagles were unfolding their heavy wings, rising one after another into the air, and slowly flapping away across the steppe.

One day the boys revealed to me the secret of Fo-Fo's perpetually well-groomed hair.

'You see,' Seryozha explained to me, 'it isn't really hair at all. He wears a wig.'

'Yes,' Ilya went on, 'one night I woke up and I saw him standing there bald as an egg. He was shaving his neck. When he noticed I was awake he scolded me and told me to go back to sleep. I was scared and hid under the bedclothes . . .'

'Just take a good look at his parting,' Seryozha said. 'There's a seam. And you can't see any skin.'

This revelation made an enormous impression on me. I had never heard of wigs before and didn't know such a thing was possible. From then on my eyes were constantly riveted on our unhappy German's scalp. And eventually I came to the conclusion that my brothers were right, that Fo-Fo did undoubtedly wear a wig.

13

Papa did everything he could to keep us children and mamma entertained, because he was only too aware of the fact that we were all there on his account. He often took us on outings to the neighbouring villages, some Russian, some Bashkir.

Most often we went to Gavriloka to visit Vassili Nikitich, a peasant papa knew there. He was a wise, very phlegmatic old man, and papa used to discuss religion with him, especially all the various different sects with which the district abounded.

We children didn't really understand very much of what the grown-ups were talking about, but we loved drinking the delicious tea our friendly hosts provided. It was sweetened with clear, scented honey, and accompanied by cherry cakes that were also a great treat.

'Your tea is a great remedy,' Vassili Nikitich would say as he sipped the scalding liquid out of his saucer.

He had one eye covered with a white film, a ginger beard, and big liver spots all over the backs of his hands. He would listen attentively as my father talked, nodding his head approvingly and saying again and again:

'It's true . . . it's very true . . .'

One day papa took us to a Bashkir village to see a mullah (7). The place was called Karalyk. Papa had already been there during his previous visits to Samara and knew a lot of the Bashkirs there.

The road to Karalyk dipped down into a hollow, where to my utter delight I saw a real Russian birch tree for the first time since our arrival, with a proper white trunk and shiny scented leaves. But how tiny it was! No taller than a man, and as crooked and gnarled as a hunchbacked dwarf. Never mind, even looking like that I was as delighted to see it as if it had been some long-lost friend. I pulled off a sprig or two so as to sniff the smell of them and remember Yasnaya Polyana on Trinity Sunday, when the house was full of birch branches . . . At the same spot we picked some amazing flowers, something like verbena but bright, bright red, of a kind I'd never seen before.

The Bashkir village was on the bank of a little stream. Except that one couldn't really call those little round ponds with dry ground between them a stream. The Bashkir houses were solidly built, clean and well kept. The mullah we had come to visit greeted us with cordial hospitality. Before long some of papa's former acquaintances arrived, in particular a very merry old Bashkir who was referred to in the Russian fashion as Mikhail Ivanovich, and who promptly challenged papa to a game of draughts. The challenge was accepted, and the two of them settled down one on each side of the board. Whe he was perplexed over a move Mikhail Ivanovich would scratch his forehead and say:

'I must have bi-i-i-g thinking here.'

While the game was in progress our host's manservant was sent out to slaughter a sheep. And in the meantime we were offered tea and kumiss.

When the meat was cooked, the servant carried in a big dish piled with pieces of stewed mutton. I had heard that among the Bashkirs it is absolutely not done to refuse an offer of food, because it is taken by the master of the house as a grave insult. I had been told that if a guest did refuse the meat offered him, then the host would pick up a piece and smear it all over the offender's face, after which the guest was still obliged to eat it up anyway. As a result, when the Bashkir took some morsels of meat from the dish and offered them to me I took them with great alacrity and ate them without leaving a scrap. Not that I found it very hard, because the long journey had given me a tremendous appetite and the meat was tender and tasty. In those days I had not yet become a vegetarian, indeed none of us had even heard of vegetarianism.

Papa could always find things to talk about that would interest the various people he met. With the mullah he discussed religion, with Mikhail Ivanovich he joked, and with the peasants he talked about spring sowings, horses, the weather . . . And they all responded with trust and simplicity.

After the meal we went for a walk round the village and admired the flocks and horses. Mamma expressed particular praise for a pretty light-bay mare, remarking that it was her favourite colour. And papa agreed that the animal was a particularly fine specimen.

As we walked past the the tiny lakes of the Karaly river I caught sight of some white water-lilies. I was delighted by the sight of the water and the pretty flowers floating on it, but when I tried to pick one I couldn't reach it. Without a moment's hesitation the mullah's son, young Nagim, slipped off his boot-covers, then his supple green leather boots, tucked up his breeches, and waded out into the water. Having gathered a whole armful of water-lilies he returned to the bank and presented them to me. I was not accustomed to such gallantry and blushed scarlet as I stammered out my thanks.

Late in the afternoon we took leave of our kindly hosts as we waited for our pletushkas to be brought round. The pretty light-bay foal mamma had admired was tethered to the back of the vehicle in which my parents had arrived. The master of the house was making a present of it to his lady guest. In the East it is the custom to make a gift of anything a guest has praised. Mamma was greatly embarrassed.

'I really don't know what to say!' she cried. 'But why? If I had only known I would never have praised your horse . . .

She wanted to give the foal back to its owner, but papa prevented her, since he knew that it would give offence. He thanked the mullah warmly, shook him by the hand, and gave the signal to set off. The foal trotted along merrily behind the carriage while mamma loudly lamented her folly in forgetting all about these eastern customs. At the first opportunity papa reciprocated the Bashkir's courteous gesturing by offering him several gold coins as ornaments for his daughter's dress.

14

At that time my father owned huge herds of horses. He had set his mind on crossing his little steppe horses with the great European breeds in the hope of combining the strength, stamina, and spirit of the former with the beauty and size of the latter. He had engaged a whole team of keepers, trainers, and grooms to assist in the task.

I loved horses, so I did my best to make friends with all those involved in taking care of them. I got on particularly well with Lutai, a herdsman to whom papa had given the job of second coachman because of his skill at controlling even the wildest of horses.

When we were due to go on a drive somewhere, and Lutai was given order to harness a carriage, he would take a lasso and a bridle and go out into the steppe where our horses were grazing. He stood for a moment until he had picked out the animal he wanted, then began moving towards it, lasso in hand. The horses, still half wild, would back away as he came near, pressing against one another and snorting. Lutai would cast his lasso over the animal's head and pull it tight so that the horse couldn't shake it off. The beast would shy, fall, scramble up on to its knees, then collapse again, before finally calming down and lying quietly on its side as though dead.

Then Lutai slipped a bridle on the horse—he even twisted the lips of animals that were very recalcitrant—and gradually loosened the lasso. The horse's energy seemed to rekindle, and it would rise to its feet. The moment it did so Lutai leapt nimbly up on to its back, and there ensued a series of desperate efforts on the horse's part to rid itself of its rider. It bucked, kicked, came to total and abrupt halts, or galloped like a thing gone mad . . . But Lutai seemed to have been welded on to his mount, and the creature was quite powerless to unseat him. After a few minutes of this wild behaviour the horse finally wore itself out, and became so docile that Lutai was able to ride over to the herd and round up the other two horses he needed for his team.

Before long he was riding triumphantly up to the house leading two of his captures by their bridles and riding the third. Then, with the aid of our grooms, he harnessed them to the waiting lineika. When that was done, Lutai clambered up on to the driver's seat, told the grooms to take a horse each, stand in front of it, and hold it by the bridle. The animals were very restive, snorting, panting, stamping and shaking to rid themselves of flies. As soon as Lutai was firmly in the seat he shouted:

'Hey, Tanya, get in! Styopa, up! Seryozha, Ilya, up quick!'

We hurled ourselves into the lineika. Lutai shouted to the grooms: 'Stand back!'

The three men leapt aside. To begin with Lutai let the horses gallop at will, and they flew along the flat, smooth surface of the road like the wind. The lineika hurtled through the steppe at an incredible speed. Often I didn't even have time to seat myself properly and was still lying flat on my stomach, clutching the seat, as the horses flew off in their mad gallop. Then I just had to stay in that position until they had tired themselves out and slowed to a trot. After that, with my brothers' help, I was able to sit up.

As soon as the horses had quietened down Lutai took up the reins and was able to do just as he pleased with them. He would turn round to us, face beaming, and say with a jerk of his head at his now docile team:

'You saw?'

And his Mongol face lit up in a broad smile.

15

On June 13th 1873 Hannah at last arrived from the Caucasus. How I had waited for her! How my heart beat when I heard the wheels of the carriage! With what joy I threw myself into those arms where I had so often found tenderness and comfort. I was unable to restrain my tears. Mamma and the boys ran up. We were all so happy to see her, and she had a special word for each of us.

They handed down her luggage. I would have known it anywhere! We carried it into the room prepared for her, which until then I had been occupying alone. After unpacking her bag and unstrapping her travelling rug we put all her things away in a cupboard.

Hannah had arrived still weak from a recent bout of illness and saddened by the death of her little pupil, my cousin Dasha Kuzminski, whom she had just had time to get to know and love. During the last moments of her life, Hannah told me, Dasha had displayed very special qualities of soul.

'We prepared her for the Lord,' Hannah said.

And we wept gently together as we thought of her.

Hannah began her kumiss cure very conscientiously straight away, because she wanted to get back her strength in order to continue being of use to aunt Tanya. There was no question of her returning to us. I had another governess now, and the climate in the Caucasus was so much healthier for Hannah than our very cold winters at Yasnaya Polyana. I consoled myself with the hope that Hannah would come and visit us every summer with the Kuzminskis. 'My lessons and all the other things I have to do will help me get through the winter,' I told myself. 'For now I must just enjoy her company and not think about having to say goodbye again.'

With Hannah's arrival my life changed. She was able to find something of interest in everything she saw, and to make me share it. She made me aware of the unique beauty of the steppe.

'Look,' she would say, 'those vast flocks of sheep make one think of the Bible. And Mahomedshah, our Bashkir, doesn't he look just like a biblical patriarch with his white beard, his long, brightly-coloured garments, and his grave, courteous manner?'

We often ventured out for long walks together. We went as far as the Shishkla and climbed right up to the top. It wasn't easy either, because it was so high and steep: we had to crawl up the last bit on our hands and knees. As we stood on the top a light breeze sprang up, something that never happened down on the steppe. All around us we could see only infinite space fading away into a blue mist of distance.

On the slopes of the Shishkla we gathered lots of curiously shaped fossils, mostly shells of various sorts and devils' fingers.

Sometimes, in the evening, we walked out on to the steppe to admire the beauty of those limitless spaces. At night the steppe presented a picture of particular majesty. The vault of the heavens and its multitudes of stars seemed like a vast bowl upturned above us. And we humans, how tiny, how insignificant we appeared beneath that sky!

Where the steppe hadn't been cultivated vast stretches of a grass called stipa grew, its flower-plumes white and light as down. On moonlit nights, when it waved in a passing breath of wind, the whole steppe seemed to have been spread with silver velvet. We gathered great bunches of stipa to decorate our rooms.

During the day we sometimes went out into the bakchas, the fields where melons and huge watermelons lay ripening in the sun. The man who tended the fields, old Babai, picked out the really ripe ones for us. And since we had no knife we split the watermelons open by throwing them on the ground. Then we sank our teeth into the sweet, juicy flesh. The juice ran all down our chins and we got pips in our mouths, yet even as we ate we were already casting our eyes around to see if there was another ripe enough to eat.

After dark, old Babai used to drum on the bottom of an old rusty bucket as he sang strange, wavering songs.

Here and there out on the steppe we saw herds of horses guarded by argamaks, stallions specially trained for that purpose. The argamaks were very vicious, and quite capable of biting a man to death if he tried to steal one of their herd. There were also massive, slow-moving oxen, hung with tinkling bells and chewing meditatively at their cud out in the pastures. The shepherds lit fires while one of their number played a plaintive air on his pipe.

During the day, harnessed in pairs, five in line, the oxen went out to plough the rich, black steppe earth. When the ploughman cried 'Tsob' (right) or 'Tsobay' (left), they obediently veered in the direction he wanted. The heavy plough turned over clod after gigantic clod of earth as its blade drove through the virgin earth.

This ploughing was in preparation for the autumn harvest. The spring wheat was already ripe, and on our estate the first harvest had begun. The harvesters hired for the summer lived out on the steppe in their tents. Many had come with their families, and the women did their cooking in cauldrons out in the open.

In the evening, after sunset, we would see the men and women coming back from their harvesting work in the fields to their tents, where they lit fires and began to prepare their evening meal. A smell of smoke and cooking food floated in the air. The harvesters seated themselves ceremoniously around the steaming cauldron and proceeded to consume their meal in silence, each dipping into the big dish in the middle with his wooden spoon. The black sky sparked with stars. The steppe stretched away to infinity as the horizon melted into the rising dark.

Having swiftly harvested the wheat in one field the workers immediately hurried on to the next, leaving a large number of ears ungarnered among the stubble. Hannah was shocked by such waste.

'It is a great sin,' she said. 'All that has taken work to grow, and nothing ought to be wasted. Think how many people could be fed with what has been left lying there!'

Whereupon papa, who had overheard these comments, said to her:

'Then that's something for you and the children to do: go out and collect up as much wheat as you can and I'll see it's threshed.'

This suggestion appealed to us greatly, so we set about picking up the fallen ears with great enthusiasm.

'This too makes me think of biblical times,' Hannah said. 'For Ruth, you remember, went gleaning.'

Backs bent to the burning sun, we gleaned away, ear by ear, until we had collected several sheaves, which were then carried in to the threshing floor.

In Samara the wheat was threshed in the following time-honoured fashion: several horses were arranged in a circle, each with its bridle attached to the tail of the animal in front, then a man in the centre set them trotting in a ring like a merry-go-round. The sheaves of wheat were then thrown under the horses' hooves, which pounded them until all the grain was separated from the chaff.

Our gleanings produced almost a pud [about 36 lb.] of grain per head. We were very thrilled with our prowess as harvesters.

16

Meanwhile papa, Styopa, Hannah, and even little Masha, were all conscientiously drinking their kumiss every day. Each morning they trooped over to the kibitka where old Mohamedshah, always so noble looking and so courteous, made them welcome. Sitting cross-legged on the rugs and cushions spread over the floor of the tent, he began by mixing the kumiss in a leather vessel, then, with a ladle made out of Karelian birchwood, he dipped some out into a bowl and proffered it to one of his guests with a bow.

Papa always took the bowl in both hands and emptied it at one go, without taking his lips away from it once. It was a big bowl that held a whole bottleful, if not more. As soon as papa had finished, Mohamedshah, who had been waiting for this moment, ladled him out a second bowlful. Sometimes papa drank it, but sometimes he thanked his host and said he'd had enough.

I didn't drink any kumiss. I didn't like its sour taste. And since I was in excellent health no one tried to make me.

While the men were drinking their kumiss I slipped behind a cotton hanging into the part of the tent where Mohamedshah's wife Alifa and Hadya his grand-daughter lived. Alifa was a very friendly old woman, just as courteous and composed in all her movements as her husband. Hadya was a very pretty girl, slender, with rather prominent cheekbones, magnificent black eyes, and a charming smile.

The women weren't allowed to let men see their faces, so when Hadya passed through the tent in front of the kumiss drinkers she swathed her head in a fold of her black velvet caftan as she glided swiftly toward the door.

In the women's quarters behind the curtain I helped them make the kumiss. First the mare's milk was poured into long leather containers made out of horse's skin, then some already fermented kumiss was poured in to start the fresh milk fermenting, and finally the liquid had to be stirred with long sticks. The more thoroughly the kumiss was stirred the better it was. I stood on tiptoe beside one of the big burdyuks—which is what they called the leather mixing vessels— seized hold of the stick and tried to copy the way the Bashkir women stirred it. But I could never make the same soft and regular lapping noise they made.

The Bashkir women wore long flowing garments made of striped cotton. The bodice was ornamented with ribbons of every imaginable hue, sewn on all around the neckline and decorated with pierced Russian or Turkish coins. The young Bashkir girls also ornamented their long braided hair in the same way.

I also used to go out with the women to help milk the mares. I can still see Hadya's slender figure, her boots, her velvet caftan swathing her head, and the end of her long black braid decorated with coins that tinkled as she walked. I see her still, her bucket held in one hand, her eyes searching the steppes for her mares. They were never far away, because their foals were tied up only a few yards from the kibitka.

These foals always aroused a deep feeling of pity in my heart. There were ten or so of the poor creatures, all tethered by very short horsehair ropes to equally short stakes driven into the ground. This was done in order to keep their heads down and so prevent them from sucking the milk from their mothers, who were grazing nearby.

I can still see those poor foals too, their little heads pulled down, their bodies quivering with the incessant bites of horse-flies, warble-flies, and other insects. The grass was all torn up around them by the stamping of their restless hooves. The sun beat down, and it was not until nightfall that the Bashkir women came to free their captives. Then they untied them and let them run off into the steppe. It was wonderful to see the joy with which those foals galloped off toward the mares, and the way each infallibly recognized its own mother and nuzzled up to her to begin sucking.

17

One day when we were out for a walk with Hannah I spied something white in the distance, half-hidden in the grass. I ran over to look and found a little white lamb. I was enchanted.

'Hannah! Look! A lamb! Can we take it home? The shepherds must have left it behind!'

'Yes, I think we may take it with us,' Hannah said. 'No one is going to come out looking for it. There are so many sheep here that the loss of one lamb won't even be noticed. If its owner does turn up we can always give it back to him.'

I didn't much like the bit about giving it back, but that didn't stop me picking the lamb up in my arms and carrying it home with us. It must have been quite exhausted, because when we arrived at the house and I put it down again it was scarcely able to keep on its feet. I asked in the kitchen for a saucer and filled it with milk, but the lamb was still too young to drink it.

'Dip your finger in the milk and let it suck the milk off it,' Hannah said. 'It's used to sucking its mother, you see, so it hasn't learned yet how to drink with its tongue.'

I did as Hannah said, and to my great joy I felt the lamb fasten its mouth round my finger and begin vigorously sucking at it, while at the same time shaking its little tail vigorously to and fro. By this method I very gradually got my little Motka—for that was the name I had given him—back on to his feet, and soon he was growing stronger and bigger every day. He learned to drink out of a bowl. When he was hungry he came up and butted me with his curly head. During the daytime I gave him a drink every two or three hours, and even in the night-time I had to get up to give him his feeds.

As I lay asleep I would become aware of something pushing at me. I'd wake up and see my little Motka rubbing his head against me. So I got up, gave him a kiss on his pretty little pink nose, poured some of the milk I'd put ready into his bowl, then got back into bed and went to sleep again while he stood drinking and wagging his tail.

Motka followed me everywhere like a dog. He knew his name too, and when I called him he rushed over to me, making a terrible clatter on the floor with his little feet.

I have rarely loved any animal as much as I did Motka. And ever since then the sight of a white lamb has always made me think of my little foundling who brought me so much joy.

18

Another day when we were out walking with Hannah we met a very curious looking group of people. A thin, raggedly dressed Tartar was pulling a handcart on which lay a tiny baby. Beside him was a Tartar woman, equally ragged, covered in dust and leading a dirt-smeared little girl with an unkempt mane of hair by the hand. The whole family presented a picture of squalid, grimy exhaustion.

As they came abreast of us the Tartar asked:

'You wouldn't have any work for us? My wife works too.'

I knew that papa was looking for fieldworkers, so I sent them to the house.

'Tell them to speak to the master about you.'

As I had expected, the Tartar and his wife were taken on to work in the fields. They all four took up residence under the overhang of one of the barns, more or less in the open air.

Hannah was very concerned about their children. 'They are so hungry all the time,' she said; so we often went out with things to eat for them. At first the little girl was afraid of us, but then she got used to our coming and stopped hiding as soon as we appeared. She was like a little wild animal. I never succeeded in getting her to talk or play: her main concern in life was food.

When I was in our room with Hannah I would suddenly hear a little voice under the window.

'Lady! Lady! Give a biscuit me!'

'Wait there,' I told her.

I went into the dining-room and brought back whatever I could find. She would snatch the food out of my hand and gobble it down without even pausing to thank me.

I tried to get her to join in my games, but it was wasted effort. One of my pastimes was making gardens in miniature on the bed of our dried up pond. I stuck plants in the ground, scratched out paths, then dug holes and filled them with water to represent lakes. Needless to say the water soaked away into the soil immediately, leaving nothing but darker patches where it had been. The little Tartar girl watched me at my game, but when I invited her to share my activities she just burst into wild peals of laughter and rushed round ripping all my plantings out of the ground. Then she went searching for the holes where hairy tarantulas crouched in the centre of their webs, pointing at them and saying something in her own language. She was probably warning me that the creatures were poisonous and that their bite was dangerous. I knew that already, because papa had warned us, and my terror of the big spiders was such that I always gave the horrible holes where they lurked the very widest possible berth.

The Tartar and his family remained with us all the rest of the summer. Then, when the work in the fields was all finished, they departed as they had come, the man pulling their handcart with the baby on it, the woman leading their little wild girl by the hand.

19

The peasants of the Samara steppes often found ancient weapons and silverware in the ground, and one day they came to show us some of these things. Papa gave them a small sum of money in exchange for what they had brought, even though he was not really very interested in such things. Of all the antiquities unearthed nearby the only thing that mamma actually kept was a small lance covered in verdigris. These objects were found for the most part beneath the burial mounds.

We were also told that a few versts away some children had uncovered a Scythian grave. From the position of the skeleton and various other indications it was thought to be that of a mounted warrior who had been buried with all his weapons. Mamma was intrigued by what she had heard, and one day took us over to the village where these remains had been found. In the hole that had been dug out we saw some bones, a few fragments of a saddle, a pair of spurs, and one or two weapons. As soon as any of it was touched it crumbled into dust.

Disappointed at not having found anything we could take back with us, we soon decided it was time to start for home. Mamma was still breast-feeding Petya then, and by now it was almost time for his feed. We drove out of the village in our light pletushka, drawn by a pair of frisky little steppe horses, and were soon bowling along the beautifully smooth road. Then we noticed a big bank of black cloud building up threateningly on the horizon. Before long it was covering half the sky and had hidden the sun. The cloud was so low that we felt we were driving along inside a great vault. The sound of the horses' hooves and the wheels on the dusty road had become abnormally loud.

We were worried, expecting the storm to break at any moment, but no one said anything. Just then the driver reined the horses to a walk and began looking all around him with a bothered expression on his face. It wasn't Lutai who was driving but a Russian coachman who'd come with us from Yasnaya Polyana.

'What's the matter?' my mother asked in alarm.

'I'm just wondering if we're on the right road,' the man answered in embarrassment. 'I have a feeling I've taken a wrong turning somewhere. How can you ever tell in this steppe of theirs . . .'

Then he stopped altogether. We in the back were all for getting away as quickly as possible from that black cloud hanging over our heads, but the coachman turned the pletushka round and drove back the way we had come, looking for his turning. I was tense with fright and anxiety by now, but I said nothing so as not to panic mamma, who was already quite nervous enough.

'Oh Lord, lord! What are we to do?' she lamented. 'My poor Petya, he must be so hungry by now. And papa will be fretting. We're already late for dinner!'

Suddenly I spied a strange figure on the steppe, just off the road and standing quite motionless. I pointed it out to mamma.

'Look, what is that near the road over there?'

'It must be one of the local children. Lost like us I expect.'

Strain my eyes as I might I simply couldn't make out for sure what it was. It was true that it did look rather like a child, perhaps wearing a dark caftan, but the head was so small, and such an odd shape. Abruptly the figure broadened, as though it had lifted a big cape with its arms. Then, waving its cape, what I had taken to be a little boy rose slowly into the air:

'An eagle! An eagle!' we all cried.

Vast wings spread wide, the bird flapped ponderously away, while we stared up with tilted heads as the black shape against the leaden sky rose higher and higher before finally vanishing from sight.

The coachman was peering around as though once more doubtful of being on the right road. Thunder, distant as yet but nevertheless impressive in volume, rolled on the horizon. The sky was solid lead, the air unbreathable, the heat overwhelming. Suddenly a lightning flash zigzagged from one side of the sky to the other. We all waited as though petrified . . . A few seconds of tense silence, then brrrrrooom! . . . It was as though something just above our heads had been torn violently apart. The carriage was now bowling along at top speed, but we were still unsure whether we were going toward the house or away from it.

Two minutes later another flash of lightning rent the sky, followed by an even more violent thunderclap that took much longer to die away. Heavy raindrops began thudding into the dust, and soon the rain was pouring down in torrents.

At that point the coachman decided to leave the horses to their own devices in the hope that they would take us back to the house of their own accord. It was a wise move. They changed direction two or three times, but eventually we caught sight of Shishkla in the distance. Our driver had been right to trust to the horses: their instincts had not betrayed them. We would soon be home!

The rain stopped as abruptly as it had begun. Soaked to the skin, ravenous but in the best of spirits, we all ran to our rooms to change. Mamma was already unhooking her dress as she hurried in to Petya, who was yelling his head off for his feed.

And I had Motka waiting for me. As soon as I appeared he rushed toward me, beating a joyful tattoo on the floor with his little hooves. He was hungry too. I poured some milk into his bowl and began crumbling bread into it. But Motka couldn't wait. He hurled himself on his food even before I'd finished getting it ready, his tail waggling in a positive frenzy. My lamb attended to, I pulled off my shoes, my frock, and the wet underwear clinging to my body, then prepared to tuck into a really hearty meal.

20

Someone had told my father about an old hermit who lived in a cave near Buzuluk, and who was regarded as being so holy that people came from all over the place to visit him. My father had always been fascinated by people who make their religion their whole life, and since he also had business to attend to in Buzuluk, apart from his desire to visit the hermit, he decided to make the journey over there.

'Take me with you,' I pleaded.

'You can't be serious! It's seventy versts away. You'd get far too tired.'

'No, I wouldn't. Please! I really wouldn't be too tired. It's two hundred versts to here from Samara and I wasn't tired at all then . . .'

Lunch in the garden at Yasnaya Polyana
'*Conversations don't help to establish good relations, on the contrary they damage them. We should talk as little as possible, especially with those we set store by.*' (Tolstoy)

Tolstoy playing chess with his son-in-law, M. Sukhotin
'*We are evenly matched. Only he plays so calmly, whereas I, being so young, get carried away.*' (Tolstoy)

Left: Tatyana and Alexandra Tolstoy
'*Tolstoy's daughters are most engaging. They adore their father to the point of fanaticism . . . If he weren't sincere and beyond reproach his daughters would be the first sceptics.*' (A. Chekhov)

Right: Tolstoy and his grand-daughter Tanya (1909)

Tolstoy and his grandchildren Sonya and Ilya (1910)
'*Once upon a time there was a little boy who found a cucumber . . . as big as that . . . Whereupon Lev Nicolayevich would demonstrate the size of the cucumber with his two forefingers.*' (V. Bulgakov)

'Yes, but we stopped for the night, didn't we? Well, if mamma says you can then I'll take you.'

To my great delight mamma agreed. I forget who else came with us. I remember that Ilya didn't, because he had something wrong with his eyes, and he cried a lot because he had to stay behind. Hannah didn't come either.

The hermit lived all alone in a cave on whatever people brought him. He spent all his time praying and talking with his visitors.

I remember the awe and dread I felt as I walked into the dark, low, dank cave. The hermit gave us each a little taper to light our way. He showed us the cells that he and his predecessors had carved out of the walls, and the tombs of the other hermits who had died there. And in his gentle old voice he spoke a few kindly words about each of their lives. He himself had been living in the cave for twenty-five years.

Then there was a tomb he passed by in silence.

'Who is buried there?' my father asked.

'That is the resting-place prepared for the next,' the old hermit said calmly as he continued on his way, head bowed.

When we emerged from that dark cave with its earthy smell the daylight dazzled me. The old man had escorted us outside. After taking our leave of him we went back to the inn where our horses were waiting.

After a long silence my father asked me:

'Did you notice how he said "the next one"? Did you understand who it was he meant?'

'Himself?'

'Yes, and how tactfully he put it.'

I realized that papa had been very impressed by the hermit's answer.

Having concluded the business he had come for, papa ordered the horses to be harnessed and we set off back. Even though I had promised papa I wouldn't get tired I felt very sleepy, and I was very glad to get back to the house.

21

Before going home to Yasnaya Polyana, papa decided to give the Bashkirs a feast, and to use the occasion for testing the mettle of the

E

steppe horses at the same time. So with that in mind he also organized a big race.

A date was set, and the news was spread all through the district that everyone wanting to enter a horse in the race was to present himself at our house on a given day. The Bashkirs were very enthusiastic about the notion and immediately set about training their best horses and the lads who were to ride them. Whenever you looked out across the steppe you were sure to see groups of wildly galloping horses being ridden by little boys of about ten years old.

Papa had also announced the prizes for the winners. The first prize was to be a gun of some foreign make, the second a silver watch. Then there were several of the loose silken garments that Bashkirs wear, plus scarves, and a number of other things.

Several days before the race a whole encampment began to mushroom around the house. Sheep were slaughtered and roasted, the visitors' mares were milked, and kumiss-making was soon in full swing. Papa had also contributed the carcase of a two-year-old English horse that had broken a leg, and that too was butchered and put to stew in the camp cauldrons. The Bashkirs sat in circles on their carpets drinking kumiss, playing draughts, singing and dancing.

Merry old Mikhail Ivanovich arrived with his three wives and a great many mares. The wives were always squabbling. Mamma and I often had to lend sympathetic ears to all their complaints about one another. But Mikhail Ivanovich remained completely impervious. He just played draughts with papa, tapping his forehead when he was hard pressed for a move and repeating his favourite phrase:

'I must have bi-i-i-g thinking here . . .'

Not that it seemed to matter very much how big he thought, because papa almost always won.

The oriental music sounded strangely in our European ears. The tunes were always melancholy, played in a minor key with narrower intervals than those of the scale we were used to. It was eerie, throbbing music, played on the flute, the zurna [a wind instrument], and other curious instruments, and the Bashkirs also performed slow and graceful dances to its rhythms.

There were also some who made 'throat music'. This is a very curious method of producing musical sounds, and those highly skilled at it were highly regarded by the Bashkirs on account of their rarity. One of these virtuosos had come to watch our race. When he performed everyone was very quiet. He sat on a carpet, crosslegged, face tense, and the strain involved made a vein stand out on his forehead, while the sweat trickled down on to his nose. His features remained completely still, his lips didn't move, and yet it was as though a little organ of some kind was playing in his throat. The sounds were pure, transparent, and very melodious.

The last sound he made, as his performance came to an end, was quite different, a half-groan, half-sigh that came from his chest. The audience remained silent, still under the influence of the music.

'Well now,' papa said, 'why don't you show us what it is you have hidden there in your throat?'

The Bashkir shook his head with a weary smile. He was handed a wooden jar full of foaming kumiss. He drank avidly, then laid his hands in his lap and rested. The jar of kumiss was passed from hand to hand.

In the middle of another circle two Bashkirs were engaging in a trial of strength: they sat down facing one another so that each had the soles of his feet pressing against those of the other. Then they each took one end of a thick staff and pulled to see who was the stronger. It is a contest that requires as much skill as strength. You have to bend your knees slightly, pull with your arms, and at the same time try to straighten your legs. As soon as one of the contestants succeeds in straightening his legs the other is forced upright and has to acknowledge the other as the victor.

Papa joined in these contests, and to my great pride not one Bashkir who came forward was able to defeat him. No sooner did he grip the staff than the man challenging him was pulled to his feet.

But then there came a Russian, a soldier, gigantically tall and very fat to boot, who stepped out of the crowd and challenged papa to pull him up. Papa accepted. The soldier, puffing and blowing, plumped down on to the ground facing papa. Then they both arranged their legs so that each had the soles of his feet pressing against the other's. And finally they each gripped the staff with both hands and began to pull.

Papa's neck turned purple, his arms muscles swelled up and quivered with the strain, but the soldier would not give way. As soon as papa managed to pull him off the ground a little way he was able to get the upper hand again by using his vast weight, so that he thumped heavily back on to the ground while papa was lifted up slightly in his turn.

'Come on, come on,' I whispered, every muscle in me straining, as though that was helping my father somehow. 'Come on, come on, just a little bit more . . .'

Finally the soldier made a supreme effort, tugged with all his might, and snapped his legs straight. Papa was yanked to his feet and obliged to acknowledge defeat. He was smiling, but I could see he wasn't too pleased. Seryozha, Ilya, and I weren't either. Our hearts boiled with fury against the victor. After a brief discussion we came to the conclusion that it was solely the fact that he happened to weigh two hundred and fifty pounds that had enabled him to get anywhere near beating our invincible father.

I lingered a long while in the Bashkir camp, watching their dances and listening to their music. But when the dish of stewed mutton appeared I slipped discreetly away, dreading the sponge of greasy meat that might be wiped over my face if I refused to eat it. I had once seen the jovial Mikhail Ivanovich rub a young Bashkir's face with such a hunk of mutton, to the great humiliation of the youngster and the great amusement of those watching, so I had no wish to have that particular joke repeated at my expense.

22

More than twenty horses had been entered in the big race. A flat piece of steppe had been selected and a circle five versts in circumference marked out on it with a plough. The competitors were to make this circuit five times, which meant they had to cover twenty-five versts non-stop in all.

On the day, the steppe was black with people. There were thousands of Bashkirs, Kirghiz tribesmen, Cossacks from the Urals, Tartars, and Russians.

Mamma felt sorry for the Bashkir women because of the way they were condemned to perpetual seclusion and never saw anything apart from their mares and the inside of their own kibitkas. So she had our huge landau harnessed up and invited a few women to watch the race from inside it. The carriage was soon packed to bursting. Apart from Mikhail Ivanovich's wives, one of whom was very stout indeed, there were two Bashkir women who worked for us and several other women just visiting for the occasion. Wound in their velvet caftans to conceal themselves from male eyes, they followed the spectacle outside with passionate intensity.

Mamma, the boys and I drove out in a pletushka. But we watched the race itself standing on the roof of the landau. There was an enormous crowd of people in multicoloured silk robes, Circassian tunics, and all sorts of other national costumes.

When all the horses had been brought up, papa signalled that the race was about to begin. The crowd froze in expectation. But before the actual starting signal could be given all the horses had to be lined up. It took more than one attempt. The mounts, being half wild, pushed against one another, reared their heads, walked too far forward, or else began backing, while the boys riding them all struggled to hold them still.

Papa waved a handkerchief and shouted:

'Off!'

The horses shot away and were soon running at breakneck speed. The boys were all riding bareback. Each had a brightly coloured kerchief knotted round his head so that he could be recognized. They were all yelling and yelping, and the longer the race went on the more frenzied their yells became. Each time they passed the furthest point of the circuit and began circling back towards us, so their high-pitched yodellings grew louder and louder again as they approached. And the crowd, every time the horses hurtled furiously past us, added their frenzied yells to the clamour as well.

After the first few circuits some of the horses were so far behind that they were forced to drop out. Less than half the runners finished the course. The winners had run twenty-five versts in thirty-nine minutes. Exuberant and delighted, they were presented with their prizes, which they handed over to their fathers. One of our own horses had come in fifth.

Next day the visitors began to leave. They all came to thank papa for the pleasure he had given them. And for a long while afterwards, all over the district, people still remembered the race and the merrymaking at 'the Count's house'.

What is more, measures to preserve law and order had proved totally unnecessary throughout the festivities. Everything went off in an atmosphere of calm, courtesy, discipline, and also gaiety. There was not the slightest discordant note, not a hint of dissension. Excluding, that is, the set-to's among Mikhail Ivanovich's wives. But then they all took place in the privacy of their kibitka, behind closed curtains, so that the general harmony of the occasion was never at risk.

23

The grown-ups now began to talk about returning to Yasnaya Polyana. It was at this point that I began to grow uneasy: what was going to happen to Motka? 'How can I persuade papa and mamma to let me take him with me?' I asked myself. 'I can take care of him myself as far as Samara. I know he'll sit quietly on my lap. But what about after that? On the boat? On the train?' Sadly I told myself that they would certainly never allow it. 'But if I leave him here, who will look after him, who will take care of him the way I do? No one will love him as much as me.' Even in thought I did not dare to envisage the notion that Motka might suffer the same fate as the sheep that were consumed in such vast quantities out on the steppe. To kill Motka and eat him, was such a thing possible?

I covered his little milky-smelling pink nose with kisses, and asked him with brimming eyes: 'Ah, poor little Motka! What am I to do with you?' And my tears dropped down on to his uncomprehending head.

A tight band round my heart, without much hope, I went and asked my parents for permission to take my beloved lamb with me. I was astonished at the lack of importance they attached to my request. I had spent days working out exactly how to phrase my plea, yet how curtly and offhandedly they dismissed it:

'I never heard such silliness!' mamma said. 'Wanting us to take sheep on top of everything else. There are plenty of sheep for you at Yasnaya Polyana.'

It was useless trying to insist. I went to see our cook, who wasn't going with us.

'Advotya,' I said to her. 'I'm giving Motka to you. But please, you must be sure to look after him properly. You will, won't you? And . . .' I shied away from a direct expression of my fears '. . . do take care no one hurts him . . .'

The cook gave me her word. But there was insufficient conviction in her voice to satisfy me. I was afraid that once I'd gone she would go back on that word.

I had another source of sorrow besides Motka. A worse one still: the time had come for Hannah to leave too. I would have been utterly unable to resign myself to our parting at all had it not been for the hope of seeing her again at Yasnaya Polyana the following year, with aunt

Tanya and my cousins. The kumiss had done her a lot of good. She had put on weight and stopped coughing. She was returning to the Caucasus with renewed vigour and the intention of helping aunt Tanya bear the great misfortune that had struck all of them there.

I said goodbye to her until the following spring. I wept scalding tears as I parted from her. My grief and loneliness prevented me from sleeping for many nights. The room where I had slept with Hannah seemed so empty now, so gloomy . . .

'She'll come back, we'll see each other again,' I whispered to comfort myself.

24

It was early August by now. Once again all the rooms were piled with trunks, suitcases, and skips, while mamma ran from one to another packing away everyone's things.

We rode back to Samara just as we had come, in our great big 'sleeper' and several pletushkas. This time the journey seemed to me shorter and less tiring than it had been coming. But the boat journey was not as enjoyable as the time before. The river level had fallen during the summer and the boat had to be handled with extreme care to avoid running it on to sandbanks. The pilot was constantly measuring the depth of the water, calling out the number of fathoms as he pulled up the line.

'Five and a ha-a-a-alf!' the singsong voice would call. 'Four and a ha-a-a-lf!'

At night we didn't move at all, because unfortunately for us there was such a thick fog the whole time we were on the river that the captain was afraid of colliding with other vessels in the pitch darkness. It took us four days to get from Samara to Nizhni-Novgorod, as opposed to the twenty-four hours of a normal run.

In all, the journey home took eight days. What joy when we at last got back to Yasnaya Polyana! 'We arrived home during the evening of the twenty-second, just in time for my birthday,' mamma wrote to aunt Tanya on August 25th 1873. 'I won't give you an account of our life in Samara. Hannah will be able to describe it all much better to you in person. How do you find her? She drank her kumiss right up to the last moment. and thought of only one thing: being strong enough to be able to help you, to make life easier for you, share your work, and ease your grief. She has become very fond of you, and thought so often of Dasha, because she still can't get used to the idea of her not being there any more. What is admirable in her is her heart: the thought of relieving you of your burden was always with her . . .'

The same day my father wrote to Fet: 'Despite the drought, the losses, and the discomfort, we were all pleased with our stay, even my wife, but we are even more pleased to be back in our old surroundings . . .'

25

When I said goodbye to Hannah I had no suspicion that I would never see her again. When she returned to the Kuzminskis in the Caucasus she continued to supervise the education of my cousins Masha and Vera. Even though, as she herself put it, the one she loved most had vanished with Dasha, she nevertheless quickly became attached to the two younger girls entrusted to her care.

She wrote to us often, and we noticed no change in the tone of her letters. Then suddenly, in the spring of 1784, we received a letter from her sister Jenny telling us that Hannah was marrying a Georgian nobelman, Prince Nachutadzeh. This news filled us with utter astonishment. What! Hannah getting married! We had never even imagined such a possibility. And we didn't know whether to be overjoyed for her sake or grieve for our own.

An exchange of letters followed. Hannah told us how she had become engaged, and invited us to visit her in Kutais. Naturally we promised to do so, and in our turn invited her and her husband to visit Yasnaya Polyana.

As we learned later, the early days of Hannah's marriage were by no means easy ones for her. Her husband's parents were very displeased at their son's alliance with a penniless foreign girl. The young prince had defied them and married without their consent. Since the old prince and princess had then retaliated by cutting off their son's allowance, the young couple were obliged at first to live extremely frugally. Moreover Hannah was deeply upset at having come between a son and his parents.

The birth of the first child brought a general reconciliation. When the old parents learned that they had a grandson, and came round to seeing that Hannah was a good, modest, and loving wife, they invited the young couple to visit them, made up the quarrel, and suggested eventually that they move into the family home.

The Nachutadzehs lived on the outskirts of Kutais, where they owned a goat-cheese concern. Once she had settled in with them Hannah began to take an active interest in this family business, which prospered so well that the old parents eventually turned the running of it entirely over to her. It was on their estate, near Kutais, that Hannah spent the rest of her life.

During the years immediately following her marriage we exchanged many letters. She sent us a photograph of her second child, a daughter who bore a striking resemblance to her mother. Subsequently the letters became rarer, but we never ceased to correspond altogether.

Hannah wrote that she hoped one day to see 'dear old Iassnaya' again, and to bring her daughter with her. But none of our plans were ever realized. None of us ever saw her again, with the exception of Seryozha, who did have that joy . . . When he was already almost an old gentleman he had cause to go to the Caucasus on business and did in fact pay a visit on our former governess.

I envied him, and never lost hope that I too might see her again one day. Then the news came that she was seriously ill and some time afterwards we heard that Hannah had departed this world. She was not old when she died. She must have been just a little over fifty.

26

Back home at Yasnaya Polyana we resumed our lessons. The school year was beginning. I felt I was alone again, but somehow it made me less sad now. Perhaps this was because I was taking more of an interest in my studies. Perhaps too because I still remembered the hermit of Buzuluk, whose life I now held up as an example to myself. But whatever the reason, I was able to face up to life more bravely than the year before.

I took up drawing. The first spur was provided by a visit from the painter Kramskoy, from whom Tretyakov, the owner of a Moscow gallery, had commissioned a portrait of papa. [This was for a *Gallery of famous Russians*. Ivan Nicolayevich Kramskoy (1837–87) was the first artist to paint a portrait of Tolstoy, and it is still to be seen in the

Tretyakov gallery to this day.] I found it fascinating watching him paint, even though my shyness made it a torture for me to go into the room, since I was obliged to say good day to him and curtsey. I watched him at work with devouring curiosity. I had never seen anyone paint properly before, and I found it totally engrossing to watch the way Kramskoy mixed the oil paints on his palette, then applied them with tiny deft strokes to his canvas, till suddenly a living face emerged from it. There were papa's own eyes, grey, serious, attentive, just as they really were. What a miracle!

Kramskoy had taken up residence about five versts away from Yasnaya Polyana with two friends, the painters Savitski and Shishnin. He came over every day for the sittings. And he was painting two portraits at once, because mamma had asked him to do one for her too.

They both came off extremely well. Kramskoy allowed mamma to choose which one she wanted. The one she picked is still at Yasnaya Polyana, the other is in the Tretyakov gallery in Moscow.

After Kramskoy's visit I applied myself to my drawing a great deal more. I copied a picture of a little boy sitting on a tree trunk. I was pleased with my work and showed it to my parents, who praised and encouraged me:

'You must have drawing lessons,' papa told me.

He could see from the way my face went red with pleasure that the suggestion delighted me. So he went in to Tula, saw the drawing master at the secondary school there, and arranged for him to come over and give me lessons twice a week. My brothers weren't included because they had quite enough on their plates already.

I set to work with enthusiasm. My teacher, a little hunchbacked man named Simonenko—I have already mentioned him earlier—loved his art and took pleasure in teaching it. We drew busts and bunches of flowers from life. Simonenko showed me his drawings. I marvelled at their clarity and precision, and told myself I would never be able to attain such perfection. Clarity and precision aside, however, I didn't seem to learn anything from Simonenko, and he did nothing to help me understand in what the art of drawing consisted.

After that another teacher named Baranov came to give me lessons. We began to paint from nature. But he too taught me only the technical aspects of the art.

Later, when we went to live in Moscow, papa took me to see V. G. Perov, the head of the college of painting and sculpture there. This was in 1822, when I was eighteen. Perov put me through an examination then told my father:

'If she can manage to forget everything she's been taught, then she'll get somewhere, because she's very talented.'

Poor Simonenko! Poor Baranov!

It is very hard to forget things inculcated into one in childhood. Despite all my efforts I was never able to rid myself of the manner of my first teachers. Their main defect was that they allowed me to concentrate on insignificant details to the detriment of the whole. I would draw every hair in my model's beard even though the eyes weren't in the right place and the nose was all lopsided.

Later on, whenever I started a drawing, I always had to go through a quite conscious process of forcing myself to concentrate on the broad outlines and not think about details. I never really succeeded completely.

27

Until 1872 there had not been a single death in our family. But beginning in the autumn of that year, death came knocking regularly at our door.

In the autumn of 1873 my little brother Petya died. Petya was a bonny, plump little boy with huge dark eyes and sweet pink cheeks, always laughing, and very affectionate.

Some days before he fell ill I came upon him in one of the downstairs rooms, sitting on the flagged floor beside a puppy that was being treated for some ailment or other. There was a cup on the floor with bread and milk in it for the dog. The little creature didn't want to eat it, but Petya was absolutely insistent on making it swallow the soggy lumps of bread he was pushing between its jaws. And when the puppy dropped them out again Petya put them in his own mouth.

When I saw what was going on I told my little brother he mustn't eat what was in the cup. Then Petya picked the puppy up, cuddled it because he was so sorry for it, and imitated its cough:

'Heh! Heh!'

Several days later he became ill.

Mamma wrote to aunt Tanya: 'God alone knows how it happened. Croup probably. It began with a sort of hoarse whistling that just got worse and worse, and after two days of that the illness just carried him off. An hour before the end the whistling eased off, and then our fat, laughing baby died, lying there in his bed, without waking up, without even moving, as though he'd simply fallen asleep. His face stayed just as plump and smiling as when he was alive. I don't think he suffered much; he slept a lot during the illness, and there was nothing frightening, no convulsions, no pains. That at least was a consolation . . . Ten days have gone by since then, but I still haven't got over the shock, I still expect to hear his feet toddling behind me and his little voice calling me. None of the other children ever became so attached to me, none of them had his sweetness and sunny gaiety. Whenever I felt low, or when I went to rest after lessons, I'd take him with me to my room and have more fun romping with him than with any of my other children . . .'

Papa on his side wrote to Fet: 'A misfortune has befallen us. Petya, our youngest child, caught croup and died within two days. It is the first death in our family for eleven years, and very distressing for my wife. One can console oneself with the thought that if one of us eight had to be taken, then this death is the least hard for everyone. But the heart, and a mother's heart above all, that amazing and sublime manifestation of Divinity on earth, does not reason, and my wife is in great grief . . .'

At about the same time papa wrote to aunt Tanya: 'Just by not being here, our noisy little Petya—not to mention the sadness of having lost him—has left a void in the house I hadn't bargained for . . .'

Petya was buried two days after he died. It was a cold, sunny day. A little coffin covered in silver cloth that glistered in the sun was placed on the table in the big drawing-room. It was the first time I had seen a corpse. Every detail of it remains engraved in my memory. I can still see the blackened nails on the tiny waxlike hands that someone had crossed on his chest. I can see the curves of his closed eyelids, his black lashes, the golden hair on his temples and forehead, the rigid body under the white cloth.

Around me I was aware of silent coming and going, people consulting one another in low voices, whispering, bringing things into the room. I stayed rooted where I was, in front of what two days before had been a laughing child bursting with the joys of life, and I couldn't tear my eyes away.

Suddenly I heard the front door open and someone come in. Something was carried inside, then lots of people were talking all at once. I left the big drawing-room, looked down the stairs, and saw that some visitors had arrived. The newcomers removed their coats, the servants hung them up for them then began taking their luggage. I saw mamma come out to greet them. She kissed them, said something to them, and wept. It was my godfather Dmitri Alexeyevich Dyakov with his daughter Masha and her governess. They had broken their journey to Moscow in order to pay us a visit, completely unaware of our misfortune.

Mamma came upstairs with them and explained what had happened. Her eyes were red with weeping and her cheeks were aflame. I realized that this visit from our old and faithful friends, far from putting her out, was a solace in her grief. They knew how to listen, and their sympathy with our sorrow was so sincerely expressed that I felt no need to conceal my joy at seeing them either, and threw my arms around their necks.

I felt like crying, but I didn't. My godfather didn't tease me as he usually did, but just tapped me kindly on the cheek.

I don't remember either the closing of the coffin or the burial itself. I know I didn't go with my parents to the church. Mamma wrote to aunt Tanya: 'the very day of the funeral, even before we had closed Petya's coffin, the Dyakovs arrived from Cheremishnya, not knowing anything, just out of the blue. They showed themselves such good, sincere friends. Dmitri Alexeyvich came with us to the church for Petya's funeral . . .'

28

My years as a young girl were painful ones. All sorts of absurd, distressing ideas troubled my still unformed mind. After a childhood wholly without problems suddenly the whole vast field of thought, concealed from me till then, opened up before me. I began asking myself questions that had never entered my head as a child. There were the problems of life and death, of one's position with regard to religion, to one's country, one's parents, one's brothers, sisters, friends, and servants; the problems of money, art, relations between the sexes . . . I was determined to sort it all out. And what was more to sort it out on my own, without anyone else's help or experience to guide me.

In our first youth we feel ourselves to be all-powerful, and in our arrogant presumption we do not wish for advice or directives. We want to solve everything ourselves, we won't accept that the human spirit and mind have limitations. Then eventually we come up against an impassable wall, we despair, then continue our search, refusing to believe that there is no answer to the questions we are asking . . . And when once we do become convinced of that fact, then we tend to lose all wish to go on with a life that is apparently without meaning. The idea of suicide presents itself. And if we do not act on that idea it is either from cowardice or else because we still go on confusedly hoping that some solution does really exist, and that we may even yet be lucky enough to find it (8).

Sometimes I was gripped by nameless anxieties. I was hungry for new sensations. I dreamed of a man who would love me. And I wasn't quite sure whether I was attracted or repelled by that possibility. I was aware of an unhealthy curiosity. But I was ashamed to ask questions, so I waited for chance to confirm what I was vaguely sensing.

The child in me was dying, the adult was being formed. And like all states of transition it was a painful one.

Remembering that disturbed time in my own adolescence, I always do my best to employ the utmost tact and delicacy when dealing with young people of either sex. I know with what sincerity, with what honesty, they are seeking answers to the great problems with which life is facing them. I realize that they are striving, with greater seriousness than any adult, to picture the future that awaits them, a future so complex, so rich in insoluble enigmas and temptations.

I know how difficult it is to be open at that age, and I respect their reticence. I simply try to let them know, as gently as possible, that they have my sympathy. I also know that if we are to help them, if we are to hand on even a tiny fragment of our own experience, then it must be done with infinite precautions and immense love. From Tolstoy's *Anna Karenina;* 'The child knows its own soul, loves it, and protects it as the eyelid protects the eye. Without the key of love it will let no one enter . . .'

Flashes of Memory

When you are besieged by memories

A Paris newspaper once ran a series of articles in which people were asked how one can best recognize the onset of old age.

One of the answers given was: when you are besieged by memories.

For some time now I have been acutely aware of this happening to me. When I am alone I see fragments of my past played back before me. I see a certain sceue again, I can almost hear the voices . . . For the most part these memories involve my father—the dearest and most luminous being in my life. I cannot always connect these scenes with the events that preceded or followed them, or put a date to them. Yet the incident itself I see again as though it happened yesterday.

I write down these 'flashes of memory' as and when they occur.

Where Tolstoy was born

When anyone asked my father where he was born he used to point to the top of a tree that grew between our house and the separate smaller house often occupied by my aunt Tanya and her family. 'Just up there,' he would say. 'That's where my mother's bedroom was, and it was up there, on the leather sofa now in my study, that my mother brought me into the world.'

The house where my father was born no longer existed by then. In his youth, at a time when he was in financial straits and away from Yasnaya Polyana, he had written to his guardian asking him to sell off some of his property. It may have been with my father's consent or it may not, but the guardian, deciding that the two little brick houses flanking the main house were quite sufficient to house my father and his aunt Tatyana, sold the big house to a neighbour, who had it removed to his own estate about eighteen miles or so distant from Yasnaya Polyana.

Oddly enough, the house was never lived in after the move. The owner lived some considerable distance away, and after his death the heirs sold the whole property, including the house, to the estate peasants, who shared out the land, demolished the house, and used the beams, planks, and bricks from it to build themselves isbas.

Later on my father regretted having sold the house. His mother had spent her whole life there. He had been born and spent his childhood in it. When he was old he made a pilgrimage to see it and noted on his return: 'Went over to Dolgoyeh. Very moved by the sight of the ruined house. A swarm of memories . . .'

I too remember that house, which I visited one day with my brothers and sister. All forty rooms were uninhabited. The caretaker lived in a little cubby-hole on the ground floor. For us it was the Rostov family's house in *War and Peace*. We imagined we were exploring the rooms my father had described in his novel, and we argued passionately over exactly which room had been used for what, as though the Rostovs had been actual people who really lived there once.

That house, together with all the other buildings at Yasnaya Polyana, had been built by my great-grandfather Prince Nicolas Volkonski, commander of Paul I's armies, who had resigned from his post in 1799 and settled down at Yasnaya Polyana with his only daughter, Marie, and her French governess.

Here is what my father says about him in his *Recollections;* 'My grandfather had the reputation of being a very hard master, but I never heard it said that he descended to the kind of brutality so prevalent in those days . . . The quarters he had built for his servants were extremely fine architecturally, and he always saw to it that his people were not only well fed but also well clothed, and that they did not want for entertainment. He organized festivities for them, games, fancy-dress parties, and dances.

'He must have possessed an acute sense of beauty. Everything he had built is not only solid and comfortable but extremely elegant, and the same is true of the park he had laid out. People said that he loved music, and it is certainly true that he built up a small but excellent orchestra entirely for the entertainment of himself and my mother . . .'

Prince Nicolas Volkonski and his daughter Marie served as prototypes for old Prince Bolkonski and Princess Marie in *War and Peace*.

My grandmother, Marie Volkonski, was extremely well educated. Apart from Russian, which contrary to the custom of the day she both spoke and wrote correctly, she knew four other languages: French,

English, German, and Italian. She played the harpsichord extremely well, and there were some who still remembered her wonderful gift for telling stories, which she made up as she went along.

A woman friend of hers recalled that quite often, in her youth, my grandmother would wander off during a ball to some secluded room, taking a few other girls with her, and then start telling them stories so completely riveting that they all quite forgot about the dancing. The band continued to play, and the young men all began to wonder where their partners could possibly have gone.

While still very young, Marie Volkonski had been engaged to marry a Prince Galitzin, who died of typhoid before the marriage could take place. Long afterwards, when she was already thirty-two, she married my grandfather, Count Nicolai Tolstoy, four years her junior. The marriage had been 'arranged' by the two families. My grandmother, who possessed a large fortune, was an orphan, but not pretty and no longer young. He was a young officer, very popular in society, bursting with high spirits, who had been ruined by his parents, both of whom were so extravagant that our grandfather inherited far more debts from them than he did possessions.

Old Agafia, who had once worked for them, told me that her master and mistress used to send all their laundry to Holland, because in their opinion Russian laundresses were quite simply not good enough. So once a year they sent carriage loads of dirty linen off to Holland, and after several months it would come back duly washed and ironed.

There was no passion in the love between my grandparents. It was an attachment compounded of friendship and mutual respect. Nevertheless, my grandmother did write the following poem—in French, naturally:

O amour conjugal, doux lien de nos âmes
Source, aliment de nos plus doux plaisirs,
Remplis toujours nos coeurs de ta céleste flamme
Et au sein de la paix couronne nos désirs!

Je ne demande au Ciel ni grandeur ni richesse
Mon sort tranquille suffit à mes voeux.
Pourvu que mon époux, me gardant sa tendresse
Autant qu'il est chéri, soit toujours heureux.

Que notre vie s'écoule comme un ruisseau paisible
Qui ne laisse de traces que parmi les fleurs.

Qu'au plaisir d'aimer toujours plus sensibles
Nous fixions près de nous le fugitif bonheur.

Oui, mon coeur me le dit, ce destin qu'on envie,
Le Ciel dans sa bonté l'a gardé pour nous deux.
Et ces noms réunis, Nicolas et Marie,
Désigneront toujours deux mortels heureux.

(for translation, see Appendix)

Their marriage produced five children: four sons, of which my father was the youngest, and one daughter, the youngest child of all. A few months after the birth of this daughter my grandmother died of some strange and ill-defined illness. She suffered from mental troubles— once while giving her eldest son a lesson she was observed to be holding her book upside down—and sometimes her mind wandered. Old Agafia, who was young at the time, had another explanation for her death. She told us that one day, when my grandmother was being pushed on a swing by some women servants, they pushed her so high that she banged her head against a beam. It was an extremely violent blow, and my grandmother remained for a long while unable to move, lying with her head clutched in her hands. The servants were extremely frightened and afraid they would be punished, but she reassured them by promising never to tell anyone. From that time onward she suffered from constant headaches, and eventually died of meningitis, or brain fever as they called it then.

Was it because she knew she was less than pretty that my grandmother never had her portrait painted? At all events nothing had come down to us but one tiny black silhouette. My father claimed that he was really rather glad, because it meant he was free to picture her not as a real flesh and blood person but as a pure spirit.

It has often been asserted that great men have invariably had remarkable mothers, exceptional not only in their intellectual qualities but morally as well. This was certainly true in the case of my father. Of all her children my grandmother lavished her love particularly on her first-born, Nicolai, and on the youngest son, Lev, my father. She called him her Benjamin, and felt a very special tenderness for him.

'Everything I know of her is fine and noble,' my father wrote in his *Recollections,* 'and I don't believe that those who spoke to me of her were deliberately choosing to tell me only the good things. She was undoubtedly a woman of great virtues.'

He also said that she had possessed those character traits dearest to his own heart: indifference to the opinion of others, and a modesty so great that she always attempted to conceal her qualities of mind, education, and character from others. She even seemed to be ashamed of them.

Even though he did not remember her, Tolstoy continued throughout his long life to regard this dead mother as the dearest and holiest of beings. He said himself that her memory was a religion to him, and as late as 1908 he was noting in his diary:

'This morning walked in the garden, and as always thought of my mother, of "mamma", of whom I have not a single memory, but who has remained a sacred ideal for me. I have never heard the slightest ill spoken of her. One day, crossing the birch drive before turning into the hazel walk, I saw the imprint of a tiny female foot in the mud, and that made me think of her, of her body, and I realized that I simply couldn't imagine her as flesh and blood. Anything fleshly would have sullied her. How fine the feeling is I have for her! How I wish I could have similar feelings toward all women, and toward all men too!' He also wrote: 'I cannot speak of my mother without tears coming into my eyes . . .'

He also used the memory of his mother as a haven and a support in the darker moments of his existence. Whenever he found himself experiencing animosity toward someone, he would say to himself: 'Stop. Try to look for what is good in him. Try to see him in the same light as the being dearest to you in the whole world. And in my case that was my mother . . .'

Some years before his death, in a moment of depression and loneliness, he noted—not in his diary, which was being read and copied out every day as he wrote it by his over-zealous disciples, but on a scrap of paper just for himself: 'All day a feeling of gloomy dread. Toward evening this state of wretchedness was transmuted into a feeling of deep tenderness, into a desire to be caressed, comforted. Like a child, I long to press myself against some loving, sympathizing being, to shed tears of love and affection, and to feel myself being consoled. But where is the being with whom I can find such a refuge. In my mind I go through all those I love—not one is what I need. To whom am I to turn my affection then? Should I become a child again and hide my head against my mother as I picture her? Yes you mamma, you whose name I never spoke, because I was still too young to talk . . . Yes you, the highest ideal of pure love I have ever succeeded in imagining, of human, warm, maternal love. That is what my weary soul cries out for. You, mamma, you, comfort me, console me . . .'

That cry of love was uttered by an old man of seventy-eight. He ended this love letter with the words: 'All this is madness . . . And yet it is true.'

War and Peace

My father said that it took him 'five years of unremitting and single-minded labour' to write *War and Peace*. He made few notes during that period, since he was reserving all his energies for the novel itself, with the result that there is only the scantest documentation available to anyone wishing to reconstruct the creation of *War and Peace*. Nevertheless one does find, scattered here and there in his diary and letters, just a few precious indications of the way in which Tolstoy was envisaging the problems of writing at that time. For instance: 'It is better to eliminate everything that might provoke indignation' (Diary, March 29th 1869). Or again: 'It is only with the epic that I really feel at home' (Diary, January 3rd 1863).

In a letter he also states his view that 'literary problems are incommensurable—as the mathematicians put it—with social problems. The writer's aim does not consist in resolving the questions posed, but in instilling a love of life in all its innumerable and inexhaustible manifestations. If someone were to tell me that it lay in my power to write a novel explaining every social question from a particular viewpoint that I believed to be the correct one, I still wouldn't spend two hours on it. But if I were told that what I am writing will be read in twenty years' time by the children of today, and that those children will laugh, weep, and learn to love life as they read, why then I would devote the whole of my life and energy to it.'

In 1863 he wrote to his cousin Alexandra: 'I have never felt my spiritual and even moral energies so untrammelled and ripe for employment. It is a novel about the years between 1810 and 1820 that has been occupying my whole attention since the autumn . . . I am now a writer with all the force of my soul. I am writing and thinking as I have never written and thought before in my life.'

In 1864, while out hunting, he fell from his horse and broke an arm. Complications ensued and it was many long months before he was back to normal. It was during this period of enforced idleness that he conceived the largest part of his novel.

On January 23rd 1865 he wrote to the poet Fet, his friend and faithful correspondent: 'Let me tell you something amazing about myself. After my horse had thrown me, breaking my arm, my first thought when I regained consciousness was that I was a writer. Yes, I really am a writer, but a solitary writer, a silent writer. Soon the first part of *The Year* 1805 [Tolstoy's original title for *War and Peace*] will be out. I want you to write and tell me what you think of it, and in detail. Your opinion, and also that of a man whom I like less and less as I grow older—Turgenyev—, are both precious to me. I regard everything I have published up till now as being mere pen-sketches, rough drafts. What I am about to publish at the moment seems feeble to me just now—which is inevitable in the case of an introduction— and yet how frightening. Write and tell me what they are saying in your circles.'

On March 7th of the same year he noted in his diary: 'I write, I scratch out. Everything is clear, but the enormity of the labour to be got through appalls me. I must make a plan so as to avoid getting bogged down over tiny details and changing them all the time, and to keep the important passages ahead in my mind.'

And on March 19th: 'I have been reading the accounts of Napoleon and Alexander with ever increasing interest. I am overflowing with joy at the idea of being able to bring off a great work, a work of psychological history: the novel of Alexander and Napoleon. I shall put all men's cowardice, madness, and contradictions into it; that of their followers and that of the two men themselves as well . . .'

The following day he wrote: 'Wonderful weather. Am in good health. Rode over to Tula. Thinking on a really big scale. My plan of the story of Napoleon and Alexander becoming clearer.' And finally, on March 23rd: 'Wrote only a little during the evening, but quite well. I may get there.' Toward the end of the year he wrote to Fet: 'Every day I think: *ars longa, vita brevis*. If only one could accomplish a hundredth part of what one has conceived! But one never brings off even a thousandth! All the same, that feeling of knowing we have the power to create, for us writers that's happiness. You know it, that feeling. This year it is particularly strong with me.'

He worked at *War and Peace* with unparalleled ardour, ecstasy, and love, neglecting everything that was not his novel. He who in his old age was to say that 'a man's most important work is his life,' wrote in his notebook on November 27th 1866: 'The poet extracts what is best from life and puts it in his work. That is why his work is beautiful and his life bad . . .' And in a letter to Fet on July 28th 1867: 'The strength of poetry resides in love. Without love there is no poetry . . .'

That is more or less the whole of what the writer had to say during that period on the subject of his work and his ideas on literature.

It is equally difficult to pinpoint the various materials that Tolstoy made use of in composing his epic. In the library at Yasnaya Polyana one finds a whole series of historical works: memoirs, descriptions, letters, and notes by Russian and French authors of the time. In addition to these, however, my father also delved into every other source of material available to him. For instance he often went to Moscow to consult the archives in the national museums.

'I can't explain to you,' he wrote to his wife after he had been studying some freemason manuscripts in the Rumyantsev museum [now the Lenin Library], 'why my reading has plunged me into a state of such depression that it has lasted all day. The sad thing is that those masons were absolute idiots.' And next day: 'I was back at the Rumyantsev museum first thing. What I found is really riveting. I've spent three or four hours there for the past two days and not even noticed the time passing.'

He also visited the battlefield of Borodino and explored it in minute detail. He was most put out when he was told that the keeper of the monument, an eye-witness of the battle, had just died. He went round the sites of all the individual engagements twice, taking notes and making sketches of the troop movements. 'I'm extremely satisfied with my excursion,' he wrote. 'If God gives me the health and strength I need, I shall produce a description of the battle of Borodino such as there has never been . . .'

The newspapers of that time were also of invaluable assistance to him. He consulted them at length in various libraries. Indeed, wishing to have a set of his own always at hand, he even inserted the following advertisement in the *Moscow Journal*. 'Wanted, for 2,000 silver rubles, complete set of *Moscow Gazette* for 1812.' He gave the address of a Moscow hotel, but as far as I know he received no replies.

The archives and oral traditions of our own family provided him with the material for his descriptions of the Bolkonski and Rostov families. Thus the letter Princess Marie writes to her friend Julie is almost an exact reproduction of a letter from his mother to one of her friends. As for the characters of *War and Peace* generally, they are composite portraits derived from a variety of my father's ancestors, friends, and acquaintances.

'Who is Prince André?' he wrote in one letter. 'No one, like the hero of any novel, unless the novelist is a mere memorialist or biographer. I would be ashamed to have my work published if all my labour had consisted merely in painting portraits from live models . . .'

However, despite the author's insistence on his right to freedom in depicting his imaginary characters, he permitted himself no play of fancy in his description of the historical figures involved. 'Throughout my novel,' he wrote in an explanatory note published after the appearance of *War and Peace,* 'whenever historical characters act or speak I have invented nothing, but based everything upon documents, which as my work progressed gradually acquired the dimensions of a veritable library. It seems to me unnecessary to list all their titles here, but I am ready at any time to provide references to the works I used.'

Probably the only character actually drawn from a single living model—and this is something my father himself did not deny—was that of Natasha, who was a portrait of his wife's younger sister, Tatyana Behrs. At the time when he was writing *War and Peace* she was still unmarried, and my father, in whom she habitually confided, was extremely fond of her. Moreover he predicted her future: she married Alexander Kuzminski, a good, very kind man, whom she loved without being in love with, and subsequently settled down to a quiet life of domesticity, becoming rather plump in the process, exactly like Natasha after her marriage to Pierre . . .

Marcus Aurelius

Could the emperor Marcus Aurelius ever have imagined that his *Thoughts* would one day bring spiritual support and comfort, nineteen centuries after he wrote them, to a lowly peasant woman in far-off Russia?

During the eighteen-eighties my father started a company to provide books and pictures specifically for the people. With this end in view he had entered into an arrangement with a publisher who had already succeeded in creating a simply enormous market in this field, for his books, despite their mediocrity, had met with great success among the uncultured public they were aimed at.

My father's idea was to replace this wretched stuff with a better quality of reading matter that would do some good. He asked our best writers and painters for their collaboration, and they all gave it gladly. Within a few years there were tens of millions of these booklets, costing no more than a few kopeks, to be found in homes all over Russia. And that figure is not an exaggeration: I remember quite clearly that at the time I was involved with *Posrednik*—the name given to the collection as a whole—the number of copies printed had already passed the eight million mark.

My father handed these booklets out right, left and centre. Every isba in Yasnaya Polyana had dozens of them.

One of the books—the *Thoughts* of Marcus Aurelius—found its way into the hands of a little boy in the village who proceeded to read it out aloud to his parents. Since my father had seen to it that everything published in the *Posrednik* collection was written in a language access-ible to the people, young Petya's parents were able to appreciate the work's beauties, and this particular booklet became the mother's favourite reading matter. Since she was herself illiterate, however, she had to rely on her son to read it to her, and in moments of doubt, or when she felt her faith in God weakening she would call out to the boy:

'Petyushka! Find the Marcus Aurelius book—it's over there, under the ikons—and read me a bit.'

Petya would take the book, and Anushka, cheek on palm, would listen and weep as he read. By what mysterious path had the thoughts of the great Roman sage found their way so directly to Anushka's heart, when so many people, undoubtedly much more cultured than she, were quite indifferent to them?

'Well, Anushka, and how are things?' my father asked when he met her one day. 'Has Petya been reading you any Marcus Aurelius lately?'

Anushka, aware of the hint of mockery in my father's voice, took offence.

'Lev Nicolayevich, the man who wrote that book must have been a great saint. The other day, when I felt my faith slipping a little, I called Petyushka in to read me Marcus Aurelius's book. And little by little I felt my faith coming back, till there I was happy as the day is long again.'

Your Plays are even worse than Shakespeare's

My father loved Chekhov both as a writer and a man. I myself remember him still, that modest man with the attentive eyes who always listened more than he talked. He had hesitated for a long while before visiting Tolstoy. Knowing how precious time is to a writer, he was afraid of being a nuisance. From their very first meeting, however, the fellow-feeling between them was so unmistakable that even Chekhov, for all his modesty, could not help but become aware that his visits gave Tolstoy great pleasure.

Tolstoy much preferred Chekhov's stories to all his other works. Quite often, at Yasnaya Polyana, the whole family would sit round the great circular table, lit by a big white lamp overhead, while he read them to us. And though he was an excellent reader, I am afraid that when reading Chekhov my father was sometimes quite unable to go on, so infectious did his helpless fits of laughter become.

'Oh how charming that is!' he would exclaim as he laughed till he cried. 'How is it Chekhov can't see that the most priceless part of his art is the humour? A humorist like him is the very rarest of things.'

And when Chekhov began writing for the theatre my father was in fact disappointed. Nor did he conceal his lack of appreciation from the younger writer:

'As you know,' he told him, 'I really don't care for Shakespeare's plays. But yours are even worse . . .'

Humour

When my father was eighty, if he was a little below par and someone asked him how he felt, he replied:

'As if I were eighty.'

Of an egocentric fellow far too fond of himself, he said:

'That man has one great advantage: he fears no rival.'

If something he had asked for was difficult or impossible to obtain, he would withdraw the request with the words:

'I was only joking. I didn't really want it at all . . .'

When deferring some enterprise he felt might be too much for him, he would say:

'I'll do it when I'm grown up.'

And if it was some object that had proved impossible to obtain for him:

'You can give it to me when I'm grown up.'

The Bicycle

My father loved all sports. Toward the end of the last century, when they first came into vogue, he bought himself a bicycle. And since it was mid-winter he used to go off to the Moscow Riding School to practice riding it indoors.

'The queerest thing keeps happening to me,' he told us. 'I have only to catch sight of some obstacle to find myself being drawn irresistibly towards it, and eventually crash into it. And it happens particularly, I'm afraid, in the case of a certain fat lady who is there like me learning to ride her bicycle. She wears a feathered hat, and I have only to see those plumes of hers waving in the wind to feel my bicycle steering itself irrevocably in her direction. When she sees me coming she begins to utter piercing shrieks and does her best to escape from my path, but all in vain. If I don't have time to put a foot down and stop myself there is nothing I can do to avoid her, and I knock her over. So just now I'm trying to visit the Riding School only at times when I hope she won't be there . . . And I can't help wondering,' he added, 'if it is not an ineluctable law of nature that the things we seek to avoid are always precisely those that really attract us most.'

'Womanophobia'

My father did not hold women in high esteem. Sometimes his attacks on them were just intended to tease, but on other occasions his misogynist pronouncements were quite serious and meant to carry conviction. At home we used to accuse him at such times of 'womanophobia'. It sometimes happened that he and his friends, finding themselves alone, indulged themselves in tearing us women to pieces.

After such sessions my father would say 'we've been doing a bit of "womanophobing" in there.' When in a more serious mood, he would put forward his true views on women. He insisted that the Christian woman—a woman who lives in accordance with the laws of morality and religion—merits all our esteem. In every woman there are extremely precious qualities to be found not possessed by men, but it is wrong of any woman to try to rival men in spheres to which she is not fitted.

As for the woman who employs all her charms to seduce men, and to that end decks herself out in costly and often immodest garments, who regards sexual relations merely as a source of pleasure, who avoids motherhood in order to preserve her beauty, such a woman is a contemptible being and a public danger.

'When I encounter a woman of that kind,' he said, 'I want to cry out: "Thief! Thief! Help!" and send for the police.'

I have heard my father reply to someone who defended the rights of women, and who claimed that both sexes possess the same gifts and abilities:

'No, even if I were to admit that women have the same abilities as men, I would still have to recognize that they have one we men do not possess.'

'What is that?'

'The ability to bring children into the world . . .'

When my father was writing his essay on art I often did his copying for him. One day he asked me for permission to use a passage from my private diary in the book. I agreed, and he quoted it as being the words of 'a friend' possessing an acute artistic sensibility. When I returned the fair copy of that section I said to him: 'I can see why you didn't give my name, but why have you allowed the reader to assume that this friend of yours is a man?'

'Well,' my father answered in some embarrassment, 'it's simply so that the reader will attach more importance to your opinion.'

The little green wand

Do you know why my father is buried under a little mound in the shade of some old oak trees, there in Yasnaya Polyana wood? It is because that spot conjured up for him a childhood memory particularly dear to his heart. The oldest of the Tolstoy children, Nicolai, who had a great influence on all his brothers, and particularly on my father, had told them that just there, in that particular part of the wood, he had secretly buried a little green stick on which he had carved a magic spell. Whoever found that wand would become its master, and would have the power to make everyone in the world happy. Hatred, war, disease, grief, and misfortunes would disappear from the face of the earth, all men would know happiness and become 'Muravei Brothers', or in other words 'Ant Brothers.' 'That phrase appealed to me particularly,' my father remarked later, 'because it made me think of all the members of an anthill living together in perfect harmony.'

It is also possible that what Nicolai actually said, or at any rate meant, was 'Moravian Brothers', a sect practising and preaching love of one's neighbour whose story had left a deep impression upon him. Whatever the truth of the matter one thing is certain: that this precept of loving one's neighbour as oneself had struck a deep answering chord in the young Nicolai's loving and unassuming nature.

As a result, the Tolstoy children also invented what they called the Ant Brothers game. By pulling together a few chairs, then draping them with shawls, they would build themselves a house. Then they snuggled together inside it and promised never to quarrel any more and to love one another for always. My father told us that his liking for this game sprang from the feeling of tender love and affection it aroused in him. 'We thought of it as a game,' he said, 'but I realize now that it is everything else in my life that has been a game, everything except for that feeling of love and togetherness I felt, in earliest childhood, snuggled up beneath those chairs and shawls . . .'

As children we knew all about the little green stick and the Ant Brothers game. We also knew that in memory of his favourite brother my father wanted to be buried where the little magic wand was supposed to be hidden. And indeed he reminded us of it from time to time.

One winter day, two years before his death, I went for an outing with him in Yasnaya Polyana wood. He was on his favourite horse, with the rather pretentious name of Délire, while I brought up the rear in a light sleigh drawn by a pony. It was a magnificent December day, with the frost-covered trees all sparkling in the bright sun. The cold pricked our cheeks, the runners of my sleigh squeaked over the frozen snow. My father, despite his eighty years, still rode tall in the saddle and trotted so quickly that my pony had difficulty keeping up.

When we reached the spot where the little green wand was buried, he turned round pointing to the mound:

'You remember?' he called.

'Yes,' I answered, 'I remember.'

Nothing more was said and we continued on our way.

When he died, on November 7th 1910, in the stationmaster's little house at Astapovo, a long way from the house where he was born, we brought his body back to Yasnaya Polyana to bury him where the little green wand with the magic spell for universal happiness lay hidden.

In his declining years my father explained the mystery of the 'Muravei Brothers' in this way: 'The ideal of the "Ant Brothers" who huddled together in love, not just under chairs covered with shawls, but under the vault of heaven, that ideal of love for one's neighbour has remained my ideal too. And just as I believed then in the existence of the little green wand and its hidden power to eliminate evil and bring mankind the greatest of blessings, so I believe today that such a truth does really exist, that the time will come when it will be revealed to them and keep its promise.'

My father bequeathed me that faith. And I believe as firmly as he did that 'the time will come'.

When did he understand women?

My father was still unmarried when he wrote his novel *Conjugal Happiness*.

'I believed at the time that I knew all about women,' he told me one day. 'Even before my marriage, however, it had dawned on me that I knew nothing about them whatever, and it was only through my wife that I got to know them.

'But now,' he added, stroking my hair, 'now that I have my grown-up daughters taking me into their confidence, talking with me heart to heart, I realize that I knew no more about women after my marriage than before it, and that it is only now, at long last, that I am just beginning to comprehend them . . .'

The Stolen Samovar

One winter night in Moscow, during the eighteen-nineties, papa and I were left sitting alone together in the big drawing-room. And as we sat there beside the cold samovar, near a table covered with the remains of cakes, fruit peelings, and used crockery left by our many guests that evening, we fell to talking about the people who had just left. Among them were two of my father's friends, both professors, who were frequent visitors to the house. One, Ivan Yanzhu, a portly, pleasant-looking man, taught law; the other was the philosopher Nicolai Grot, editor of the review *Philosophical and Psychological Questions* to which my father was a contributor. A number of my friends, young people of both sexes, had also been present. They included two young men, also frequent guests of ours, who were both paying me assiduous court.

Papa questioned me, wanting to know what I thought of them both. As always I answered with total frankness.

'Do you think they want to marry you?'

'I sometimes think so . . .'

We compared the advantages that marriage to each of them would bring, discussed their virtues and defects, and speculated as to which one was most likely to bring me happiness.

'But let us not be too hasty,' my father suddenly said. 'Perhaps we are attributing intentions to them that they have never entertained.'

'Perhaps,' I agreed, without much conviction.

At that moment we heard mamma coming to see why we were sitting up so late.

'What are you two talking about there like conspirators?'

'We were wondering, Tanya and I,' papa said, 'whether or not Grot and Yanzhu are entertaining an intention to steal our samovar.'

My mother failed to see the point of the joke.

'What new silliness is this?' she said. 'Don't you know it's after two in the morning? I can just imagine what time Tanya will be getting up tomorrow!'

Papa got up, and I with him. I wished them both good night, and as I kissed papa I whispered in his ear:

'But our samovar isn't going to let itself be stolen . . .'

The Chicken

In early autumn it was customary for my mother to leave Yasnaya Polyana for Moscow, taking with her all the children who were still attending school. My father, my sister, and myself stayed on at Yasnaya Polyana for a few more months, and during that time, following our father's example, Masha and I led a Swiss Family Robinson sort of existence, doing the cleaning ourselves, since the servants had all gone, and cooking our own meals, which were of course strictly vegetarian ones.

One day we received a message announcing the imminent arrival of one of our relatives, an aunt of whom we were all particularly fond. Knowing that our aunt enjoyed good food, and meat in particular, we were quite at a loss as to what we should do. The idea of cooking 'corpse'—which is how we referred to meat—revolted us. And while my sister and I were arguing the pros and cons our father came in. Having had our difficulty explained to him, he reassured us, and promised that he would attend to our aunt's bill of fare.

'You two just get dinner as usual,' he told us.

Our aunt, beautiful, gay, bursting with vitality as always, arrived later in the day. When dinner time arrived we all went through into the dining-room, and what did we find? Beside our aunt's place at the table there lay a gigantic kitchen knife, and attached to the leg of her chair by a length of string was a live chicken. The poor creature began fluttering in fright and dragging the chair across the floor.

'Since we know how you enjoy eating living creatures,' my father said, 'we arranged to have this chicken for you. However, since none of us has a taste for murder we have also placed this assassin's knife at your disposal so that you can perform the deed yourself.'

'Oh Lev,' my aunt exclaimed through her laughter, 'not another of your awful jokes! Tanya, Masha, untie that poor thing at once and take it outside, please.'

We speedily did as our aunt had requested. And the chicken once more at liberty, we all sat down and helped ourselves to what Masha and I had made for dinner: macaroni, vegetables, and fruit. Our aunt tucked into everything with a healthy appetite.

I am bound to add, however, that she did not profit from the lesson her brother-in-law had administered as much as she might, and remained an ardent carnivore to the end of her life.

Papa's tip

It is about a hundred and twenty miles from Moscow to Yasnaya Polyana, and my father sometimes made the journey on foot. A haversack on his back, he set off along the high-road and mingled with its nomadic society of pilgrims, who were a source of perennial fascination to him and talked to him more readily when he was just one more anonymous fellow-traveller. It took him about five days to cover the distance home, and he used to break his journey in isbas or cheap inns for a night's sleep or a bite to eat. And if he passed near a railway station he would go into the third class waiting-room for a rest.

During one of these halts, as he wandered along a platform at which a train was just on the point of leaving, he heard someone calling to him.

'Old man! Old man!' a lady was shouting as she leaned out of a carriage window. 'Would you just run to the ladies' wash-room for me and bring me my handbag. I've left it behind in there. But do hurry, the train will be leaving at any moment.'

My father duly hurried into the ladies' wash-room, fortunately found the bag still there, and restored it to its owner.

'Thank you so much,' she said. 'Here's something for your trouble.'

She held out a large copper coin, which my father calmly slipped into his pocket.

'Do you realize who it is you've just given five kopeks to?' a fellow traveller asked her, having recognized the old dust-covered pilgrim as the author of *War and Peace*. 'That is Lev Tolstoy!'

'Oh my god,' the lady cried, 'what have I done! Lev Nicolayevich! Lev Nicolayevich! For pity's sake forgive me, and give me back those five kopeks I so stupidly gave you.'

'Why should I?' my father answered. 'You've done nothing wrong. I earned those five kopeks. And I intend to keep them . . .'

The whistle blew, the train began to move, carrying with it the lady still shouting apologies and begging Tolstoy to give her back the five kopek piece.

My father, a smile on his face, stood and watched the train disappear into the distance . . .

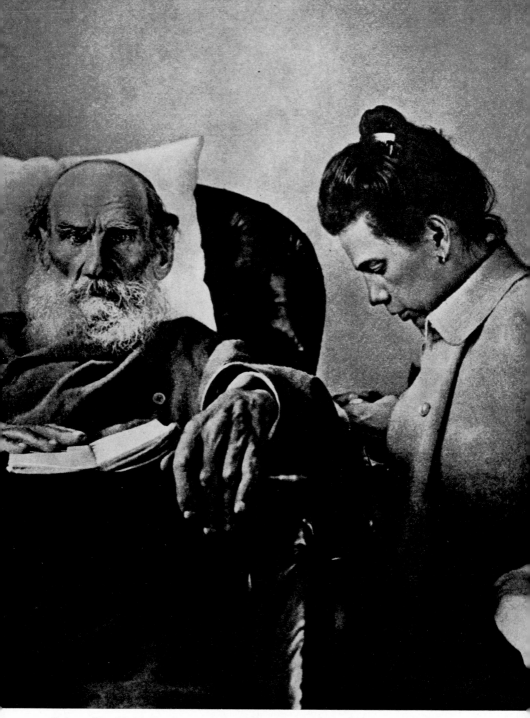

Tolstoy ill, with his daughter Tatyana (Crimea 1902)
'*Illness has withered him even more, burnt something out in him; inwardly too he seems lighter more transparent, nearer to life itself. His eyes are even sharper, his gaze more piercing.*' (M. Gorki)

Tolstoy's grave at Yasnaya Polyana
'*I came back through the forest . . . just at sunset. Grass fresh underfoot, stars in the sky, scent of laburnum in flower . . . And I thought of death, and it came to me quite clearly that it would be just as wonderful . . . on the other side of death.*' (Tolstoy)

Tatyana Tolstoy (Rome 1946)
'*My mother's old age was serene and happy. To give and to go on giving was what mattered most to her in life. She asserted that in growing old she had attained an inner joy such as she had never known in her youth.*' (Tatyana Albertini)

Was Tolstoy Superstitious?

If anyone had asked my father whether or not he was superstitious I am sure he would have denied it firmly. And yet, throughout his life, I frequently observed him yielding to certain superstitions. More than once, for example, I have felt his powerful hands gripping my shoulders as he forced me round so that I shouldn't see the new moon from the right. And if, like the good king Dagobert, 'he put his trousers on all back to front,' he was always put out and spent the rest of the day anticipating some mischance. I also often heard him say: 'If such and such a thing happens, I will do this or that; if it doesn't I won't.'

One day we were riding over together from Yasnaya Polyana to my uncle Sergei's place about twenty miles away. We had to pass through several villages. Russian villages usually consist of a single street, always very wide and sometimes stretching for well over half a mile. Well, we were riding along one of these village streets at a brisk trot when suddenly my father pulled his horse's head to the right, guided it through a narrow gap between one of the isbas and a big water-cart that happened to be standing in front of it, then turned back on to the road and continued on his way as briskly as before. As we left the village I caught him up and asked him:

'Why did you turn off like that?'

'Didn't you notice?' he answered. 'A black cat crossed the road in front of us and ran underneath the water-cart.'

'Do you mean you turned aside just to avoid riding over the place where the cat crossed the street?'

My father made no reply, and we trotted on our way.

A Hoax

There was a great deal of discussion at Yasnaya Polyana over the ideas of the great American economist Henry George. He had sent copies of all his books to my father, who duly read them and as a result became an enthusiastic admirer of the simple, yet just and moral solution they offered to the agrarian question. My interest aroused by the conversations I heard on the subject, I too read Henry George's books. Then, having grasped his theory and become in my turn an ardent supporter of it, I began to feel that it ought to be made familiar to everyone. I was convinced that no sincere and unprejudiced person could fail to be won over by its impeccable logic. Every great idea, I reasoned, is based upon a moral principle that at the same time renders it practical. And I was quite sure in my own mind that no agrarian system could be more practical, or in other words profitable, than the great American's. But how was the knowledge of it to be spread? Henry George's writings were so voluminous, and I knew from my own experience that for people without a basic grounding in political economy they were far from easy to understand. I therefore decided to produce a work of vulgarization summarizing his ideas. After having recast the first section of this work several times, I typed it out, then decided I would like my father to see it. But would he feel free to judge it impartially if he knew it was I who had written it? I thought not, so I signed both my article and the covering letter with a pseudonym, the first that sprang into my mind: P. Polilov. And I also gave an answering address.

At this time I was living at my husband's place some sixty miles from Yasnaya Polyana. I sat tight and waited with great impatience for my father's reply. After a while, when it still hadn't arrived, I decided to go over to Yasnaya Polyana myself and investigate. I knew that copies were made of all my father's letters, and that if he had answered me there would be a copy of that answer in the files. Having arrived at Yasnaya Polyana, and not wanting to disturb my father at his work, I went straight in to see my sister.

'So what's been happening at home since my last visit?' I asked. 'What have you had in the way of letters?'

'There was one letter, with an article, that caught papa's interest no end,' she answered. 'It was from a certain Polilov, some fellow no one's ever heard of. Papa was so taken with it that he's written back at great length, almost an essay in fact. He even rewrote it several times.'

On the envelope of my own letter my father had scrawled: 'Interesting'. Then under that: 'Answered'. I asked my sister for the copy of his reply. Heart pounding I read it through. I had to turn my face away so that my sister shouldn't see my joy.

Here is a summary of what my father had written:

Your article and letter have given me great pleasure . . . The agrarian question, that of the power of land, generally regarded as a political one, is as you so very rightly say a moral question, a violation of the most elementary laws of morality. You may therefore imagine the joy I felt in reading your admirable article, which expounds so clearly with such intelligence the essence of the question . . . I am very grateful to you for the pleasure you have brought me. Please keep me informed of your work's progress. I shake your hand in friendship and gratitude.

Leo Tolstoy

I was at the same time wildly elated at my father's appraisal of my work and seized with remorse at the trick I had played on him. It was only then that I realized how disappointed my father was going to be when he found out that this advocate of Henry George's ideas was not a new find but someone from his own circle.

With great trepidation I waited for my father to emerge from his study. Eventually he did so, in very merry mood, and sat down immediately to eat—he always ate lunch alone after everyone else had finished. As he ate he told me about the mail he'd received that morning, and laughingly described a letter from a young friend who had just married and was very amusing on the subject of his young wife. 'She understands nothing whatever about my ideas,' he had written, 'but my socks are always darned. She despises the friends who share my convictions, but my dinner is always on time . . .' And so the letter went on, all in much the same vein.

'Ah, women!' my father exclaimed, his voice a blend of contempt and indulgence.'

After a pause I asked him:

'And were you pleased with Polilov's article?'

'Yes, delighted. Do you know him?'

'Yes. Did you know it's a pseudonym? Polilov is in fact a woman.'

'Impossible!'

'But true.'

'Who is she?'

'Me . . .'

'Impossible!'

So then I told him everything: the thinking that had led to the article, and the reason why I'd sent it to him under a pseudonym. As was customary with him, he expressed no reproach, but I could tell I had been right in my predictions and that he was feeling let down.

163

Not that he allowed anything to show, but even the slightest disappointment can always be sensed if people are as close as we were.

We then went on to a serious discussion of my book, and I explained the general plan of it to him. The first part, the section I had sent him, dealt with the moral side of the question: the inequity of private ownership of the land. The second was to be devoted to an exposition of existing agrarian programmes together with a critique of them. This was where I was running into problems: what and how much should I select from the confused mass of works on the subject generally accepted as important? The third and last part was to be a clear and simple exposition of Henry George's theory, an easy enough task for me, since my knowledge of it was fairly complete.

As the conversation came to an end my father began to chuckle and said:

'But how sad about poor Polilov! And I'd formed such a clear picture of him too: he wore dark blue jacket, really very dapper, in early middle age . . .'

Then stroking my hair he added:

'Well, if you don't finish your book, then we shall be able to say you are a true woman.'

Alas, I was to prove that I was indeed an authentic member of my sex. Like a true woman I have left my book unfinished to this day . . .

Contradiction

During the Russo-Japanese conflict in 1904–5, my father followed the fortunes of the war with passionate interest. When the Russians surrendered the fortress of Port-Arthur to the enemy he was unable to conceal his indignation.

'We would never have done such a thing in my day,' he said.

'What would you have done?' asked a tolstoyan who was present.

'We'd have blown the place up rather than surrender it.'

'You mean you would have sacrificed the lives of all the men in it?'

The tolstoyan was apparently shocked by the Master's words.

'What do you expect? If you're a soldier you've a job to do. And you do it properly.'

The disciple couldn't understand that. And I myself wondered if my father's words had come, not from the logic-loving moralist, but from the old soldier.

The Village Idiot

My father used to say of Parasha that she possessed both of the two fundamental Christian virtues: she never took care for the morrow, and she wished everyone well. Her big, fleshy face had a smile for everyone. When she laughed, her fat red cheeks bulged upward and almost obliterated her little grey eyes.

'Are you still alive?' she would ask everyone she met. And without waiting for their reply she would burst into laughter and cry: 'Well keep on living! Live forever!'

It was her task to tend the village calves, and she performed it most efficiently. We often glimpsed her, stick in hand, chasing after a calf to drive it back into the meadow, or chatting to one of her favourites. She often came up to the house, and our cook Semyon would give her some titbit to eat. Whenever she met me, after her customary 'Are you still alive?' she would add:

'Give me a kopek.'

'What for?'

'To buy some sunflower seeds.'

One day I showed her a big five kopek piece, a silver twenty kopek piece, and a gold five ruble piece.

'Which do you want?'

'This one,' she answered as she snatched the big copper coin.

Once when I came on a visit to Yasnaya Polyana alone, without my husband, Parasha immediately asked:

'Where's your sweetheart?'

'I've left him,' I said jokingly. 'He beat me.'

'Ah, then you must forgive him,' she told me without hesitation.

A guest who had overheard this exchange was quite delighted by it.

'Only at Yasnaya Polyana could one ever hope to meet a village idiot of that calibre!' he crowed.

Returning to Yasnaya Polyana after several months' absence, I went into the kitchen as usual to visit my old friend Semyon. I found Parasha there.

'Are you still alive? Give me a kopek.'

'What for?'

'The baby,' she said, and her little eyes went into total eclipse as the fat cheeks shot upward in a beatific smile.

'The baby? What baby?'

Semyon intervened:

'Haven't you heard, Tatyana Lvovna? She is pregnant.'

'Pregnant? Parasha? But in heaven's name by whom?'

'A cooper who lived in her mother's isba for a while as a lodger. And this is the result! She's torn up her only halfway decent skirt to make swaddling clothes. And her mother's in despair.'

Parasha listened to Semyon with a beaming smile that seemed to be saying: 'So you see, I'm just the same as everyone else.' When I turned to her she took my hand and laid it on her belly.

'Feel how it moves, my little pup!'

I gave her a few kopeks.

'I'll buy some nice biscuits with that,' she said as she knotted the coins into her kerchief.

Poor Parasha! As her term drew near I watched the maternal instinct bud and blossom in her poor simpleton's soul. But why shouldn't she too have the right to fulfil her woman's life, I asked myself, just like all her sisters, who may be more richly endowed with intellectual qualities but less, perhaps, with moral ones? She sometimes asked me for scraps of material for her baby, and when I brought them out to her she would stroke them lovingly, already imagining her child clothed in those odd-shaped remnants.

I waited with a certain apprehension for the birth. How would it go off? At last her sister came up one day to tell us that the pains had begun. My sister Masha, who often nursed people in the village when they were ill, gathered a few medicines together and set off to Parasha's home. She found the local midwife already there with Parasha's mother. Parasha was moaning gently: the birth did not seem to be all that imminent.

'Forgive me, Masha,' Parasha said as she saw my sister come in.

And then, turning to her mother and sister:

'And you, little mother, forgive me too. And you, Olga. All of you forgive me.'

'May God forgive you, Parasha,' her mother replied as she clambered up on to the stove. 'And when you are up there and meet the Lord, put in a good word for us. You are a half-wit and the Lord will listen to you.'

At that the old woman wrapped her blanket around her and fell asleep. As for the midwife, convinced that the baby wasn't due for a long time yet she left. Masha stayed on alone with her patient. Eventually, since the pains were becoming more and more violent without any movement of the child, she decided she had better call in a doctor. She asked a peasant who lived next door to go to the station and telephone to Tula for a good midwife and a doctor.

It was almost morning before a professional nurse and an obstetrician arrived, bringing the appropriate instruments and medicaments. They had supposed that they were being summoned to Yasnaya Polyana house, and were somewhat disconcerted to find themselves in an isba at the bedside of a poor simple-minded peasant girl. To their credit, however, that did not prevent them from treating her just like any other patient, and they both did their very best for her.

They say it takes intelligence even to bring a baby into the world. Parasha lacked it, and they were obliged to use forceps. The episode came to a sad end with a little still-born daughter.

A few days later Parasha was back tending the village calves and asking passers-by for a kopek to buy sunflower seeds.

'I shan't do it again,' she said with her big smile. 'Masha's told me I mustn't. Next time I'm going to punch the fellow's nose in . . .'

The Italian Straw Hat

There was a period in my father's life when he took a great interest in the theatre, and one evening during this phase, at a time when he was writing his own comedy *The Fruits of Enlightenment,* he went to see Labiche's very amusing play *The Italian Straw Hat* at Moscow's Maly Theatre. During the interval he went out to take a turn in the foyer, where he bumped into a professor of his acquaintance who seemed rather embarrassed at having been caught by Tolstoy attending so frivolous an entertainment.

'Ah, Lev Nicolayevich,' he said with a forced laugh, 'so you've come to take a look at this tomfoolery too, have you?'

'All my life,' my father replied, 'I have dreamed of being able to write something of this sort. But I just lacked the talent.'

David Copperfield

We were talking literature at Yasnaya Polyana:

'If you were to put the whole of world literature through a sieve,' my father said, 'and keep only the very best, you would be left with Dickens. If you had to do the same with Dickens, you'd be left with *David Copperfield*. And if *David Copperfield* itself were put through the sieve, then you'd be left with the storm at sea . . .'

The Art of Being a Bore

Generally speaking, if every detail is included in a painting, a play, or a book, it soon becomes tedious. If, on the other hand, the artist presents only the broad outlines, leaving the task of imagining the rest to the spectators or readers, then he awakens their interest: they have the feeling of collaborating with the author. On condition, of course, that those broad outlines are such as to excite their imagination, their interest, their curiosity.

'The writer who wants to make gold,' my father used to say, 'must amass vast piles of raw material then sieve it all really thoroughly through his critical faculties.' He also liked quoting Pacal's postscript: 'I have made this letter so long only because I lacked the time to make it shorter.'

In Shakespeare's day they didn't bother very much about scenery: they made do with a placard on which they wrote out where the scene was supposed to take place. And as far as we know the audiences didn't enjoy his masterpieces any the less because the period and location of the action were not reproduced in microscopic detail.

One day, as an example of all this, my father presented us with two descriptions, one a failure and one a success. In some French novel he had found a description of the smell of roast goose that covered several pages.

'It's quite true,' he said, 'that by the time you get to the end you can smell that goose. But that's not the best way of imprinting things in people's minds. Do you remember, for example, the way Homer conveys Helen's beauty? With these simple words: 'When Helen walked in, at the sight of her beauty old men rose to their feet.' One pictures the radiance of that beauty right away. No need to describe her eyes, her mouth, her lips. Everyone is left free to imagine Helen in his own way, but everyone is struck by this beauty that draws old men to their feet at the mere sight of it.'

And my father concluded with this quotation from Voltaire: 'The art of boring people is to tell them everything.'

Ganya the Thief

Yasnaya Polyana village, like all villages in central Russia, is in the form of a single street about half a mile long. In those days it had about fifty isbas on each side of the street, and my father knew the inhabitants of every one of these little dwellings, in which he had watched several generations grow up.

The village school stood at the far end of the street from our house. The schoolmaster, a very good and admirable man, was blind in one eye. He often consulted my father on the subject of educational methods, and my father on his side always took a great interest in our conscientious teacher's work.

One winter evening my father set off to visit him. To reach the school he had to walk the entire length of the village. The lights were already out in all the houses: the evenings were long and paraffin expensive, so people went to bed early in the winter.

However, as he passed one tiny isba my father noticed a light. It came from the window of an unmarried woman well-known both for the looseness of her morals and for being a thief. Her name was Ganya, and the village people all sneered at her in the street.

My father went over to the window and glanced inside. Ganya was saying her prayers. Her lips moved from time to time, she emitted great sighs, she kept crossing herself over and over again, and then, throwing herself down on the floor, she began banging her forehead against it. 'What prayer can that unhappy creature be offering up?' my father wondered.

Having drawn back from the window he continued on his way to the schoolmaster's, spent some while in conversation with him, then set off back home. As he retraced his steps through the village he saw that Ganya's light was still not out. Again he went over to the window and looked in. Ganya was still on her knees, praying and crossing

169

herself. My father watched her for a little while, then returned home and told us what he had seen.

'Have we the right to destroy faith like that?' he asked when he'd finished. 'That loose woman's prayer may be wholly without meaning, but it is also possible that it is the one gleam of light in her sullied soul. It is not for us to judge which prayer is most pleasing to God . . .'

Art and Chance

It was at the time when Tolstoy, by then an old man, was writing his last great novel, *Resurrection*. I went into his study one day and saw him at his desk dealing out the cards for a game of patience. It was something he often did to give himself a rest, or to enable him to mull over what he had just written. Sometimes he even used the cards to make decisions for him: if the game came out, then he would do such and such a thing. If not, then he would do such and such.

Aware of this habit, I asked:

'Are you thinking of anything in particular?'

'Yes . . .'

'What?'

'Well,' he said, 'if it comes out, that means Nekhyudov is to marry Katyusha. If it doesn't, then they stay unmarried.'

When the game of patience was over I asked:

'Well?'

'Well,' he said, 'it came out . . . But the snag is that Katyusha can't marry Nekhyudov . . .'

And then he told me a story about Pushkin, one he had heard from Princess Mescherski, a friend of the great poet.

'One day Pushkin appeared at the princess's. "Do you know," he said to her, "that Tatyana of mine—meaning the heroine of *Eugen Onyegin,* which he was writing at the time—has shown Eugen the door. I simply wouldn't have believed her capable of such a thing." '

'The terrible thing for the writer,' papa added, 'is that once his characters have been created they begin living lives of their own, independent of their author's will. And once that starts to happen he just has to go along with his characters' moods. That is the reason why my Katyusha and Pushkin's Tatyana act as they see fit and not as their creators please.'

'But then,' I thought to myself, 'in order to "create" characters rather than just "inventing" them, you have to be Pushkin . . . or Tolstoy.'

Workers and Singers

One evening at Yasnaya Polyana we were discussing the division of labour. At that time my father was at work on his essay *What then must we do?*, a work full of passionate protest against the exploitation of the workers by the privileged class, and exposing the injustice of what is termed 'the division of labour'.

'Manual labour is always necessary,' my father said, 'whereas our kind of labour, whether scientific or artistic, is more often than not useful solely to the small social group we call the privileged class. As far as peasants and factory-workers are concerned our work is almost invariably useless. Yet we, without their work, would be quite unable to subsist, let alone go on producing all the hollow scientific or artistic products that are such a source of pride to us and no good whatever to the labouring class.'

The painter Repin, our guest at the time, broke in:

'If you will allow me, Lev Nicolayevich, I would like to tell you about something I once saw. As you know, I live on the outskirts of Petersburg near the naval shipyards. I often see the workers there hauling away at big hawsers, manoeuvring sections of the ships on the stocks into position. And one day, because the load they were dragging was much heavier than usual, one particular team seemed to be on the point of giving up out of sheer fatigue. At that point I saw two men leave their positions in the group, jump up on to the big girder they were pulling, and launch into a rousing song, really letting rip in virile, ringing voices. And the sheer vigour of their song had such an effect on their comrades that they seemed to be galvanized with new strength, and found their task had become light again.'

'And so?' my father said, having listened to the painter attentively and now eager to hear his conclusions.

'Well,' Repin went on in a modest tone, 'I think that those who are able to lighten the workers' load through their art should also be allowed the right to exist. They have a part to play as well. I myself feel that I am one of those people. I want to be one of the singers . . .'

'Very well put,' my father said with a laugh. 'The only snag, unfortunately, is that there are too many people wanting to jump on the girder and not enough pulling it. That's the problem!'

Tolstoy's sneezes

When papa sneezed it was like a bomb going off, and you could hear it all over the house. When it happened during the night it always woke my mother up with a great shock, and being of a nervous disposition she then found it impossible to get to sleep again. So eventually she said to him:

'If you feel a sneeze coming on in the night, just wake me up very gently before it happens. That way I shall be able to get back to sleep.'

My father promised he would do as she asked. And one night, when he felt a sneeze coming on, he very gently woke my mother up.

'Sonya,' he whispered, 'don't be afraid. It's just that I'm going to sneeze.'

My mother woke up and lay there waiting. Two minutes went by, then three, then five. Not a sound! She leaned over her husband and listened to his slow, regular breathing. He was asleep. The need to sneeze had subsided and he had dozed peacefully off again.

Paolo Trubetskoy

One evening I heard from my friends the Trubetskoys that they were coming on a visit and bringing their cousin, the sculptor Paolo Trubetskoy. I had already heard people talking about this somewhat eccentric person, who although he had spent his childhood and youth in Milan, and indeed been brought up exclusively in Italy, had never set foot in a single one of that country's museums to look at the sculptures. I also knew that he was a convinced vegetarian, that his mother was South American, and that he spoke not a word of Russian. He was said to be very talented and was already quite famous abroad.

Since I was interested in everything to do with the arts, I looked forward to his visit with curiosity. Eventually he arrived, and what I saw was a tall young man, rather shy and taciturn, whose eyes seemed to actually fasten themselves on to anything he looked at.

The first conversation between Trubetskoy and my father was a rather odd one.

'I haven't read any of your books,' Trubetskoy confessed.

'Then you've done the right thing!' my father answered.

'But I did read your article about tobacco, because I wanted to stop smoking . . .'

'And?'

'Well, I read the article, and I'm still smoking . . .'

They both burst out laughing.

From the very first moment of their meeting Trubetskoy was so totally fascinated by my father's physical appearance that he kept an intense and continual watch on his slightest movements, gestures, and changes of expression. The artist was studying his model. But my father, being by nature shy and retiring, felt extremely embarrassed at the way his guest's eyes were riveted on him the whole time.

'I understand now what you women feel,' he whispered in my ear, 'when some fellow is madly in love with you. It's very embarrassing.'

To escape his guest's searching gaze, my father decided it was time he paid a visit to the public baths [in those days few Russian houses were equipped with their own bathrooms, so that visits to the public baths were a frequent occurrence] and announced his intention to the assembled company. Trubetskoy's face immediately lit up, and leaning towards my father he said:

'Lev Nicolayevich, I shall accompany you, if you have no objection.'

The opportunity to observe his model undraped was a hitherto unhoped for prospect that inspired his artist's soul with joy. My father, however, became quite panic-stricken.

'Uhhh, no,' he said, 'no, on second thoughts I don't think I really ought to have a bath today. I'll have it another time, it's far too cold this evening.'

Trubetskoy did of course make several busts and statues of Tolstoy. And they are undoubtedly that great artist's greatest masterpieces.

The Lunatic Asylum

My father was extremely interested in mad people, and never missed an opportunity of observing them. He used to say that madness was egoism carried to its ultimate conclusion.

The garden of our Moscow house bordered on the grounds of a lunatic asylum. There was only a board fence between them. Through the gaps in this fence we were able to watch the mad people walking in the grounds. We even struck up an acquaintance with some of them. They used to hand us flowers, and snatched the opportunity of brief conversations with us when their keepers' backs were turned.

One of these unfortunates had lost his reason after the death of his only child, a boy about the same age as my little brother Vanya. He became very attached to Vanya, waited by the fence with the greatest impatience for him to come out into our garden, and picked all the best flowers in the asylum flower beds to present to him. It has to be said that Vanya was in fact a most exceptional and very charming child who displayed the greatest love and attention to everyone he met, and thanks to him this poor man in fact recovered his will to live. After his discharge from the hospital he wrote my mother a most touching letter. In it he told her that he had learned from Vanya that love and affection still existed in this world, and he thanked her for having brought so enchanting a being into it.

One unfortunate inmate succeeded in escaping from the asylum and hiding in our garden. A number of orderlies came running round to our door, and after asking permission started a systematic search all round our house. They finally found the poor fellow hiding behind a tree.

My father knew the asylum's principal medical adviser, a Professor Korsakov, who was very well known in those days for his research into nervous and mental illnesses. My father used to enjoy talking to him a great deal, and one evening Korsakov invited us to an entertainment being given in the asylum. Both cast and audience were to be made up of inmates.

The actual entertainment provided was completely indistinguishable from any amateur entertainment of the kind given by members of Moscow society. It consisted mainly of a series of sketches and one-act comedies, all most amusingly acted by performers who gave no signs whatever of being anything but perfectly normal people. But the same could not be said of the audience. I remember one young girl in particular, seated not very far away from me, who despite the tremendous efforts she was making was unable to prevent herself from laughing. Her face became quite scarlet, and then suddenly the laughter would come bursting out, a terrifying cachinnation that was hard to distinguish from sobbing. Others muttered under their breath all the time. And some, with orderlies or nurses stationed on both sides of them, paid no attention at all to what was happening on the stage, but kept flashing malevolent glances around them the whole time.

During the interval a number of people came up to my father and engaged him in conversation. Suddenly we caught sight of a man with a black beard hurrying over toward us, his eyes sparkling with delight behind his glasses. It was a friend of ours who had been taken into the asylum to be treated for *delirium tremens*.

'Ah, Lev Nicolayevich,' he exclaimed delightedly, 'how very glad I am to see you! So you're here now, are you? How long have you been with us?'

He was very disappointed when he discovered that my father had only been invited in for the evening.

Twenty Eight

Tolstoy was born on August 28th 1828. He left to join the army in the Caucasus on a 28th. The letter written by the editor of *Sovremennik* accepting his first work, *Childhood,* for publication, arrived on a 28th. His first son was born on a 28th. My father never failed to comment on any recurrence of that figure himself. 'Ah, the 28th again,' he would say. Last of all, he left his home for the last time on October 28th 1910. When I went to see him in the little house at Astapovo station where he completed his final journey, he said to me:

'Just look in *A Circle of Reading* and read what it gives for October 28th.' (*A Circle of Reading* was one of my father's last books. It is a selection of thoughts and maxims culled from the works of various wise men of all countries and ages and arranged in the form of a calendar.)

I took up the book and read the page for October 28th aloud. All the thoughts allotted to that date were concerned with the necessity for suffering as a precondition of progress along the path of perfection. Here are three of them:

Tolstoy: 'Just as pain is a sensation necessary for the preservation of our body, so suffering is necessary for the preservation of our soul.'

Kant: 'Suffering causes us to act, and is that which makes us aware of our existence.'
Schiller: 'Do not let yourself become accustomed to happiness, for it passes; let he who possesses it accustom himself to the idea of losing it, and he who is happy to that of suffering.'

'I didn't read that page before I set off,' my father said.
He lived for 82 years: the same two digits reversed.

Eyes Like Drills

My father loved all mankind, and every human being seemed to him worthy of interest.

'One day when I was at the Tolstoys',' Turgenyev once recounted, 'I noticed that among the many people also present there was one young girl who seemed to be of particular interest to our host. He kept staring at her with those penetrating eyes of his, without realizing that he was making her extremely ill at ease. His eyes simply kept up their piercing scrutiny like a pair of drills, boring deeper and deeper into her very being, till I began to think I could actually see them coming out on the other side of the poor girl's head. Yet Tolstoy himself remained completely oblivious of the embarrassment he was causing her, and just kept on staring and staring at her.'

My father, who had been listening to all this, began to laugh.

'But why ever didn't you make some sort of signal to me on the quiet? Then I might have realized how very rude I was being.'

Mamma's Laugh

Mamma laughed rarely, and probably that was why her laugh lent her such a singular charm. I remember two occasions in particular when she laughed quite uncontrollably, and both times it was a remark of my father's that had provoked her hilarity.

My mother adored babies, and once we were all grown up, so that we no longer needed her to look after us, she often felt at a loss. As a result, and by way of compensation, she was always on the look-out for opportunities to mother any baby she could lay hands on. One day she was looking after a little child from the village:

'I am going to have a rubber baby made for you,' my father told her, 'one that will have constant diarrhoea. And then I shall expect you to be totally happy . . .'

My mother burst into a fit of loud laughter, and covered her mouth with her hand, as though to staunch that untypical flood of merriment.

On another occasion, as I arrived at Yasnaya Polyana on a visit, my father said:

'Take care! Mamma has just bought the most enormous quantity of gloss paint, and is busy painting everything she can lay her hands on. Though in all justice I must admit that so far at least she has spared the living.'

Mamma, happy to sense a kind of affection in his teasing tone, began to laugh. She seemed embarrassed, and somehow astonished too, at being unable to restrain herself. As for papa, delighted at having amused her, he simply gazed at her with great gentleness.

The Police Officer

My father always travelled third class. One day he had to go out to a small town about thirty miles from Moscow to look out some material he needed for his work, and stayed the night with his brother-in-law, who was a municipal official there. Having made the notes he needed, and anxious to get back to Moscow, my father returned to the station escorted by my uncle and his family. They were received on the steps with great ceremony by the police officer on duty—in full dress uniform—, who had been informed that Count Tolstoy, the celebrated writer, was coming to catch a train there.

My father had scarcely begun moving toward the ticket office when the policeman leapt forward, clicked his heels, saluted, and said: 'His Excellency must not bother. If His Excellency would permit me to buy his ticket for him. Is His Excellency travelling first class? Or second class?'

'Second class,' my father answered in a cowardly murmur.

Back home again in Moscow, my father proceeded to give us a self-mocking account of his pitiful showing in this encounter. He just couldn't forgive himself. He despised himself. And this little incident upset him so much that I heard him recounting it to innumerable other people too.

Yet it seems to me that it was not in fact cowardice at all that made him permit the policeman to buy a second rather than a third class ticket, but simply his reluctance to disappoint the man. For my father always did everything he could to avoid hurting people's feelings, and it was clear to him that if he had asked for a third class ticket the policeman would have been shocked. I ought also to add that my father was always prepared, at the least opportunity, to accuse himself of every conceivable failing you could imagine.

The Chopin Waltz

As children we were all given piano lessons. My brother Ilya had no aptitude for music whatever, and his French tutor claimed that whenever he began to play the dogs all howled and ran away. But one day, when my father was in his study, he heard Ilya attacking a Chopin waltz with the most amazing and uncharacteristic brio. Keeping his foot hard down on the pedal, utterly undeterred by all his wrong notes, he swept on through the piece at a truly awe-inspiring fortissimo.

My father got up, tiptoed over to the door, and opened it slightly so that he could see into the room where Ilya was playing. It became immediately clear to him then why Ilya had so abruptly acquired the manner of a great virtuoso: our carpenter, Prokhor, was in the room putting up the inner windows for the winter. We were all of us very fond of old Prokhor, and Ilya was a particular friend of his. He often used to visit him in his workshop, where he had learned a great deal about the techniques of carpentry, as well as how to turn little wooden ornaments on the lathe. Indeed, there could be no doubt that his talent for woodwork exceeded by far his very meagre gift for music. Papa understood immediately: it was to impress Prokhor that he was massacring poor Chopin like that. Papa silently closed the door and retreated, but later told us all what he had seen.

Ever since then, whenever one of us was attempting to show off or impress someone, another member of the family would invariably murmur: 'Ah yes . . . that's for Prokhor.' And that little phrase was always enough to deflate us.

Everyone who is afraid of death

One evening at Yasnaya Polyana when there were a great many people to dinner, not only our immediate family and our aunt Tatyana's but a great many guests and friends as well, including Turgenyev, the conversation turned to death and the fear it inspires.

'Everyone who is afraid of death put up his hand,' Turgenyev said, raising his own.

He looked round: his large, beautiful hand was the only one raised. There were many of us at the table, my brothers, my sisters, my cousins, and I, who were still all under twenty at the time. Who fears death, or anything else, at such an age?

'It would appear then,' Turgenyev said sadly, 'that I am alone.'

At that my father put his hand up as well.

'Me too,' he said. 'I'm afraid of death.'

At that point our aunt Tatyana's beautiful clear voice rang out:

'What kind of subject for conversation is this? Can't we find something less macabre to talk about?'

'But Tanya,' said my father, who never missed an opportunity to tease his sister-in-law, 'don't you realize that you're going to die as well, even you?'

'Me? Die! Oh Lev, another of your silly jokes!' my aunt exclaimed without a moment's hesitation.

Everyone laughed heartily and we began talking about something else.

An Incomprehensible Sect

One of our friends, a man of great culture and broad intellect named Basil Maklakov, said once apropos of Tolstoy's disciples: 'Those who understand Tolstoy don't imitate him. And those who imitate him don't understand him.'

I often had occasion to observe the accuracy of this observation. Of the innumerable visitors who poured in from all over the world to see my father many were tolstoyans only in name. They limited themselves to imitating the Master's manner and appearance without any comprehension of the deeper meaning of his ideas. As for those who did understand, they had also grasped that Tolstoy left everyone free to live his own life and resolve his own problems as he saw fit. Consequently they never sought to imitate the externals of his behaviour, which in their eyes had no importance.

One day, among the group surrounding my father, I noticed a strange young man in a Russian smock, baggy trousers, and topboots.

'Who is that?' I asked my father.

Papa leaned toward me, put his hand in front of his mouth, and whispered in my ear:

'He is a young member of what is to me the world's most strange and incomprehensible sect: the tolstoyans.

You are just an ignorant lout

My father laughed till he almost burst when he told us this story . . . He had gone out, as he often did, for a walk along the main road. It was what he ironically referred to as his 'grand tour'. As he made his way along the road—the main Moscow–Kiev high-road—he used to meet and converse with pilgrims, peasants on the way back from market, and a whole variety of other passers-by.

On this particular day having walked rather further than was usual, my father began to feel tired on the way back. He hailed the first vehicle that came along, which happened to be a sleigh drawn by a well fed pony and driven by a man snugly wrapped in a big cape. The man very affably invited my father to get in beside him. As they continued on their way they fell into conversation, and my father learned that his companion was from Krasnoyeh, a village about fifteen miles from Yasnaya Polyana.

'Ah, then it was in your village that they nearly buried the sexton alive,' my father said. 'They say it was only as he was actually being lowered into the grave that anyone noticed he wasn't dead.'

The man went scarlet with rage.

'You are an ignorant dolt!' he cried, trembling with fury. 'Yes, despite your grey hairs I tell you that you are an ignorant dolt, just an ignorant dolt . . .'

It was the sexton himself!

Why should being reminded of this incident, of which he had not the slightest need to be ashamed, have made him so extraordinarily indignant? Did he think my father had already recognized him and was deliberately mocking him? We never found out. For reining his pony to a halt he made my father leave his sleigh, repeating the whole time:

'An ignorant dolt, that's what you are! And I say it again, despite your grey hairs: an ignorant dolt!'

Stupider than you?

In my youth, as is frequent at that age, I tended to be arrogant and to judge others more harshly than I did myself. This pained my father, and he hit upon a tactful way of correcting this defect: every time I came out with some sweeping condemnation on the lines of: 'How stupid that person is!', he would interrupt me by innocently inquiring:

'Stupider than you?'

If I said that some man was boring or that a woman was plain, he never failed to ask:

'More boring than you? . . . Plainer than you?'

I understood the lesson he was trying to teach me perfectly well, but I refused to accept it and would answer back insolently:

'Yes, stupider than me! More boring than me! Plainer than me!'

But the lesson went home all the same. The proof being that I still remember it.

Life in accordance with the laws of nature

In 1892, the year of the great famine, my father, my younger sister, and I were all a long way from Yasnaya Polyana, in the province of Riazan, one of those most badly afflicted by the disaster, where we had gone to provide aid for the inhabitants. As a result of a collection taken up among society people we had considerable funds at our disposal. My father, without ever deceiving himself that it was anything other than a palliative, had felt unable to refuse his aid in that time of distress, and did everything within his power in the circumstances.

In addition to the various people who flocked in from all over the place to offer us their help, we were also visited by numbers of journalists and others who were mainly interested in observing Tolstoy in action. Among this latter group was one of the oddest men I have ever known, a Swede by the name of Abraam von Bunde.

Here is how my father described his arrival to my mother: 'Three days ago a seventy-year old Swede arrived here, a man who has lived for thirty years in America, as well as visiting China, Japan, and India. He is short, fair-haired, with a big yellowish grey beard, wears an enormous hat, and dresses in rags. He looks rather like me. He is an apostle of "life in accordance with the laws of nature". He speaks fluent English, is extremely intelligent, original, and interesting. For instance, he wants to teach people how a single individual can produce sufficient food for ten off a plot of only about ten acres, and that without livestock and using a spade as the only means of cultivation . . . Every evening he treats us to a long discourse. He is a vegetarian, denies himself even eggs and dairy produce, and prefers his food raw. He goes barefoot, sleeps on the floor, and uses a bottle by way of a pillow . . .'

In June we returned to Yasnaya Polyana. Prospects for the coming harvest were good, our co-workers had taken over the responsibility of dismantling our food centres, and we all felt we had certainly earned a little rest after so many months of hard work under very arduous and often dangerous conditions. My father had invited the French journalist Jules Huret, who had come to Russia to interview him, to spend a few days with us at home. As for our Swede, he had been absolutely insistent upon accompanying us, but my father had finally prevailed on him to follow on the next day.

'I find it embarrassing enough travelling alone,' papa told us, 'because people recognize me and stare so. But travelling with my double—and a double in rags—I have to confess I just didn't have the courage.'

The Swede duly arrived at Yasnaya Polyana and settled himself in as though intending to spend the rest of his days there. He was continually preaching 'life in accordance with the laws of nature', and critical of everything that infringed those laws, such as meat, wine, and tobacco.

One evening, after dinner, we were taking our coffee outside under the trees. Jules Huret, impeccably dressed, was chatting with the ladies while Abraam sat darkly glaring at him. While talking, Huret felt in his pocket, took out a cigar, and with the ladies' permission lighted it. The Swede's expression grew still blacker. He turned to me, and speaking as usual in English, he said:

'Ask that man if he wants me to spit in his face.'

My mother flashed me an admonitory glance that clearly meant: don't translate that. But I was young, and took a mischievous pleasure in the thought of setting two such totally different men at odds. I glanced over at my father and caught an answering glint of mischief in his eye. Spurred on, I turned to Huret and said in the most civil of tones:

'Monsieur, that gentleman is asking if you want him to spit in your face.'

Huret started, then wavering between politeness and anger replied: 'Oh, and can you tell me why?'

I translated for the Swede.

'Tell him that the smoke he is spreading makes me sick.'

I translated again.

'Ah,' Huret said, his anger getting the upper hand now, 'then will you tell him, please, that these ladies have given me their permission to smoke. And as for him, please say that I am doing my utmost to ignore his presence, particularly since the mere sight of his filthy feet would make me sick.'

I continued translating.

'He's a liar,' the Swede said calmly. 'Just tell him he's a liar. The sense of sight cannot produce nausea, whereas smoke is unhealthy and can certainly induce vomiting.'

My mother's desperate signals had no effect, I had no wish to put an end to a dialogue that was causing papa such amusement. Huret, becoming angrier every moment, said that if it weren't for the presence of the ladies he would slap the old Swede across the face. My mother, deciding that Abraam had gone too far, felt obliged to defend her French guest. She told the Swede, rather sharply, that it would be best if he left Yasnaya Polyana. Bunde, phlegmatic as ever, replied:

'But you know, with my five acres of land . . .'

My mother didn't let him finish:

'Yes, yes, I know!' she said. 'So please go and live on your five acres.'

'I have worked it out mathematically,' Abraam went on imperturbably. 'Every man has a right to five acres of this earth. And I intend to take my five here.'

'You'll do no such thing, because I won't have it!' my mother exclaimed. 'You may take them wherever else you wish, but not at Yasnaya Polyana.'

'Very well,' the Swede said gently. 'If you do not wish it then I won't take them here. But you cannot refuse me the tiny piece of earth my two feet take up. About this much.' And he laid his hands flat on the table to demonstrate eactly the area of land he was laying claim to.

By this time, however, my mother had heard quite enough, and she was adamant that Abraam had to leave Yasnaya Polyana. After his departure we found his watch, together with a few small tools attached to the chain. I made a package of them and posted it off to the forwarding address in Sweden he had left us. A few weeks later the package was returned to me: addressee unknown. Where had he gone? In what far-off region was he wandering? Did he live on for many years after leaving us, or was he already dead by then? All questions to which we never received any answer.

As for Jules Huret, after spending several days at Yasnaya Polyana, collecting all the information he required, he went back to Paris, where his impressions of Tolstoy and the Russian famine were published in *Le Figaro*.

The Old Mujik

My father always wore a traditional mujik's smock, with a tulupa over it in winter when he went out. The reason he dressed in this way was so that he could feel free to approach the poor people he met and be treated by them as an equal. But his simple apparel did sometimes lead to misunderstandings.

I witnessed one such incident myself. It happened in Tula, our regional capital, where a performance of his play *The Fruits of Enlightenment* was being mounted to raise funds for a home for the children of criminals. Since I had been asked to take part in my father's play, I was going in to Tula fairly regularly in order to rehearse. During the course of one particular rehearsal the hall doorman came in to tell us that there was someone outside asking to come in.

'It's an old mujik,' he said. 'And no matter how many times I tell him it's impossible he keeps on insisting. He must be drunk, I just can't get him to understand that he has no business coming here.'

I realized at once who the old mujik was, and to the doorman's great displeasure told him to send the visitor in immediately. Shortly afterwards I saw my father walk in, still chuckling at the mistake his clothes had caused.

Papa's lady friend

'Guess which lady I escorted past the house a moment ago.'

The question was put to us one evening by papa when he returned from his usual stroll through the Moscow streets. There were a great many ladies in Moscow he might well have given his arm to, but why had he so specifically said 'past the house'?

'Because "past the house" is precisely where I escorted her . . .'

We went through all the ladies of our acquaintance who might conceivably be eligible, but papa shook his head at them all.

'No, not her . . . No, not her either . . .'

We gave up.

'All right then, I'll tell you. Do you remember the old dear who collects for the parish charity fund outside the church round the corner? Well, it seems that earlier this evening she managed to break open that collecting-box of hers. And she then proceeded to get so drunk on the money inside that she couldn't walk a step. So since her house is just at the end of our street . . .'

'So it was her you were escorting!'

'What else could I do? Her legs kept giving way, so she asked me to see her home. Could I refuse?'

I desire all I have

During the early years of my father's marriage the writer Sologub came to see him at Yasnaya Polyana and found him wholly contented with his lot.

'What a fortunate man you are!' Sologub said to him. 'Life has brought you all you desire . . .'

'No,' my father replied, 'it's not that I have all I desire, it's that I desire all I have.'

My father's death

Author's Preface

I *have often been reproached for failing to protest against the impostures, the plagiaries, the counterfeits, and the slanders that have appeared from time to time in print throughout the world, and that are still appearing, associated with the name of my father, Leo Tolstoy.*

In keeping silent I have been following his example; my father made it a rule never to protest against any infringement of his literary rights, or to answer any slander on his private life.

If I am breaking my silence now it is because certain books have been published, originating with friends of my father, that give a false picture of the relations between my parents, and a portrait of my mother distorted by prejudice. The facts related in those books are for the most part correct, and yet, to use an expression of our own Nicolai Gogol, there is nothing worse than a truth that isn't true.

As the eldest daughter, I have come to the conclusion that it is my responsibility to defend the truth. I owe it to my parents' memory now to break my silence. It is a painful duty, however, since it will force me to reveal many things of a kind not ordinarily mentioned outside a family's private circle.

But my family was not an ordinary one. We belonged to the category of those who live in glass houses, and our home was open to all who chose to visit it. Anyone and everyone was free to see everything, to penetrate the most secret regions of our family life, and to display the results of those observations, truthful or otherwise, in the market place. Our only protection lay in the discretion of our visitors.

My father was never afraid to talk about himself, whenever he felt that it was necessary, and made no secret of his life. He himself wrote A Confession, in which he laid bare all the secrets of his heart with an unflinching sincerity.

I have now decided that the time has come when I must share with all those interested in Tolstoy everything that I myself experienced during a lifetime spent very close to him. I have my own opinion on the relations between my father and my mother, and on their relations with us, their children. I am a witness. I wished to address myself in the first place to my Russian brothers and sisters, among whom my father still has many friends. But today I am addressing myself to a wider readership that also, I am quite sure, includes many friends of Tolstoy. As for myself, I have nothing to hide from those friends. I wish them to judge for themselves. I simply want to put before them, seen from a new angle, some aspects of my father's life. I shall speak to them truthfully and trustingly, and if I do not say everything I could say on the tragedy of my parents' life, it is because too many people were involved in that tragedy, and for some of them it would still be too soon.

On a dark autumn night, that of October 28th, at three in the morning, my father left the house at Yasnaya Polyana where he had been born and where he had spent the greater part of his life.

What were the motives that led to this departure—I might even say, this flight? Do we know, shall we ever know?

It is easy to say that Tolstoy ran away from his wife because she did not understand him and made life difficult for him. Or that the relative luxury in which his family lived was distressing to him, and that he wished to live a simple life, out of society, among the peasants and workers. But there is never in any man's life a single reason that drives him to perform one particular action rather than any other. Any given action invariably derives from a whole network of motives, all intermingling, conflicting, contradicting or reinforcing one another. And this was particularly the case with my father, because his nature was so rich, so passionate, and so complex.

I witnessed my father's life during both of its broad phases: that before his religious crisis and that after. I should add that I was a particularly well qualified witness. I was associated more closely than any other person with his inner life. For the thirty-five years before my marriage I always lived at home. My father confided in me a great deal, especially with regard to my mother. He knew I loved them both, and that I would always be ready to do everything I could to bring peace between them.

My mother also confided her secret troubles to me, as well as letting me share her joys. I was her eldest daughter, only twenty years younger than herself. And over the years the difference in our ages gradually dwindled in importance, until quite soon she was treating me almost as her friend and equal.

To understand the tragic situation that built up imperceptibly over half a century and led to my father's departure, then to his death in the stationmaster's little house, one first needs to understand how Tolstoy became the man he was, and also what kind of person his future wife, the young Sofia Behrs, had once been.

I have before me as I write the personal diary my father first began to keep in 1847. He was at that time nineteen years old and a student at the university of Kazan. I also have that begun by my mother in 1862. She was then eighteen and very newly married. Any attentive reader of these two documents will be able to discern in them the seeds of both my parents' characters in their maturity.

First the man: constantly wrestling with his passions, constantly analyzing himself, judging himself with implacable severity, insisting on the highest standards both in himself and others. At the same time an incorrigible optimist, never complaining, finding a way out of every difficult situation, searching for a solution to every problem, a consolation for every misfortune, every setback. He could find compensation even in a toothache. He notes in his diary: 'Toothache brings a greater appreciation of health.' And again: 'My illnesses have certainly been a source of great moral profit to me, I therefore thank God for having sent them.'

The leitmotiv of his entire life is 'making himself better'. On March 24th 1847 he wrote:

'I have changed a great deal, but still not attained the degree of perfection I would have liked.' Then immediately went on to list a number of rules of conduct.

He set himself too many tasks, and since he was never able to perform them all was perpetually dissatisfied with himself.

On April 7th he wrote:

'I leave in a week for the country. What ought I to do during that week? I'd like to take advantage of it to study English, Latin, Roman law, and to concentrate on the rules of life I want to lay down for myself.'

At the end of the week he noted:

'How shall I make use of my time in the country during the next two years? 1. Continue my law studies in order to pass my final exam at university. 2. Study the rudiments of theoretical and practical medicine. 2. Study languages: French, Russian, German, English, Italian, Latin. 4. Study the theory and practice of agriculture. 5. Study history, geography, and statistics. 6. Study mathematics (the Gymnasium course). 7. Write a dissertation. 8. Try to perfect myself in music and art. 8. Get down my rule of life in writing. 10. Acquire some knowledge of the natural sciences. 11. Write something on all the subjects I study.

The following day he realized he was being excessive, and on April 18th noted:

'I have laid down a great many precepts for myself and tried to carry them all out at once. I am not up to it.'

Two months later he observed:

'Ah, how hard it is for a man to become better when he is subjected to nothing but bad influences . . . Will I ever succeed in freeing myself from my circumstances? That is what perfection means, in my opinion.'

Later he came to see that 'self-perfection' and 'self-improvement' are different things, and on July 3rd he was to write:

'My chief error was to aim at perfecting myself instead of just improving myself. One might begin by understanding one's self and one's failings thoroughly, then go on from there and strive to correct them, instead of aiming at perfection, which is not only impossible to achieve from the very low level I am on, but which . . . robs you of all hope of ever attaining it . . .'

He continued this struggle with himself indefatigably. He never lost hope. From time to time he recorded advances he made along this path of self-improvement. He wrote that he was 'taking great strides forward'. He was delighted with the rapidity with which his 'moral improvement is progressing'. And he was tireless in pursuing that path. One day he set himself the following task:

'One good action every day.' Then added: 'That's enough.'

'I am firmly resolved to devote my life to my fellow-man. For the last time I tell myself: if I don't do something for others during the next three days, I shall kill myself.'

And a month later: 'If I don't do something tomorrow, I shall kill myself.'

Many years later, looking back at those years of inner struggle, my father wrote:

'. . . My only sincere faith at that time was a faith in self-perfection. What the aim of it was I had no idea . . . With all my soul I longed to be good, but I was young, I had my passions, I was alone, absolutely alone, in my search for the good. Every time I expressed my most secret desire—to be morally good—I met with scorn, mockery. While the moment I abandoned myself to sinful passions I was given praise and encouragement.'

Then came his marriage.

On September 12th 1862 he noted: 'I am in love as I never believed it possible to be. I am a madman, and I shall put a bullet through my head if it goes on like this.'

On September 16th he handed the young Sofia Behrs a letter in which he requested her hand. In his diary he wrote: 'Hand requested. She: yes. She, like a wounded bird. Useless to write. Impossible to forget or record it.'

A week later—on September 23rd—they were married. Two days later, he noted:

'Immense happiness . . . It is impossible that it will all end only with death.'

What did marriage mean for Tolstoy? An interlude of love, a means of putting an end to the temptations that assailed him; a stage in his life, but one that did not make use of his spiritual and mental energies to the full. Before a year had passed he was already realizing that the first nine months of marriage had been for him a period of moral hibernation. His egotistic life filled him with remorse. His idleness had become a burden to him and robbed him of his self-esteem. The joys of family life were absorbing him too completely and making him forget 'the higher regions of truth and energy' he had once known. On June 18th 1863 he noted:

'Where has my self gone? The self I once loved and knew, that sometimes jetted out of me with such eruptive force, to my own pleasure and terror? I am small and insignificant. And what is worse, I have become so since I found myself married to a woman I love . . .'

And he concluded that day's entry with the prayer:

'Oh Lord, lend me grace and succour me . . .'

Now the woman. Who was she when she met, loved, and married Tolstoy? The second daughter of Doctor Behrs, physician to the Imperial Russian Court, brought up in exactly the same way as all the other young ladies of her class and time. In those days the goal of every young girl was marriage. And my mother was also drawn to that ideal by instinct. To her, marriage was a sacrament. Her entire education had been a preparation for life as a wife and mother, and she brought to that family life all the treasures of her virgin body and soul.

Unlike her husband, however, she was of a pessimistic nature. She often lost heart, and was easily reduced to despair. To her, it seemed as though everything around her had been designed deliberately to make her unhappy. She saw herself constantly as caught in some imaginary and insoluble dilemma, and instead of searching for a way out she would lament her lot, by turns reproaching herself and finding excuses for herself. She felt at once responsible for all the misfortunes surrounding her and guilty at her inability to remedy them.

The first great sorrow she experienced was the discovery of her husband's past life. Right up until her death she was still unable to come to terms with the idea that she had given him all her love while he had loved other women before her. She wrote in her diary:

'His whole past is so terrible to me that I don't think I shall ever get over it . . . He doesn't understand that his whole past, his whole life, with its thousands of good and bad feelings, can no longer belong to me, just as his youth, spent God knows on whom and on what, cannot belong to me. And he doesn't understand either that I have given him everything, that none of my life had been spent at all, that there is only my childhood that didn't belong to him . . . And even that childhood belonged to him too . . . He would rather I had lived the same life as him, experienced evil as much as him, so that I too would understand the good better. He feels an instinctive anger because happiness came to me so easily, because I just put out my hand and took it, without thought, without suffering . . . I cannot forgive God for arranging things so that men have to go through such experiences before becoming properly behaved people.'

So happiness had come to her, but she was unable to enjoy it. Even when there was no reason for her not to be happy she went out of her way to fill herself with doubts and presentiments.

'When he's unwell I think: what if he should die? And that means three hours of gloomy thoughts. When he is in high spirits I say to myself: if only these high spirits last . . . When he's out or busy I am obsessed with the thought of him, I am perpetually listening: can that be him? And when he is with me I keep a constant check on his expression . . .'

She was jealous of everything and everyone.

'He makes me sick and tired with his people. I feel he will have to choose between me—me as representing his family—and the people and this fervent love he feels for them. It's just selfishness on my part. But I don't care! I live only for him, through him. I demand the same thing for myself . . . I have read the first things he wrote. Whenever there is any mention of love, of women, I feel revulsion, distress. I would have liked to burn it all, so that there would be nothing to remind me of his past. And I would have had no pity for his distress, because jealousy makes me appallingly selfish. If I could kill him then create another just like him, I'd have done so with pleasure.'

Poor child! All these incoherent notions she invented were simply a form of self-torture that only increased her suffering. She couldn't grasp that the source of that suffering lay in the incompatibility between her idea of marriage and reality. For her, the ultimate end of everything was family life: to be a loving and faithful wife and a devoted mother, that was the duty she had imposed on herself. And God knows she performed that duty loyally throughout her long life. And she wanted Tolstoy to feel and act as she did.

Yet how was he to limit his interests to the needs of a family? How could he be merely a husband and father?

Because of the great love that united them, the seeds of discord already present in the earliest days of my parents' marriage remained dormant for about twenty years. Until the moment of what is termed Tolstoy's conversion or religious crisis, though he himself called it his second birth, the first twenty years of their marriage were happy ones.

As I have said, my mother was only eighteen when she married my father. She was beautiful, of delicate build, dark-haired, and passionate. She had never lived in the country. And now this girl from the city, this child almost, was obliged to say goodbye to the merriment of life as part of a large family, and to all the excitements and entertainments of a great city. One dark September night, in one of the great composite carriages of that time called 'sleepers', she set off with her husband for Yasnaya Polyana, where she was to find just one old aunt, Tatyana Alexandrovna, who lived there alone apart from a number of rather queer characters one of whom was no longer in her right mind. The young bride was frightened: instead of the bright lighting of the Kremlin, where she had lived with her parents, there was the thick darkness of a country courtyard; instead of a stream of delightful visitors she saw only the humble pilgrims from the high-road to whom the doors of her house were always open. These new, totally unfamiliar surroundings seemed to her odd, foreign, and rather frightening. And her husband slept on a divan, head resting not on a proper pillow but on a leather cushion—without even a pillow case!

The young wife had some difficulty in adapting to a way of life so utterly new to her. Yet the deep love she and her husband felt for one another eclipsed everything.

My father wrote in his diary:

'She is incomparably pure, good, and totally giving with me. In those moments it is not I who possess her, I would not dare, it is she who owns me utterly.'

The young Sofia on her side saw herself as far from worthy of this great man, her husband. She made constant efforts to raise herself to the high plane he occupied in her eyes: 'I never cease to be aware of his superiority in every way,' she wrote in her diary: 'superiority in age, superiority of education, of intelligence, of experience of life, not to mention his genius. I have been doing my utmost to catch him up spiritually, or if not that, then at least to get close enough to understand him. But I am so conscious of lacking the necessary strength.'

Here is what their daily life was like at Yasnaya Polyana at that time: once my father had drunk his morning coffee he went through into his study. But even during his working hours he could not bring himself to leave his wife. She would sit in there with him, quietly sewing away on the divan while he wrote. Then in the evening she would settle down to make a fair copy of the pages written during the day. This she regarded as her principal task, and she never shirked it, no matter how tired she was. Then, when she had finished, she went through into the drawing-room to sit with old aunt Tatyana.

It was not long before she was expecting her first child. When the pregnancy made her unwell she liked to rest at her husband's feet, lying on the fur of the black bear whose fangs and claws had so nearly proved fatal to Tolstoy some years before. She was able to doze there peacefully until it was time for everyone to retire for the night. My father not only required my mother to suckle this first child—my brother Sergei—but also to dispense with the help of a nurse. It was a lot to ask of a young woman with no experience of motherhood who had been brought up in a certain degree of luxury. The child was soon ailing. Yet the breast-feeding, a source of intense pain to the mother, was even then not abandoned until such a step had clearly become absolutely unavoidable. But bringing in a wet-nurse? Such a course seemed criminal to both parents. They decided the child would have to be bottle-fed. People in those days were not over-concerned with such matters as hygiene and sterilization. The baby now became seriously ill. My mother describes in her diary how my father warmed the child's milk and fed it himself, hands atremble in his anxiety over performing this unaccustomed task properly. 'As for me,' she wrote, 'I was in the depths of despair. I wept night and day. I said goodbye to the baby. I talked to it as though it could understand me, apologizing for not being able to feed it, explaining that it wasn't my fault.'

G

The father watched over his little son for nights on end. Dawn would find him still fully dressed, and then he would go back to his study to spend the day with Alexander I, Napoleon, Pierre, Prince André, Natasha, Plato Karatyev, and all the other characters of the epic he was in the thick of at that time, his *War and Peace*. But the time came eventually, despite their repugnance, when they were obliged to call in a wet-nurse.

It was not long before I followed my brother into the world. But there were no such worries after my arrival. Life seemed good to my parents, and my father wrote to his father-in-law: 'It's just as though we were beginning our honeymoon all over again, Sonya is charming with her two children.'

Eighteen months after my arrival it was Ilya's turn. Then, at intervals varying from eighteen months to two years, the family continued its steady increase. There were thirteen children in all, and eleven of us my mother breast-fed herself. As long as our life continued to be directed by a skilled and loving hand—my father's—all went well. My mother gave her husband all the best in herself: her entire energies and her total love.

We lived at Yasnaya Polyana all the year round then. My father devoted his energies not only to his literary work but also to his family and the running of the estate. He reafforested, enlarged the orchards and gardens, supervised the apiary, the cowsheds, the stables, and a whole roster of varied livestock. But his literary work took pride of place all the same, and occupied the greatest share of his time: 'I am overflowing with joy at the thought of being able to bring off a great work, a work of psychological history: the novel of Alexander and Napoleon.' That was written in his diary for 1865: it is the first mention of *War and Peace*.

And two years later my mother wrote to her sister:

'All this winter Lev has been writing in a state of emotion that often goes as far as tears. In my opinion his novel *War and Peace* is going to be something quite out of the common run. Everything he's read me from it has moved me to tears.'

During these readings my mother offered her opinions. Her husband took note of them, and sometimes made changes at his wife's suggestion. Here is a passage from a letter in 1864:

'I am writing in my study. In front of me I have portraits of you at four different ages, Sonya, my darling. How intelligent you are in every sphere, whenever you put your mind to it.'

And he goes on to analyze the kind of intelligence she had, ending with these words:

'I haven't said yet in what you are intelligent. Like a good wife you take as much interest in your husband's life as in your own, and I shall never forget how one day you told me that the whole historico-military side of *War and Peace,* over which I had laboured so hard, was coming out badly, and that the best part would be the psychological side, the characters and the picture of family life. It couldn't have been truer, and I haven't forgotten how you were able to see that and tell me, and I think of you all the time. I feel I want to cry out, as Tanya would, 'mamma, I want to go to Yasnaya,' and it is Sofia I want. My darling, love me as I love you. Nothing else matters to me and every-thing will be for the best . . .'

At that time husband and wife were both going about their own separate occupations while at the same time taking a concerned and loving interest in the life led by the other. Both were putting themselves totally into their particular tasks.

My father's was literary in nature. 'I must leave some part of myself every day in my inkwell,' he said, 'so that my work may bear fruit.'

As for his wife, it was in the nursery that she left her daily fragment of herself. She wrote in her diary:

'I love the children with a passion, so much so that it hurts sometimes.'

She was not exaggerating, for although she breast-fed her children with willing love it was a process not without pain. I can still see her, a child cradled in her arms, head thrown back, teeth clenched in her determination to conceal that pain. To her it was a mother's duty, one not to be denied: 'I'd rather die of pain than give up,' she wrote to her sister. And in another letter: 'My child wouldn't be wholly my child if it were thanks to some stranger's milk that it lived and flourished during the first year of its life, the most important of them all.'

Voluntary bondage of a mother who also wrote to her sister, after the death of a little boy at the age of ten months:

'So here I am, Tanya, free! But how hard a freedom it is to bear!'

Sometimes my father went to Moscow on business. On those occasions they eased the pain of separation with a daily exchange of letters. She wrote to him from Yasnaya Polyana:

'I am in your study, weeping. I am weeping over my happiness, over you, over your absence, and I think about the past.'

And he replied:

'The day after the day after tomorrow I shall come into the nursery and kiss you . . . My fine and sprightly wife, my darling wife.'

And note how specific he is about the place where their reunion is to occur: in the nursery. He knew only too well that no matter what time he arrived that was where he would find her.

She was sometimes alarmed by the extent to which she felt her personality was being absorbed into her husband and children. Among her diary entries for 1863 I find this: 'I think, but my thoughts are his, I see things, but from his point of view. It is distressing . . . I shan't become him, yet I shall lose my own personality.' And elsewhere: 'Even when he's not here I still live wrapped up in him, I go into his study, I tidy up, I put away his clean clothes in his drawers and hang things up, I look through his papers, and I strive with my whole being to penetrate into his inner core, so as to understand him.' She wrote to him: 'When you're not here it's as though I had lost my soul. You alone can clothe everything in poetry and enchantment, and draw me up to a certain level . . . Even when you're away I can like only what you like, and often I'm not clear whether I'm liking something myself or just through you.'

Even so, her youth and love of pleasure were still able to make their claims felt on occasion, and she could write: 'I am sent off to bed just when I feel like turning a cartwheel, singing, dancing.'

For she was still only nineteen. She felt young, and often confessed frivolous feelings to herself: 'My desire to escape from the realities of life is too strong. I mustn't. I have neither the time nor the right.' She was particularly susceptible to the charms of music, and on that account feared it more than anything.

'Mashenka played something. I hadn't heard any music for a long while, and I was transported to some other place, somewhere a long way away, a place where the things that make up my daily life don't exist: no nursery, no nappies, no children even. It quite frightened me in fact. It's so long since I stifled the voice of those strings that music or the beauties of nature set quivering within me . . . And I never want them to reawaken in me, those sensations so necessary to you, the creator and writer, but merely a source of pain to me as a mother and mistress of a household, because I cannot and must not give myself up to them.'

This inner striving, these efforts to attain self-mastery did not escape her husband. He loved her more on their account, even though he did not observe them without a certain apprehension, as one can tell from a diary entry in 1863: 'She is young, there are many things in me she does not understand, much she suppresses in herself on my account. And she will lay them at my door one day, all these sacrifices she is making.'

The day did come when my mother drew up the debtor's account he foresaw, but only much later on. At this period life was good and the road still easy.

In these early days of his marriage my father made several attempts to introduce a simpler and more austere way of life into their home than was customary among members of his class. But these attempts were ill-fated and quickly abandoned. He had wanted his firstborn to be brought up without a nurse; but my mother's ill-health had obliged him to engage one, and later on a governess was brought over from England. The first attempt at a family outing in a telega, an uncomfortable vehicle used by peasants and not far removed from a cart, was hardly a success: my mother was so badly affected by the shaking she received that she fell ill. There was nothing for it but to order a properly sprung barouche. It was not in my father's nature to dig in his heels over such things. Moreover, although his principles required that he should strive constantly to lead a better and more perfect life himself, he claimed no right whatever to impose his wishes on others. As a result, once he became convinced that it was not possible for his wife to change her tastes and habits he accepted that fact—he gave way. And it was relatively easy for him to do so at that time, since in those days his desire for simplicity was merely a matter of personal inclination rather than a deep-seated conviction. And besides, life at Yasnaya Polyana was even so a very simple affair.

A relative luxury was not introduced into the house until large sales of my father's works became assured. Then the resulting increase in income did lead to a change in our style of life. We had foreign governesses and tutors, plus teachers and mistresses for Russian. All these people lived in the house. And other instructors of various kinds came in from Tula several times a week. We were given religious instruction and taught the meaning of the various church services and the religious objects used in them. In addition we learned several languages, music, and drawing.

Those twenty years of happy family life were the prelude to a tragic conflict that had been building up for a long time, and that eventually threw our home into chaos.

A tragedy is a real tragedy when there is no villain, when the situation is one that leads to an insoluble dilemma. Our family found itself in such a truly tragic situation, one from which there was no way out.

It had been decided by our parents, at a time when we were still very young, that once we older children reached a certain age we were all to leave the country and go to live in Moscow. My brother Sergei was to be tutored at home for university entrance. As for me, I was to be brought out in society when I reached eighteen. That was something firmly fixed even in my father's mind. I know how worried he became on this score when I broke my collar bone. He took me to Moscow to consult the very best surgeon, and asked him most specifically if the operation would leave a scar. He wanted to be quite sure that there would be no swelling or mark visible when I began wearing lowcut ball gowns.

Shortly before 1880, however, all my father's aspirations became diverted to new goals. It was a process that began imperceptibly.

In 1877 he wrote to his friend Strakhov:

'I was present the other day while the priest was giving the children their catechism lesson. It all seemed to me so unacceptable, I saw so clearly that intelligent children must not only be unable to believe what is written in it but cannot do otherwise than despise it, that the idea came to me of using the framework of the catechism to explain what I myself believe. And I had a try at it. I realized then how difficult, and I'm afraid even impossible, what I had set out to do was going to prove. And that is weighing on my mind and making me sad.'

From that day onward my father never gave up attempting to express his faith. In *A Confession* he recounts how he became aware of the first signs heralding his conversion.

'Something strange was happening to me at that time. I experienced moments of doubt and moments when life stopped; I no longer knew how to go on living, and I was unable to satisfy myself as to what it was I ought to be doing. At those times I asked myself: But why? Where does it lead to?'

At first my father did not attach much importance to these questions, which he dismissed as futile. But they recurred more and more frequently, with ever greater insistence, and eventually set up a clamour that had to be answered.

My father then realized that what was happening to him was what happens to a man sick with a mortal inward illness. He saw that *he had to answer* those questions. He had to know, when he wrote a book, or brought up his son, or bought some new property, why he was doing it. 'Very well,' he told himself, 'so you will have thousands of acres, hundreds of horses; you will be more famous than any other poet or writer in the world. And what then? What is the point of it? What will all that bring you?'

'I felt there was nothing beneath my feet any more,' he wrote in *A Confession*, 'and that what had once constituted the fabric of my life no longer existed. And I no longer had any prop to help me live . . .

'I was a healthy and fairly wealthy man, yet I had reached a point where I felt I couldn't go on living . . .

'And it was then, despite all my outward appearance of happiness, that I reached the point of hiding a rope so that I should not be tempted to hang myself with it, in the room where I undressed alone every night, from the pole I'd had put up between two cupboards there. And I stopped going shooting, so as not to be tempted by so simple a method of putting an end to my life . . .

'My horror of the darkness was too terrifying, and I longed to rid myself of it as quickly as possible with a noose or a bullet . . .

'I told myself that there was something awry, but as for seeing exactly what it was, that eluded me. It was not until much later that the darkness began to clear, and that I was able by degrees to perceive my true state.'

Little by little my father became aware that the motive force of life resides in faith, and that the deepest human wisdom is to be found in the answers that faith alone provides.

It was then that he set to work studying all the world's religions, beginning with our own Russian Orthodox teachings. These he studied with the help of books, but also by means of contact with living people. He became friendly with believers among the uneducated, and despite finding a great deal of superstition mingled with their true Christianity he saw that their faith was for them a necessity that lent their lives reason and purpose. He learned to love such people, and the more he loved them the lighter the burden of his life became.

He understood then that life itself is not futile, not an evil, but that it was his own particular life that had no meaning and was bad.

And the words of the Gospel, when it tells us that men prefer darkness to light because their actions are bad, became intelligible and clear to him.

Everything he had come to feel led him to examine his own life more closely. This was the beginning of a period of doubts and probings, which were carried out in a state of anguish. He searched for the answers to the questions that were obsessing him in science, in philosophy, and in religion.

And so it was that in his mature years, at a time when he had acquired everything in life that a man can expect in the way of happiness, he turned his face away from that sort of happiness.

Worldly goods and all the surface attractions of life began to appear to him as shackles, and eventually became a cross he found it hard to bear. The burden they represented was to seem so heavy to him at times that he sought to slough them off, to break with his entire past, to reject the family life he had dreamed of in his youth, to give up all the wealth he had acquired, and finally to break with the Church, to which he had cleaved at first because it was the only thing that seemed to provide him with a feeling of community with the people, always so dear to his heart.

But before rejecting the religion in which he had been born he subjected it to a ruthless analysis. He scrupulously observed all the practices of the Orthodox Church, all its required abstentions and fasts, said all the required prayers, and attended all its services.

I can remember going to mass with him every Sunday. Instead of having our carriage and four harnessed up, as was customary when my mother took the younger children to communion, we made the journey on foot. My father's genuflexions were all performed with a facility acquired by long habit. And all fasts were rigorously observed, even fish being excluded from our menus. My mother wrote in her diary:

'Lev's character is changing more and more. Of course he has always lived modestly, but his gentleness, patience, and modesty become more and more marked all the time. And the ceaseless battle he has waged from his youth onward to attain moral self-improvement continues with complete success.'

Still pursuing his study of every aspect of Orthodox doctrine, my father went to Moscow to see Makarius, the Metropolitan there, visited the Laura of St Sergius, and made a journey on foot to the monastery of Optina. He also visited Kiev, because he said he felt drawn to that place. But having arrived at the famous monastery there he wrote to his wife: 'From first thing until three I visited the cathedrals, the catacombs, the monks, and am very cross at having come; it wasn't worth the bother. At seven I went to the Laura to see Antonius the Skhimnik (ascetic monks living a life governed by particularly austere rules).' And he added: 'I derived little profit from it.'

During this time my father was also studying the Gospels, and the further he progressed with his studies the more he realized how much in the doctrine of the Orthodox Church was sadly misleading. The pure teachings of Christ emerged to his eyes with ever greater clarity.

'It was by following the sun's rays that I reached the sun,' he wrote, meaning that it was via his study of Orthodox doctrine that he had arrived at his knowledge of Christ's teaching. And he was to write in *What I believe:*

'I was dazzled by the revelation of the truth, and obtained complete answers to the questions: What is the meaning of my life? And the meaning of other people's lives?'

During this period my father devoted himself totally to a titanic labour: he made a new translation of the four Gospels, compared them, and on the basis of that collation established a single text.

At the same time he continued with his *Criticism of Dogmatic Theology.* And in order to do so he was obliged, late in life, to learn both Hebrew and Greek.

I now have to explain the repercussions produced by my father's conversion on his family.

Since we were his inferiors both as regards intellectual gifts and moral strength, and had not accompanied him on his journey of inner transformation, we were unable to follow him on his new path. As a family we had been brought up in certain traditions, in a certain social climate, and now our leader, our head, was suddenly abandoning the life to which we had become accustomed and withdrawing into ideal regions far removed from all his previous conceptions of life.

Nevertheless, he did not believe he had the right to destroy at a single blow all that he himself had built up.

He had married a child of eighteen. It was he who had formed her, and his influence had put down very deep roots in her mind and personality. It was he who had never permitted her to travel other than in first class carriages, who had ordered the best clothes or shoes for her and her children from the very best shops. And now he was saying that he would like both herself and those same children to live like peasants . . . Why? Why suddenly give up a life of pleasure and pastimes at this stage for a life of drudgery and deprivation? That was how my mother formulated the problem in her mind.

At the outset she did her best to understand him. She wrote to him one day:

'Yesterday, travelling beside you, I said to myself: what wouldn't I give to read his heart, to know what he is thinking? You share your thoughts with me so little, and that hurts me a great deal. Morally it would be good for me, even essential. You undoubtedly think I am stubborn, whereas I think that slowly but surely much that is good in you finds its way into me. That thought is what above all makes life easier for me.'

I would like to stress this trait in my father's character: not only did he never preach or moralize to people, even within his family, he even refrained from ever giving them advice. He talked to us very rarely about his beliefs. His inner struggle was something he pursued alone. We had at no time been privy to its progress, and then one day we found ourselves facing its results, for which nothing had prepared us.

At that time we didn't understand him. His ideas alarmed us without convincing us.

Perhaps there was a kind of modesty in him that prevented him from talking to us about his most heartfelt ideas. Perhaps too a fear of putting pressure on us, of doing violence to our consciences? And it was more through his disciples than from him personally that we children eventually learned to know our father better.

After six weeks of marriage my mother was already writing in her diary: 'It's strange, I love him terribly, but I feel he is influencing me very little.'

The disharmony between my father and his family became particularly acute at the time of our move to Moscow. The interests of husband and wife were becoming increasingly divergent. The decoration of the house, the search for various teachers for the children, placing them in schools, the purchase of carriages and horses, the engaging of servants, all fell on my mother. Then there was clothing for us all to think about. And my mother was expecting another child very soon.

My father felt sorry for her, and even though his wife's domestic worries were of no interest whatever to him he did nevertheless make an effort to help her. He wrote to her in Moscow:

'You can't imagine how much the idea of your overdoing things torments me, and how repentant I am at having been of so little help to you, or even none at all. I am cured now of the error that made me

think that others can and must see everything the way I do. I have
been very much to blame in my attitude toward you, my dearest,
without realizing it, without intending it, as you know very well. But
to blame all the same. My only excuse is that in order to achieve the
mental concentration I need for my work, and to achieve a certain
result, I have to forget everything else. But I really have been too
neglectful of you, and I do see that. For God's sake, and that of our
love, don't overdo things. Put off as much as possible until I get there.
I'll do it all with pleasure, and do it pretty well too, because I shall
really put my mind to it.'

And my father did in fact leave for Moscow to help my mother as
soon as he could. He took over the task of seeing the boys into the
Gymnasium, arranged for me to attend art classes, and saw to a great
many other details. But living in Moscow was very distressing to him,
and his resulting state of depression affected us all. 'Even though
everyone had nothing but praise for the house,' my mother wrote, 'it
wasn't long before we sank into a mood of despondency and anxiety
that have been increasing these past three days. The house is like a
cardboard house. You can hear everything. And whether we're in our
bedroom or Lev's study there's no question of any peace. It sometimes
reduces me to despair, and the pressure never lets up all day. "Whatever
you do you must all keep quiet!" We've had it all out. Lev finally told
me that if I loved him, if I had any consideration for his spiritual
peace, I would never have chosen this vast room, in which there can
be no question of a moment's real rest, crammed with armchairs just
one of which would have made a peasant happy for life (meaning that
the twenty-one rubles each one cost would buy a horse or cow), this
room that robs him of everything but eyes to weep with. So you see
just how carefree life has become. The baby is two weeks off, and I
see no end to the worries, the irritations, the chores . . .'

During our time in Moscow we—the family—were totally immersed
in social engagements, parties, material concerns, and various aspects
of our education. My father was meanwhile making acquaintances of
a quite different kind, acquaintances that we referred to in our private
language—to distinguish them from the people we ourselves were
meeting in society—as 'the dark ones'. He would go off with sawyers
into the Moscow suburbs, out to Sparrow Hill, where Napoleon had
once stood and gazed out across the city. In order to get to know these
new companions better he crossed over the river every day to go and
work with them.

My mother noted one day: 'At that time he went visiting prisons and houses of detention, sat in on all the cases being tried by our district courts and justices of the peace, and watched soldiers being recruited. It was as though he was deliberately going everywhere looking for places where he could see human suffering and violence being done to people . . . It was as though he was turning his face away from everything in the world that is joyful and happy in order to see only the opposite.'

Which was true, and he could not have done otherwise. He had adopted wholeheartedly the Christian doctrine of loving one's neighbour: he had to search out all those whose distress he might be able to alleviate. He was more and more tormented by the fact that he was a possessor of wealth, and began entertaining dreams of sloughing it off. 'To give away what I have,' he wrote, 'not in order to do good but in order to become less guilty.' He took to handing out large sums of money right and left. That terrified my mother. 'Lev's new state of mind also expressed itself in a sudden tendency to give away large amounts of money. I tried to make him see that it would be wise to exercise a little method in the distribution of these gifts, to consider to whom and for what reason he was making them. But he just dug in his heels and quoted the Gospel: "Give to him that asketh thee".'

She didn't understand that to her husband giving away everything he possessed meant freeing himself from a sin, the sin of ownership, which had become intolerable to him now that his intense inner struggles had led him to adopt and profess certain principles.

During his first winter in Moscow an event took place that had a profound emotional effect on my father. This was the 1882 municipal census. My father had put his name down as a voluntary official, and asked to be assigned to the district that included Moscow's 'lower depths', its doss-houses and dens of vilest debauchery.

For the first time in his life he saw real poverty, and was able to observe the moral deterioration that overtook those who had slipped down into society's sumps. He was shattered by the experience, and then, as always with him, subjected his reactions to the most ruthless analysis. What was the cause of this appalling poverty? Why did these vices exist? It did not take him long to reach his answer.

If there are people in poverty it is because others have more than they need.

If there are people living in ignorance it is because others have too much useless knowledge.

If there are some bent beneath the yoke of appalling labours, it is because others are living in idleness.

And when he went on to ask the question: who are these others?, the answer was ineluctable: myself, myself and my family.

It was something he had been aware of to some extent for a long while. But all that he had now witnessed forced him to assent to it with the full force of his nature.

People like my father react with very much greater sensitivity than the average person. He had the gift of being able to relive with exceptional intensity all that a fellow being had gone through. And having observed a sin for which he was partly to blame, his only course was to attempt to expiate it by putting a stop to it.

As he quickly realized, however, this was no easy task. We were living at that time in a house that he himself had bought for us. We had no idea when he did so what a sacrifice he had been making for his family. And my mother wrote to her sister, Tatyana Kuzminsky, somewhat ingenuously:

'The other day Lev informed us that Moscow is nothing but a vast open sewer, a stinking cess-pit. Having obliged me to agree to this point of view, suddenly he is adamant that we can't go on living here, so he begins rushing feverishly up and down every street and alley looking for a house or lodgings for us. I defy the wiliest philosopher to make head or tail of it . . .'

My brother Sergei was attending university. I was coming out in society. It was my father who took me to my first ball. And he introduced me to various people of his own class with whom he had kept up relations.

Here is what our life was like. Having got up late, my mother and I would spend the day paying or receiving visits. In the evening we set out again, either in the carriage or a sleigh, to attend a ball or party. Sometimes my mother took pleasure in this kind of life, at others she was conscious of its utter emptiness. Thus she wrote to her sister: 'I think we are well and truly launched in society now. To tell the truth, at the moment I'm not deriving a great deal of pleasure from it all. We have announced our at home day: Thursday. So on that day we wait in, sitting around like idiots. My son Lyova keeps watch at the window to see's who's turning up. Then tea, grogs, fancy cakes, sandwiches, all of which are consumed with great gusto. Then on other days we are entertained in like fashion, and do our share of consuming at the 'teas' we attend!'

On January 3rd, again to her sister, she wrote:

'Lev is very calm. He's writing articles. He sometimes launches into diatribes about city life and the life of society folk in general. It hurts me. But I know he can't be otherwise. He's a man in advance of his time. He's out ahead of the crowd pointing the way men ought to go. But I'm just part of the crowd, I move with the main current. From my place in the crowd I simply follow the torch that every great man carries (Lev among them beyond doubt), and I recognize that it is in fact the light that *must be followed*. But it is impossible for me to move any quicker. The crowd, the circles I move in, my habits, all hold me back.'

'Lev is very calm. He's writing articles . . .' That was all she could find to say, and what she believed, since she was completely unaware of the moral torments he was going through as he examined his situation and searched for a way out. It is easy for us to understand those torments now. When he left some doss-house and returned home he would walk in to find the table laid: oranges and cakes on a shining white cloth . . . Two servants scurrying round waiting on a band of idle young blades. He looked round at the wall hangings and the carpets strewn everywhere. Enough to clothe ten people. His heart contracted with distress, swelled with indignation. He simply could not accept this life of carefree idleness we were living only a stone's throw from people who were dying of poverty.

Remember what he wrote in *What then must we do?*: 'How can a man not completely without conscience and reason go on living if he is not sharing in the struggle of all mankind for existence, if he is limiting his role merely to consuming the labour of those who are struggling—many of them destined to lose their lives in the process—and to increasing the sum of that toil by his demands?'

He understood that men must not live solely for their personal good, that they are called upon to work together for the good of others. He regarded that fact as a natural law, acceptance of which could alone assure his happiness. And he was having to watch that law being constantly violated: like bees that live by plundering other hives, some people were withholding their share of labour, they were living off the labour of others, and like such bees they were doomed by this infraction of the law. Those doomed and thievish bees, as he saw it, were himself and his family. It could not go on.

He could see quite clearly that his wife was incapable of understanding all this. The distress he was undergoing was in her eyes a morbid condition. She feared for his reason, and she had only one desire: for *all this* to blow over. That was how she talked about what was according to her a nervous 'attack', an attack that she resolutely expected to prove transitory. She failed totally to grasp the greatness of the travail in her husband's soul. And she wrote to her sister:

'Lev has sleepless nights. He sometimes paces to and fro in his room till three in the morning. But he is in such a gentle, kindly humour. God grant it may last! We are very good friends, and recently have had only one tiny little quarrel.'

They lived side by side as good friends and total strangers, each filled with a great and sincere love for the other, but also increasingly aware of the gulf between them. And the idea that had already germinated in his head was becoming ever more obsessive: he must turn his back on this life and create a new one more in conformity with his beliefs.

In 1879 my mother wrote to her sister: 'Lev never stops working . . . that's what he calls it. Alas, he is writing what you might call theses about religion, he reads and thinks till he gives himself headaches, and all just in order to prove that there is a discrepancy between the Church's teachings and the Gospels. There's nothing one can do. My only hope is that he will get to the end of this work as quickly as possible and just get over it all like an illness. As for influencing him, or diverting his mind to some other task, no matter what, no one in the world could manage that. Even he couldn't.'

As long as my father's work had been literary in its nature my mother had taken a lively interest in it. But his present labours, all so abstract, left her indifferent and hostile. She recorded her reactions in her diary:

'Savage criticism of orthodoxy and the Church, offensive remarks about the Church and its servants, remarks implying criticism of our way of life, blame directed at everything I did, everything my friends and relations did. It was intolerable. At that time I was still making the fair copies of what Lev had written or revised. But one day, I remember it was in 1880, while I was actually in the act of writing, I went red, the blood all rushed to my head, I was seized by mounting indignation. I snatched up all the pages, took them in to Lev, and told him that I would not be doing any more copying for him: I *cannot*.'

In order to ease the mutual irritation between them, my father frequently left Moscow for a while. Usually he went to Yasnaya Polyana. But sometimes he went out into the country, not far from

Moscow, to stay with the Olsuffyevs, or with his old Sebastopol friend, or even further afield still, to Samara for a spell among the Bashkirs. Even there, however, he found no peace of mind. In 1885 he wrote to his friend L. D. Urussov:

'I feel a certain distress in the country. The abnormal element in our life, this enslavement of the poor I see so clearly, the way we abuse them out of sheer thoughtlessness, is particularly painful to me. "He that endureth to the last shall be saved." That comes into my mind so often. Why? I don't know. And even though there's no reason for it I live in constant anticipation of something that will free me from the flagrant disparity between my life and my conscience.'

No such thing occurred, and he continued to live in the state of contradiction that was tearing him apart. He felt particularly alone at this period. In a letter to M. A. Engelhardt, written in 1882, we read:

'You certainly haven't realized what it is like. You can't imagine how much I am alone, how far my true self is spurned by all those around me.'

And almost simultaneously his wife was writing to her sister:

'I have felt alone at times in the past, but never as much as I do now. I see so clearly, I feel so acutely, that no one wants me, and that I am of no interest to anybody.'

My father, who suffered very deeply from the disharmony between himself and his wife, and could see how far she was from sharing his ideas, still never lost hope that one day she would come back to him. He wrote to her:

'As long as we go on living we go on changing, retain the power to change and thus, with God's grace, find our way ever closer to the truth. My whole search is to that end. It is what I desire for myself and for those dear to me, you, the children. And I do not despair. Far from it. I believe that we shall find ourselves united again, if not in my lifetime at least after it.'

And in another letter:

'You are strong, and not just physically; you are morally strong too. You lack something, a slight thing, but the most important. It will come, I am convinced. But if it is after I have gone it will cause me sadness in the other world. Many people are saddened by the thought that they will have only posthumous fame. I have nothing left to wish for on that score. And I would renounce not just a large part of my fame but all fame, if in return I could have you in communion with me with all your soul, as will happen after my death.'

Elsewhere he expresses the thought that if he is right in his thinking, then she will come round to him as others had done.

At that time, however, she was far from ready to attempt any closing of the gap between them. Her husband's way of life was causing her no less alarm than his new ideas.

'He has changed his whole way of life,' she wrote to her sister. 'Every day there is some new change. He gets up at seven when it is still pitch dark. He goes out and draws the water for the entire household. He drags it back here in a huge tank on a little sled. He saws wood. Then he chops it up with an axe and arranges it in piles. He won't eat white bread any more, and he never goes out anywhere.'

That was how they went on living, in a state of painful tension, keeping themselves to themselves, taking no part in each other's lives, while at the same time feeling that the bonds created by twenty years of love were still there between them. Interminable talks took place, long arguments that resulted in nothing but mutually inflicted wounds. During the summer of 1884 there were several painful scenes between my parents. And during the night of July 17th to 18th my father left the house with nothing but a knapsack on his back.

I can still see him walking away down the birch drive. And I can see my mother sitting outside the house under the trees, her face distorted with grief, her big, dark eyes quite lifeless as she stares unseeingly in front of her. She was about to give birth to a child, and the pains had already begun. It was past midnight. My brother Ilya went out and carefully helped her inside and up to her bed. Toward morning my sister Alexandra was born.

My father did not go far that night. He knew that my mother was about to be delivered of a child, his child. Seized with pity for her, he returned. But the situation remained so tense that it could not go on. It exploded eventually into a decisive heartbaring during which the couple made mutual confession of all their grievances against one another and brought all the torments of their daily lives out into the open. This scene took place in December of that same year. My father's patience was clearly at an end. His cup had overflowed. He was unable to contain himself, and all his reserves of inner resignation and gentleness were swept aside by an irresistible tide of indignation.

Face twisted with inner pain, he went in to his wife and informed her point-blank that he was leaving the house. Here is an extract from a letter my mother wrote to her sister:

'Lev came in to see me, nervous, as gloomy as it is possible to be. I was sitting writing. He walked in. I looked up. His face was frightening. Until that day we'd always behaved properly with one another, not a single unpleasant word had ever been exchanged between us, not one, not a single one . . . "I've come to tell you that I want a separation. I can't live like this. I am leaving for Paris, or America." . . . You can just imagine, Tanya. If the house had collapsed on top of me I couldn't have been more surprised. I was stunned. I asked him: "What's happened?" "Nothing," he said. "But you can only go on loading things on to the cart for so long. When the horse can't pull it any more, the cart stops." What exactly it is I've been loading the cart with is something I still don't know. Then came a flood of reproaches, with his voice getting louder and louder all the time. I just let him go on, and hardly answered at all. I could see only too well that he was not in his right mind. But when he said: "Wherever you are the air is poisoned," then I sent for a trunk and began packing. I just wanted to get away, anywhere, to you, just for a few days. The children ran in sobbing: Stay! That's what they begged me to do. So I stayed. But then I was suddenly taken with a fit of nervous sobbing; it was all quite simply horrible.

'You can picture the scene. Lev too was trembling and shaking with sobs. I felt a rush of pity for him then. The four children, Tanya, Ilya, Lyova, and Masha, were all weeping and wailing. I went into a fit: not a word, not a tear.

'I was almost on the verge of saying all sorts of wild things, and I was determined not to: so I kept absolutely silent for three whole hours. I'd have let myself be killed rather than speak. That was the end of it. But the anguish, the grief, the pain, the nervous distress, the feeling of rejection, all that has stayed with me. You can imagine it, the way I keep on and on till I'm almost out of my mind asking myself: what did I do wrong? I never left the house, I was working till three every morning on the new edition. I was contented. I loved them all so. I was looking after them all. What for?'

I remember that terrible winter night. There were nine of us children then. I can still see us older ones down in the hall, sitting on chairs, just waiting. Every now and then we would go over to the bottom of the stairs and listen to the sound of our parents arguing upstairs. The pitch of their voices never fell, and you could gauge the intensity of their emotions purely from the sounds that were reaching us. What was going on between our parents was clearly some very serious and decisive argument. Neither of them would budge an inch. Both were defending something more important to them than their lives: she the well-being of her children, and what she regarded as their happiness; he his very soul.

She loved her children, 'to the point of madness, till it hurt', while his love was above all for truth. We could not make out all they said, but enough filtered through for us to formulate some idea of what was happening between them. 'I cannot go on living a life of luxury and idleness,' he said. 'I cannot continue helping to bring up the children in conditions that I believe to be pernicious to them. I cannot continue being the owner of a house and estates. Every step I take in life is an unbearable torture to me.' And he concluded: 'Either I leave, or else our life has to change. We have to give away all we own and support ourselves with the labour of our own hands, like peasants.'

But she replied: 'If you leave, since I cannot live without you I shall kill you. As for changing the way we live, it is beyond me, I could not do it. And I cannot understand why it is necessary to destroy an existence that is happy in every way just for the sake of heaven knows what wild ideas.' And the argument went round and round, locked in that vicious circle, perpetually returning to the same unbridgeable gap, the same insoluble difference between them.

Did we understand what my father was saying? I certainly didn't. I believed utterly that he was incapable of being wrong. But as for the exact nature of this Truth he had discovered, that eluded me. And it seemed so far beyond the grasp of my twenty-year-old mind, so totally inaccessible to the very limited spiritual capacities of my girlish awareness, that I didn't even entertain the hope that I might come to understand it in the future. Nor did I understand my mother's attitude. It seemed to me that she ought to submit to my father's wishes, whatever they were. Bowing to the demands of a husband who loves you, and whom you love, wasn't that an easier course to take than enduring the moral tortures gnawing at his soul? I thought so, and could not understand the stand she took.

We children were not consulted. We sat in the hall, at the foot of the stairs, and simply waited for our parents to reach some conclusion. And then we saw one of the servants appear with a trunk. He carried it into our mother's bedroom, and we realized what that meant.

Fortunately we had a very good friend of the family, Mikhail Alexandrovich Stakhovich, staying with us at the time. He had been planning to leave that day for St Petersburg, but we had begged him to postpone his departure because we were so frightened of being left on our own. If mamma did decide to go, then he would accompany her. He had joined us in the hall. I can see him sitting on his suitcase, helping us to get through that long winter night.

It did end eventually, that night of anguish. But it ended without any clearcut decision, without any real conclusion being reached. From then on all painful questions were avoided, and my mother limited her concern to my father's material welfare.

He remained gloomy, silent, turned in on his own thoughts, yet affectionate both to her and us. She had been wounded by the blows he had dealt her, and that caused him pain, even though he could not have avoided what had happened. He needed to regain his peace of mind, to think, so he decided to go and stay with his friends the Olsuffyevs, who lived about thirty-five miles outside Moscow.

The little two-seater sleigh stood at the foot of the front steps. Our dear old Sultan stood waiting in his harness, looking round at me with his intelligent eyes. My mother had loaded us with coats and rugs and provisions for the journey. Now she was giving us all sorts of advice, instructing us about all the things we must be sure to do if a storm blew up, so that we wouldn't go off the road and die of cold. She was very nervous and agitated. Her face was pinched and red with the cold, her big dark eyes shining with pent up emotion.

I took the reins, the big gates out to the street were pulled open, and then I was alone with my father, gliding along the road on a fine winter's morning.

I still remember all the events of that journey. My father and I took turns driving. We overturned several times. Dark was already falling when we glimpsed our friends' house at last through a violent snow flurry. Good old Sultan, having made the same journey the previous winter, had remembered all the turns and took us straight to our goal. Well, not quite! He made a beeline for the stables where he'd stayed the time before!

On the way my father talked to me confidingly, and it was that day, for the first time, that I acquired some glimmering of his new ideas.

Then it was time to go back to Moscow. Nothing in our life had changed. It continued on exactly the same course as before. And I can say with complete certainty that not only had my parents' love for one another not in any way diminished, but that their sufferings had actually made it stronger. They were like Desdemona and Othello:

she loved him for the sufferings he had passed, and he loved her that she did pity them.

I also believe I am not mistaken when I add that out of her pity for him she did her utmost to find her way closer to him in mind and heart, to take an interest in his work and try to understand it.

My father was writing *On Life* at the time. This particular work, so sublime in its simplicity and wisdom, did find some answering echo in my mother's heart. Her correspondence with her sister makes this clear: 'I am alone, all alone. I've been writing all day. I've copied out Lev's article *On Life and Death*.' (This was the original title. But in developing his ideas my father realized that death doesn't exist, so the title was abbreviated to *On Life*.) 'He's out at this moment reading it to the Psychology Society at the university. It's a good article. Purely philosophic, without spleen, and not tendentious in any way. It seems to me profound, well thought out, and echoes my own feelings.' It echoed her feelings so completely that not only did she agree to copy the article out, she also translated it into French.

With what joy my father responded on his side to this drawing together of their souls! It was a fleeting rapprochement, one not without reservations, entailing no changes in either's ideas or actions, but at least it brought respite from rejections of his principles, negative verdicts on his ideas, and scorn for his personality. He desired complete communion with her so ardently! He so yearned to hold out a hand to her, to help her attempt a spiritual ascension that would have enabled her to understand him better. He was ready to give all the love in his heart in exchange for that. In 1891 he wrote to her from Yasnaya Polyana:

'I have retained such a joyful memory of our last talk that I only have to think of it to feel light-hearted.' And further on: 'Be assured that to the degree you need to know I love you to make you strong, that love is there, as much love as is possible. I think of you constantly, and melt with tenderness as I do so.'

In 1895:

'What I felt was a singular wave of tenderness, of pity, a quite new love for you. A love that enabled me to identify myself with you to the point of experiencing what you have experienced. A feeling so sacred, so perfectly good, that it would be better not to speak of it. But I know it will make you happy to hear of it, and expressing it cannot alter it in any way. On the contrary, even as I write I am feeling the same thing. It's strange, what we two feel. Like the westering sun. It is only now and then that the clouds of our dissensions, the clouds that emanate from you and those that emanate from me, succeed in dimming that radiance. They will clear before night comes, and sunset will bring a bright and lovely light. That is what I never stop hoping. You have been so gentle, so loving, and so gracious of late, and I see you now only in that light.'

And in 1896:

'You said that my letters were pleasant and useful to you, how much I long at every moment to do good to you, more than that, smooth out what is hard for you, act in such a way that everything shall be peace, security, contentment for you. I never stop thinking of you. I feel a sort of anxiety about you. I sense a certain weakness in you, and yet you are so precious to me.'

In 1897, in the early part of the summer, my mother managed to get away for a few days from Moscow, where she was forced to live most of the time in order to supervise her younger sons' education. She had arrived at Yasnaya Polyana unexpectedly. And it was after this brief visit that her husband wrote to her: 'Even when you had gone you left behind you such a comforting feeling, so strong and good, too good for me, for I miss you extremely. My awakening, your standing there . . . it is one of the strongest sensations I have ever experienced.'

And in a later letter:

'Lovable and dear Sonya, when I think of the tears you wept on the morning you left I cannot rid myself of a mingled feeling of sweetness and sadness. I am convinced that everything oppressing and troubling you, everything that makes me sad for you, your discouragement, that feeling of emptiness, will be overcome by what is divine in you (you are rich in that element), and that you can count on a life of happiness and tranquillity still before you. I have only one fear: as long as I am not an obstacle to it! As for helping you, I can only do so through the ever-increasing love that I have felt ceaselessly growing within me of late.'

My mother resumed the copy work she had abandoned. 'Tanya has begun doing my copying,' my father wrote, 'but she can't hold a candle to your beautiful hand.'

During this period my father also perceived glimmerings of sympathy and some signs of understanding among his children. This delighted him tremendously. When I wrote to him he answered with a long letter full of affection and a wish to help me.

My sister Sasha accepted my father's ideas totally. She was fourteen, and she and Vanichka, the youngest of the boys, were of all his children those that most resembled my father physically. Alexandra had inherited his probing eyes, so blue, so deep, so bright. I have never known a time when she was not devoting herself totally to some person or some cause.

While she lived at Yasnaya Polyana she cared for all those who fell ill, taught the children, and helped the poor. In Moscow she was perpetually busy in the city's hospitals, in which she was training as a nurse. My mother used to get very worried about her health, and about the effect upon her of all the terrible things she saw. But my father was made so happy by his feeling that she was following in his footsteps, and by the sympathy she had with his ideas as well as the part she took in his work.

My brothers too, with less constancy and in varying degrees, began to support my father in his ideas and to share in his life. Of them all, the one who came closest to my father at one point, only to move further away from him than any of us later, was my brother Lev. There was a time when his father's principles were the most important thing in his life. 'Lev had things to tell me,' my father wrote in a letter, 'he knew how to express them too, and in such a way that I feel he is dear to me, that what interests him is dear to me, and that he knows what interests me and wants to know all about it.'

At that stage in our life my father had the great joy of at last putting two of his ideas into practice: he renounced all form of ownership on his part, and he succeeded in persuading his wife to consent to his literary works being declared in the public domain, albeit with one reservation. He had no wish to make his wife and family completely destitute, so he did allow his wife to retain royalty rights on all his works published prior to 1880, which is to say on everything he had published before his 'second spiritual birth', after which he found it impossible to go on selling what he had written, since in his estimation treating one's thoughts and feelings as commodities of trade would be as shameful as selling one's body. This victory over his wife was not easily achieved. She protested vigorously before finally consenting. He begged her to think over what he was asking her very carefully, as a man on the point of death thinks in the presence of God. He wrote to her at Yasnaya Polyana:

'Do this thing without mental reservations, recognizing that you yourself find joy in this act, because in performing it you are releasing the man you love from a distressing situation; and above all do nothing grudgingly.'

She consented. She consented without understanding. Yet there was one thing she had grasped: that there existed an area in her husband's soul within which he was unable to give way, even out of love for her, because the demands of his conscience were dearer to him than life itself.

That same year he disburdened himself of all his property. My father's dream was simply to give away all his possessions and to start living the life of a peasant along with all his family. That his wife would not consent to. Some other way had to be found. So then he suggested making over all his possessions to her. She would not consent to that either. And her argument against it certainly did not lack logic: 'What,' she said, 'you tell me you think that property is an evil, and now you want to unload that burden of evil on to me!'

What was to be done? A solution had to be found. In the end it was decided to settle everything as though my father were dead: his heirs were to take possession of their heritage and divide it up among them. All the real estate was valued. It was then divided into ten lots of equal value, one for each child and one for my mother. Then we drew lots for them. Yasnaya Polyana fell to my mother and Vanya, the youngest son. This division of my father's possessions was painful for all of us. My mother felt it particularly keenly. She wrote to her sister:

'There is something deeply saddening about this dividing up of the estate, and also, as far as the father is concerned, something shocking.'

We too—the children that is—won a little victory at this time, with our father's support. My mother agreed to let us go out into the fields every summer and share the work of our peasants.

That was the most wonderful time for us! Every morning, as soon as the sun had dried the dew, my sister and I shouldered our rakes and set out with the other women for the hayfields, where the men, including my two brothers Ilya and Lev, had been scything since four in the morning. We women lined up across the field and worked down the swathes spreading them to dry in the sun, then later raked the hay into heaps and brought it in from the fields into the 'master's yard'. It was not for the master we were working though, but for the peasants, who as payment for harvesting the hay received half of every field they cut.

At noon we stopped work and ate our lunches under the trees. The children trooped out from the village with the meal their parents had left ready. And my little sister Alexandra brought us our lunch down from the house too: a frugal repast scarcely different from that of our companions. The men were always in a hurry to get back to work, and allowed us hardly any time for rest. We had barely swallowed our last mouthful before they were already shouting: 'Come on there, you women!' And if clouds appeared, if there was the slightest threat of rain, then they really drove us. We had to leap to it when they called, run for our rakes, form our line again, and work on under the scorching sun until its heat finally softened into sunset embers. What a picture it was, the Russian countryside at haymaking time! What enchantment it still holds for me when I look back, when I picture in memory the lush water-meadows beside the Voronka, our little river, and the motley crowd of peasants and peasant women toiling in the sun. In those days people were still wearing traditional costume, and in order not to stand out from the crowd my sister and I adopted it too. We trooped back at dusk, the girls in blouses and *sarafanas,* the women in *panyovi* with aprons to keep them clean, a merry procession enlivened with laughter, songs, and dancing. Masha, my sister, who walked at the head of the women, often dropped her rake, beckoned to one of the girls, and whirled her into a spirited, wild-footed jig.

Even my mother began taking part in our rustic labours. She too would put on peasant dress, seize a rake, and come out to join us. But being so unaccustomed to the steady, sustained sort of effort demanded by agricultural work, and finding the task not at all tiring at first, she went at it far too enthusiastically. As a result, having expended far too much energy early on, she suddenly had none left. In the end she made herself ill, and gave up manual labour for good.

My father was spending his days surrounded by people who loved him, labouring with the peasants and like the peasants. Labour, he believed, was an obligation for all men. Moreover he had the pleasure of knowing that his children felt some sympathy at least for the life he was leading, and for the ideas he was putting into practice . . . In those days my father was happy.

In winter he went back to his desk. By this time he already had a considerable number of disciples. Several of them became friends not only of their 'master' but of the whole family. Among those who played the largest part in our lives were Biryukov, Gorbunov, and Chertkov. Later there was also Marya Alexandrovna Schmidt, a saintly woman.

Chertkov . . . From the very outset my sister Masha and I felt that we had gained in him an exceptional colleague as far as our particular involvement in my father's writings was concerned. Chertkov very quickly provided us with a duplicator, so that from then on it was possible to keep copies of all our father's letters. Before that we had just been making hand-written copies of any that dealt with especially important topics. My father's diary was also copied, almost as soon as it was written, and the copy passed on to Chertkov. In a word, Chertkov became the kingpin of my father's life.

In those days my father's activities, which involved help from all his friends, were concentrated above all on the publication and distribution of a series of small and very inexpensive books, or rather booklets, intended to replace the often mediocre reading matter being provided for the people at that time. The general title of this collection was *Posrednik* (The Go-Between), and the various booklets produced under that title sold all over Russia in their millions. It was in this collection that some of Tolstoy's most famous stories first appeared, notably *The Powers of Darkness*. Other great writers collaborated in the *Posrednik* scheme, and the people themselves also provided their own anonymous contributions.

My mother welcomed her husband's disciples into her home with good grace: Biryukov, Gorbunov, even Chertkov. Their activities on behalf of *Posrednik* did not disturb her. And Tolstoy was delighted at the warm welcome his friends received from her:

'You have so many excellent things in you. Your attitude with regard to Chertkov and Biryukov is a joy to me,' he wrote to her. But in 1895 an event occurred that had a great and disastrous effect upon my mother's character.

The misfortune that shattered her whole existence was the death of a little boy of seven, Vanya, her last born. My mother never recovered from the blow his death dealt her.

In their declining years my parents, and my mother especially, had concentrated all the powers of love they still possessed on the person of this one child. Remarkably gifted, and also of an exceptionally loving nature, Vanya was worthy of that love, and had already revealed a great spiritual precocity. The letters my father wrote when away from home mention him often, and always with tender affection: 'I love Vanichka so much . . .' 'He is sweet, very sweet.' And elsewhere: 'He is much more than sweet, he is good.' And he was to write to the child himself: 'Vanichka, send me a letter. I love you so much. Papa.'

And now this child had died of scarlet fever, in three days. Shortly after this terrible death, in March 1895, my mother wrote to her sister:

'Tanya, I have survived Vanichka's death. In the morning, waking up after a short, agonized sleep is horrible. I cry out in horror, I begin calling him, I want to hold him, hear his voice, kiss him, and this powerlessness against utter emptiness is a hell . . . A deathly silence reigns in the house. Alexandra, frozen with grief, never budges from her corner. She weeps and gazes at me with huge, anguished eyes brimming with tears. My older daughters had occasion to make use of all the latent maternal love they have in them. Little Vanya himself had an infinite store of love in him. He made so much of everyone. Everyone had a share in his affection and everyone has lost something. It has aged Lev, he walks all bent over, gloomy, eyes pale and bright. For him too, quite visibly, the last ray lighting his old age has been put out. Three days after Vanichka's death I came on him sitting and sobbing. He said to me: "For the first time in my life I feel I am facing the irremediable." It was pitiful and horrible seeing him like that. He is broken too. The boys came. Ilya that very day. His sympathy, his tears, his kindness warmed me so much. Sergei arrived on the day of the funeral . . . Only poor Lev, and very fortunately too, was away the whole time. He is in Dr Ogranovich's sanatorium, three hours away by rail. It was God who got him away in time to spare him this grief. Lev says that often, when he saw that Vanya had turned the corner of one of his fevers, the happiness of it took his breath away . . .

'On Tuesday evening, February 21st, Masha was reading them all *The Convict's Daughter*. It's a story Tolstoy has taken from Dickens's *Great Expectations*. When Vanichka came to say good night to me I asked him about the story. He looked at me sadly and said: "Don't let's talk about it mamma, it's so terribly sad. Estelle didn't marry Pip." I tried to get his mind on to something else. But I could see he wasn't looking at all well. I took him downstairs. He was yawning. Then with tears in his eyes he said: "Oh mamma! mamma! It's coming back again." He meant his fever: temperature a hundred and four, pains, bowels terribly weak. At three in the morning he came to, looked up at me and said: "Darling mamma, I'm sorry, you've been woken up." "I've had my sleep already, my pet, we're sitting up with you in turns." "Oh, and whose turn is it now? Tanya's?" "No, it's Masha's." "Well call her, then go and sleep." And he began kissing me, holding me so tight against him, with such lovingness, putting up his dry lips and pressing me against him. I asked him: "Where does it hurt?" "It doesn't hurt anywhere." "Then what is it? Do you just feel ill all over?" "Yes, all over." He didn't regain consciousness again. The fever burned all through Wednesday: his temperature went up to a hundred and seven point six. He moaned occasionally. The rash just wouldn't come out. We wrapped him in a sheet soaked in cold water with mustard. Then put him in a hot bath. Nothing did any good. His breathing became steadily shallower. The feet and hands began to get cold. He closed his eyes and went to sleep. That was at eleven in the evening on February 23rd. Masha was with him, also Lev's sister Mashenka, who stayed there praying and blessing him, and the nurse, no one else. Tanya couldn't bear to stay in the room. Lev and I were in another room, dumb with despair.

'. . . People sent so many wreaths, flowers, posies, that the room was like a garden. No one even thought of the risk of contagion. We all had such a deep feeling of being drawn close to one another, of being bound together by our love for the lost child. We couldn't bear to be apart. Mashenka, my sister-in-law, shared it all with us, with so much kindness and heart. On the third day, the 25th, the prayers were said, the coffin nailed down, and at noon the father with his sons and Posha Biryukov took up the bier and carried it out to the big four-seater sleigh. Coffin and sleigh were both almost invisible under the flowers and wreaths. Lev and I took our places, facing one another, and the sleigh very gently moved off. A great many people at the graveyard. No wind, and it wasn't cold. Going that way reminded Lev of the days when he was first in love with me, when he used to go to Polrovskoye. It moved him, he wept and found tender words for me . . . He and our sons were the coffin bearers. Everyone wept at the sight of him, a father, already old, worn out with grief. In truth, Tanya, that we with our grey hairs should have to see that child's life snuffed out, the only bright flame left to light our future, is it a natural thing?

'How he was lowered into the grave and the coffin covered with earth . . . I remember nothing. Suddenly I felt myself losing consciousness. I could vaguely see Lev as he held me against him. Someone was trying to stand between me and the grave, someone else was holding me up. It was Ilya I discovered later. He was sobbing violently. As for me, I didn't shed a single tear . . .

'There were a lot of children. They ran and clustered round Vanya's nurse when she began handing out the rolls and gingerbread she'd brought with her in one of the sleighs . . . Lev said to me as he wept:

"And to think it was my dream that one day Vanichka would carry on the work I've begun." Seeing his grief was more horrible for me than my own grief . . .

'Vanichka and I were so close; in the evening he couldn't bear me to go. I said his prayers with him, he'd make the sign of the cross over me, then say: "Kiss me very hard, put your head close to mine so that I can feel your breath on me as I go to sleep." When he fell ill he said: "If I'm ill that's because God wants me to be . . ."

'It is a whole world, an enchanting childhood world, filled with an almost wild gaiety sometimes, that has vanished with him. Never again a child taking its first steps, no more laughter, games, lit-up trees at Christmas, painted eggs for Easter, no more skating parties, no more fervent preparations for communion (he always asked to be allowed to take communion), the end of everything that ever since my own childhood, I can truly say, has filled my life.'

My mother's despair struck so deep that she almost lost her reason. At first she went through a period of religious exaltation during which she spent a great deal of time praying, both at home and in church. My father displayed a very special tenderness toward her at this time, and since she could not bear to be left alone for a moment, sometimes he, sometimes my sister Masha, sometimes myself, stayed with her day and night. My father would go to the church to collect her, waiting for her in the porch till she was ready to be driven home. Since he himself had long since left the Church, his wife's state of mind was alien to him. And indeed he tried to take her mind off her own grief by awakening a concern in her for the troubles of others. He took her visiting prisons, and got her to choose what books to buy for the prisoners. Nothing interested her. Not even her own children, not even Yasnaya Polyana. She wrote as much to her sister:

'Can such sufferings be borne? Everything, everything has slipped away from me. The most terrible thing of all is that with eight children I still feel alone with my grief, that no matter how good and kind they are to me I still can't seem to get any purchase on their lives with my mind . . .' 'Nature, sunlight, flowers, swims in the river, household tasks, even the children, all those things no longer exist for me. Everything is dead. Over everything the horror of the grave.'

Despair had broken her. She had always been very impulsive, nervous, of an easily excitable disposition, never placid. My father was aware of her state from the very beginning. It distressed him, and he was very worried about her. 'You are so changeable,' he wrote to her, 'that your tomorrow's letter may well be completely different from today's.' And when she wrote to him confessing her fear of becoming insane, he replied: 'What you write about your psychic confusion is pure silliness.' But in reality he too was afraid. 'I am here writing to you: I worry no end about your health and above all the state of your morale. How did the journey go? You were so nervous as you left . . . I was very apprehensive about your travelling at night in your state of nerves.'

Then quite suddenly, after that terrible blow, my mother found something to occupy and distract her, something that afforded her some relief: music. It was a visit to Yasnaya Polyana by one of our friends, the pianist Taneyev, that sparked off this transformation. Eighteen months after Vanya's death my mother wrote to her constant confidante, aunt Tanya:

'Music is my whole life. It alone enables me to go on living. I study, I pore over scores, I buy new pieces, I go to concerts. And I realize that I've begun too late. I make almost no progress, and that saddens me. It's becoming something of a mania. But what can I expect of a battered soul like mine? I've never managed to get back to normal ever since Vanichka's death. Lev is being particularly kind and patient with me, and for some time now I've become aware of his influence over me, by which I mean that I can feel him encircling my soul with his protection. He has understood that I could well have lost my mental balance, and he never stops helping me with such tenderness and goodness . . .'

Such had her life become, shattered by her grief.

And he? Would he let his life be governed merely by the ebb and flow of family griefs and joys? His own strong personality and the mission he felt himself called upon to accomplish prevented that. The spiritual labour, the inner struggle with himself, continued as before: life's contingencies could do no more than slow the process down.

To go away, to leave, remained his dream. But that dream became increasingly difficult to make into a reality as his wife's inner strength declined and she became more unhappy. As she herself said, he was 'her soul's protector'. And what could she give him in return? Nothing. Locked inside her grief, she no longer occupied any place in the inner life of the man living beside her and suffering his own private sufferings. She remained completely unaware of what was going on in the depths of his soul, and took no interest in the activities by which his intense inner labour manifested itself.

It is true that she gave those we called 'the dark ones' a hospitable welcome. But she made no effort to understand what it was that drew them to her husband. At that time his life was a constant and heroic battle for self-control. It was not easy for him to reconcile himself to the kind of life that was led at Yasnaya Polyana, but he thought it his duty to accept it for as long as he could still find the strength.

What kind of life did he lead in those days? As soon as he woke up he went out into the fields and woods. As he himself put it, he went out 'to say his prayers', in other words to summon up all the best energies of his being, there in the heart of nature, in order to perform his day's work. It was rarely that he succeeded in spending those early morning hours alone. People depending on his help, whether material or moral, were perpetually there waiting for him, lying in wait inside the house or preparing to ambush him round a bend in a path: pilgrims and poor people, people begging for alms, peasants wanting to submit a request or confide some doubt; people who had come from the four corners of the earth to share their tribulations with him and ask advice, not to mention all those who came to give him theirs. Then there were three post offices that delivered a daily mound of books, letters, newspapers, and magazines: they poured in from all over the world.

He tried as far as his strength permitted to satisfy all his visitors and correspondents. Then he settled down to his work as a writer. Need I say this? He was not writing in those days to achieve fame, and even less in order to make money. He wrote because he thought it his duty to communicate to the world the Truth that had been revealed to him, and because that Truth would bring men happiness. And his work was a source of joy to him, a source of great joys. In a letter written to a young man in 1899, we read:

'You rightly sensed that I would be happy to learn that I had friends in the Far East. The important thing is that the writings that have given me so much happiness should bring the same happiness to others, however few.'

He spent his evenings with the family and any visitors. Then before going to bed he would bring his correspondence and diary up to date.

But the idea of changing this way of life was always present. His immediate circle of friends, and many more beyond that inner circle, thought that he ought to break with his family in order to go away somewhere and live a life in accordance with his beliefs. Some of those who came to see him had already formed a clear picture of Tolstoy's life in advance, on the basis of what they had read. And when they saw that his home life included servants laying tables with silver and serving meals wearing white gloves, when they were confronted with the sight of his family playing tennis, they were unable to conceal their distress and disappointment. Unaware of the principles governing all Leo Tolstoy's behaviour, they then lost their previous enthusiasm for their Master.

There were many who wrote to tell him of their disillusionment, criticizing him for what they called his 'illogical behaviour'. This caused him suffering. Yet he regarded those who wrote to him in this way as true friends, and passed even severer judgments on himself in his replies than his correspondents themselves. He said again and again to anyone willing to listen that if he himself had known a man living as he lived while preaching what he preached, then he too would have treated him as a pharisee. The judgments passed on him were a further spur to his self-scrutiny. He never stopped asking himself: Am I right to keep silent? Would it not be better to leave, to vanish? And his reply was: 'If I do not do so, then it is before all else because I would be adopting that course *for my own good,* in order to escape a life poisoned in every way. And I think it necessary that I should bear with that life.'

To a friend who pressed him on the subject, he replied:

'I can say this: the reasons that prevent me from undertaking the change you advise, and that keep me chained to my tortures, are reasons that stem from the selfsame principles of love that in your eyes, as in mine, make a change of life desirable. It is very possible that I don't know how to bring it about, that it is beyond my capacities, or, quite simply, that there are bad elements in me that prevent me from following your advice. What can I do? It is in vain that I concentrate all the powers of my intelligence on the problem, and those of my heart too, I still cannot find the way, and can have nothing but gratitude for him who is able to point it out to me. I say this in all sincerity, without irony.'

And here is another reply on the same subject:

'Your letter affected me deeply. What you advise me to do is my secret dream, but so far I have been unable to realize it. There are many reasons for this, and it is in no way a wish to spare myself that prevents me. The principal reason is this: it must not be done with a view to its effect on others, since changing others is beyond our power and ought not to be the goal of our activity. It is something that cannot and must not be done until it has become indispensable, not to any external ends I have set myself to attain, but in order to satisfy a demand from the conscience within; until remaining in the *status quo* becomes as impossible morally as it is impossible physically to refrain from coughing when one's throat is blocked. There is not far to go, and every day brings me closer to just that situation.

'As for your second piece of advice: renouncing my social position and possessions, then sharing them out among those who regard themselves as possessing a right to them after my death, that was all done twenty-five years ago now. And the mere fact that I live with my wife and family in conditions of horribly shameful luxury when we are surrounded by poverty, that is something that never ceases to torment me more every day, and not a day passes without my thinking of taking your advice.

'I thank you very much for your letter. Yours with affection . . .'

One day this thought occurred to him: 'If I leave my family, what will happen? Someone else will do the same, then another. And as a result I shall go to the aid of some other family, whose head will come to the help of mine, and so on.'

I remember one night when we were driving back home from Tula in the carriage, just the two of us. He fell to thinking out loud in front of me, as he often did. He began talking about the people we called in Russia the *yurodivyeh,* meaning rather simple but holy people. He explained to me that often these folk would deliberately behave in such a way as to suggest they were committing some particular sin, so as to incite their fellow-men to condemn their feigned wickedness. Their aim being to develop in themselves one of the most important Christian virtues: humility. And he told me that this was also the case with him, that he had given the world an opportunity to judge him for things of which he was not in fact guilty.

After my father's death a letter was found, previously known only to my sister Masha and her husband Nicolas Obolenski, written by Tolstoy to his wife on June 8th 1897:

'Dear Sonya, for a long time now the disparity between my life and my beliefs has been causing me distress. I have been unable to make you change either the way of life or the habits that I myself trained you to adopt. Nor have I been able to leave you until now, since I thought that my going away would deprive the children, while still young, of the influence, however weak, I might exercise over them, and that it would cause you pain. However, I cannot continue to live as I have lived for these past sixteen years, sometimes in conflict with you and angering you, at other times succumbing myself to the influences and temptations that surround me and to which I have become accustomed. And today I have resolved to do what I have been inwardly proposing to do for a long while: to go away . . . Firstly, because with the ever-growing number of my years this life becomes more and more distressing, and because I long more and more for solitude; secondly, because the children are grown now, so that my influence is no longer necessary to them, and because you all of you have your own interests in life, so that my absence will not be greatly noticed by any of you.

'But the main reason is this: just as the Hindus, when they reach the age of sixty, go off into the wilds, just as every aging and religious man desires to devote the last years of his life to God and not to table-talk, to puns, to gossip, to lawn tennis, so I, having reached my seventieth year, long with all the strength of my soul for calm, for solitude, and if not for perfect harmony at least for something other than this flagrant disharmony between my life and my beliefs and conscience.

'If I had left openly, the result would have been supplications, explanations, arguments; I might perhaps have weakened and been unable to carry out my decision. And it must be carried out. I beg you therefore to forgive me in your hearts if my act saddens you. And you above all, Sonya, let me go, do not look for me, do not distress yourself on my account, and do not blame me.

'The fact that I have left you does not mean that I am displeased with you. I know that you were unable—literally unable—and are unable, to see things and to think as I do; that is why you could not and cannot change your life by making a sacrifice to something you do not accept. And so I do not blame you in the slightest; on the contrary, I remember with love and gratitude the thirty-five long years of our life together, and above all the earlier half, when with the renunciation inherent in your mother's heart you were able to bear so valiantly all the burdens of what you saw as your vocation. You have given me, and given the world, what you could give: so much motherly love and self-abnegation. It is impossible not to value you on that account. But during the more recent period of our life, during the past fifteen years, our paths have diverged. I cannot believe that it is my fault, for I know that if I have changed it has not been for my own sake, nor for that of mankind, but because it was impossible for me to do otherwise. How can I accuse you in any way for not having followed me, so I thank you, and I recall, I shall always recall, with love, what you have given me. Goodbye, my dear Sonya. Your affectionate Leo Tolstoy.'

This departure did not take place. He waited another thirteen years.

The diary, notes, and letters dating from this period of his life reveal a strange state of mind: he was oscillating between suffering and despair on the one hand and happiness and joy on the other. Here are a few extracts from his letters. He wrote to me in 1902: 'I live in happiness and joy.' And elsewhere, again after 1900: 'It is strange, the older I grow the better everything becomes for me.' And in 1906: 'Although physically very weakened by my illness, spiritually things are improving with me all the time.'

Now let us turn to his diary for 1908. There we read:

'Painful, distressing state. The last few days, fever without respite. Hard and painful trying to weather it. Doubtless I am going to die. Certainly it's been hard living in the stupid conditions of luxury I've been trapped into by life, and harder still finding myself dying in the same state . . .'

'Still the same torture. Life at Yasnaya Polyana is totally poisoned. Shame and distress wherever I go . . .'

'One thing becomes an ever increasing torture to me: the lie of senseless luxury side by side with the undeserved poverty and wretchedness all around me. Everything is going from bad to worse, everything becomes more and more painful. I can't turn my mind away from it, I simply can't not see . . .'

How is one to explain these violent and contradictory emotions pulling him in opposite directions? I think that everything he experienced in the way of joys and satisfactions came from the inner spiritual processes then achieving completion within him: he was aware of the progress being made, the results of which took the form for him of new insights. At the same time, however, the external aspect of his life was becoming daily even more intolerable to him. During the agrarian riots of 1905–06, Yasnaya Polyana was given police protection. In addition, the constant stream of visitors, the malicious or futile chatter of the idle rich, always distressing to him, had now exhausted his patience completely.

He was waiting for some external event that would free him from the unbearable contradiction of his life. But nothing of that sort occurred. On the contrary, the situation got worse and worse. His wife, as though conscious of having gained a victory, had calmed down a great deal and was living a life in accordance with her own conceptions, completely oblivious of the demands of her husband's conscience. Their sons were living independent lives in which their father's ideas played no part. Alexandra, my little sister, was still very young. Masha and I had both married and gone to live with our husbands. He was left alone. 'Living without you, without my two daughters, is sometimes a sad business,' he wrote to me, and added: 'I don't say it, but I know that you understand me, and that you love not only what I love but that by which I live.'

My mother, after her terrible grief, had never really found peace again. She had searched for it everywhere that it was not to be found, in music, in painting, in new affections . . . None of these remedies proved capable of calming the morbid outbursts of that agitated heart. She lacked a certain moral resource that would have enabled her to turn her sufferings to good use. After her refusal to follow her husband's path she took a wrong turning somewhere, and as a result wandered further and further from her true way. She began increasingly to relate everything to herself, to what she felt, and became excessively preoccupied with other people's attitudes toward her.

My father was accustomed to say that disorders of the mind are simply a heightened form of egoism. And it was certainly in this form that my mother's psychological anomalies presented themselves. She who had once been always ready to give of herself totally, without any thought of self, now fell prey to a single morbid preoccupation: what other people were saying about her. What would they say about her in the future? Might they one day, after her death, treat her as a Xantippe? And she had some grounds for such fears, since she was surrounded by people who pitied her husband for all she made him endure.

Haunted by that fear, she demanded that all her husband's daily notes be revised. She wanted everything that might give a bad impression of her in the future to be excised. She took to justifying herself on every conceivable subject, and to anyone she came across—even those who had never dreamed for a moment of blaming her for anything, or of condemning her on any grounds whatever—, insisting, explaining why she hadn't followed her husband's path, proving that he was the one who had taken the wrong turning, and believing that she was thereby justifying her attempts to control his activities.

In the summer of 1909 I received an urgent telegram from my sister Alexandra. She begged me to come as quickly as I could. I set out immediately. When I arrived I found my mother in bed.

Yasnaya Polyana was in a state of crisis. My father had decided to travel to Stockholm in order to read a paper to the Peace Congress. My mother had desperately opposed the idea of this trip, which she had decided would be dangerous for her husband's health. She had resolved not to allow him to go. And when he refused to comply with her wishes she had been stunned and baffled. She had dug her heels in even harder, one moment announcing that she would go to any lengths to achieve her ends, the next lamenting that there was nothing left for her to do but die, and that they had all conspired to poison her.

By the time I arrived the peak of the crisis had passed. She was lying in bed, weak and defeated. 'My little Tanya,' she said, 'you know I suppose that I thought they wanted to poison me. Dushan (the fore-name of a Slovakian doctor, Makovitski, who was a friend and disciple of my father's) made me take some sort of sweet powder or other. Well he's not a nice person, and he loves your father. I thought he wanted to get rid of me.' I reassured her as best I could and she quietened down.

I felt so sorry for her seeing her like that, unwell, deeply unhappy, and so morally isolated. It is true that if my mother was alone she had only herself to blame, but that didn't mean she suffered any the less. My father was surrounding her with love and tenderness. I left them like that. Calm had been restored. It was over for the time being.

But clearly nothing had changed fundamentally. New occasions for bitterness were soon provoking fresh recriminations.

My mother had refused to go on helping her husband with his work as a writer, and naturally she had been replaced by others. Now she suddenly took it into her head that she was being pushed to one side: no one needed her any more, her husband was seeking assistance elsewhere, whereas previously everything had been in her hands. But how could it be otherwise? She had become a total stranger to his work, and even now was unable to revive any interest in what he wrote, so how was she to play any useful part in it? But the fact that it was so distressed her. It became a perpetual cause of offence to her that she was obliged to remain a mute onlooker, that she had no part whatever to play in the intense activity going on all around her. It became more than she could bear, and she would relieve her pent up feelings with floods of reproaches directed at the centre of those activities. But she only made things worse for herself. The others continued with their work, only now they took to concealing it from her. As mistress of the house she had put herself in an impossible situation. Whenever she walked through the typewriting room, her daughter Alexandra and my father's male secretary would simply stop what they were doing, maintain a complete silence, and on occasion, in order to avoid scenes, even hide the manuscript they were in the process of copying. She was only too quick to sense the atmosphere of suspicion that reigned in the room, and it made her furious. The seeds of the nervous instability already apparent to some extent in her youth now sprouted apace, until finally her 'nerves' had developed into real mental illness. She lost all control over herself, and her hysterical attacks became steadily more frequent.

This state of things was extremely painful for my father. He found it impossible to work, was frequently unable to sleep, and suffered a decline in his general health as a result of the moral tortures he was enduring. He tried to accept his suffering as an expiation for all the wrong he had done in his life, to use it as a spur toward greater humility. On July 16th 1910, he was to write in his diary: 'I can only give thanks to God for the leniency of the punishment.'

That summer of 1910, his last summer, every day of which brought some new suffering, my father spent almost entirely away from Yasnaya Polyana. In May he was with me, at Kotcheti, my husband's property. In June he paid a long visit to Chertkov, who was then living at Mecherski, a place he had rented in Moscow rural district. During this stay with his friend my father continued his scrutiny of the situation he had been forced into, and his search for some way out of it. 'I want to try if I can,' he wrote in his diary, 'to carry on the struggle with Sonya by a methodical application of goodness and love. At a distance it seems feasible; I shall try to act in the same way when I am near her . . . We have received only one thing, but it is a good that cannot be taken from us: love. Love, and all will become joy: joy in heaven and joy on earth, and joy among men. Yet we search for the good everywhere but in love.'

While at Mecherski my father received a telegram from his wife. It was a summons home. She begged him to come back. He did so. He found her 'worse than expected, in a state of hysteria and nervous irritability impossible to describe'.

As if that were not enough, another trial was now added to all the others: Lev, my brother, intervened in our parents' affairs, taking it upon himself to act as judge as far as his father was concerned and as counsel for the defence in the case of his mother. My father wrote: 'Lev is a sore trial, and one I find it hard to bear.'

And so day followed day. He recorded their events in his diary, noting all the changes in his wife's condition. And these notes make one fact plain: that condition was steadily deteriorating.

'Sonya has relapsed into a state of nervous irritation. It has been a very distressing day . . .'

'Sonya is over-excited again, and that has led to the same torments for us both . . .'

'The night was horrible . . . It is a distressing, frightful illness.'

Quite evidently my father regarded his wife as a sick woman. But many in his immediate circle, among them Dr Makovitski, were of the opinion that she was only play-acting, that her mind was quite normal, and that her so-called hysteria was merely a means of getting her own way. It was at this point, in July 1910, that my father made his will, the final one, the will that was eventually probated.

He had already made an earlier version of it at Mecherski, while he was staying with Chertkov. In the earlier document he had required all his works, without exception, to be declared in the public domain. But a lawyer had since informed him that such a clause could never be executed, since the law required the provision of an heir. It was the discovery of this fact that led him to name his youngest daughter, Alexandra, as legal heir to all his works. I was then named as alternative heir in the event of my sister's predecease. Alexandra was required to place all his works at the disposal of all men after his death. And the same applied to me, should I inherit. Then, in a rider to this final will, Tolstoy made Chertkov his literary executor with sole authority over the posthumous administration and publication of all his writings.

My mother was not informed of any of this. But certain allusions, certain clues, plus a kind of sixth sense, led her to suspect the existence of a will. From that moment on she kept up a perpetual search, night and day alike, for some material confirmation of her suspicions.

This meant that my father, who had once had no secrets whatever from his wife, now did have a secret from her, and one that he intended should continue to be kept from her. The consequences of this were most distressing for him. He had to hide his manuscripts, and even his diary, while she on her side was expending her entire energies trying to discover the key to this secret, the secret that he, her husband, was keeping from his wife. She took to listening at doors in order to eavesdrop on her husband's conversations. And when he was out she did not hesitate to go through his papers.

It was at this time that my father began keeping another diary 'for myself alone', as he put it. The notebook he used was small enough to permit its concealment, and he usually carried it about with him, under his smock or in one of his boots. Eventually, although it pained him, he had come round to accepting the fact that his other diary was being copied while the ink was still practically wet. There is an entry in that which reads: 'The truth is that I no longer have any sincere and simple diary. I must begin one.'

This new diary was begun on July 29th 1910 with these words: 'I am beginning a new diary, a real diary for myself alone. Today there is one thing I must write down and it is this: if the suspicions of certain of my friends are correct, then the attempt to win me over with shows of affection began today. She has been kissing my hand for some days now—something she never did before; and there have been no scenes or despair. May God and men forgive me if I am mistaken! It is so easy for me to err on the good side, the side of affection. I can love her in all sincerity.' And next day he wrote: 'Chertkov has drawn me into a struggle that is most painful and repugnant to me.'

Having made his will, my father was beset again and again by doubts. He examined his conscience continually: Had he done right? Had he done wrong?

Indeed, after a visit from Posha Biryukov, during which our friend expressed regret at all the mystery that had been created, my father immediately conceded that he was in the right. He wrote on August 2nd, after this conversation:

'Talked yesterday with Posha. He told me very rightly that my mistake was to have made the will in secret. It ought either to have been made openly, and all those concerned informed, or else I ought to have left everything as it was and done nothing at all. And he's perfectly right. I have done the wrong thing, and now I'm suffering the consequences. What was bad was acting in secret like that, imputing bad intentions to my heirs, and above all I undoubtedly acted wrongly, because of my wish to have the will drawn up in due form, in resorting to institutions controlled by the State, the very idea of which I reject. I now see quite clearly that I alone am the guilty party in all that is now happening. I should have left everything as it was and done nothing at all. The diffusion of my works will be an inadequate return for the discredit that my illogical actions will unfailingly bring upon them.'

And on that same day, August 2nd, he also wrote in his diary:

'I have grasped my error, grasped it completely. What I ought to have done was call all my heirs together and state my intentions to them, instead of acting in that hole in the corner way. I wrote as much to Chertkov. It upset him a great deal.'

Chertkov answered my father in a long letter that has recently been reproduced in the book by Goldenweiser that is one of my reasons for breaking my own silence at this point. This letter runs to eleven printed pages in the book, and in it Chertkov offers a lengthy description of what Countess Tolstoy 'was thinking'. He explains her 'intentions with regard to her husband's works'. He predicts what she and certain of her sons would have said if Tolstoy's friends had publicly announced their intention of publishing an edition of their master's works. He depicts one of that master's sons brandishing an unfinished story of his father's, *The False Coupon,* and exclaiming: 'We're going to get a hundred thousand rubles out of this if we get a kopek!'

When I questioned my brother about this myself he emphatically denied ever having done or said any such thing.

My father was deeply wounded by what Chertkov wrote about his family. And he noted:

'Long letter from Chertkov depicting everything that has happened. Reading about those things and remembering them was sad and painful for me. He is absolutely right, and I feel guilty on his account. Posha wasn't right. I shall write to them both.'

And he replied to Chertkov:

'Your letter aroused two feelings in me: disgust for the expression of grossly selfish and ruthless sentiments that I had failed to notice or forgotten, sadness and repentance for the hurt my letter inflicted on you.' (A letter I know nothing about.) And he adds that he is nevertheless still not happy about what he has done. 'I feel,' he wrote, 'that it was possible to act better, even though I don't know exactly what else could have been done.'

Once the suspicion had entered my mother's mind that Chertkov had been the deviser of the will she conceived a loathing of him. She became obsessed by jealousy, and in her madness threatened suicide unless her husband promised to sever all relations with Chertkov. My father gave way to her. Not out of weakness but from a sense of duty.

No longer being able to see his friend was not only a source of great sorrow for Tolstoy, it also hindered his work and proved an added drain on his energies. Since all the considerable material labours entailed by his work as a writer were concentrated at Telyatinki, two miles away from Yasnaya Polyana, instead of his being able to meet those involved and talk over decisions face to face, everything now had to be done in writing. Whereupon this constant correspondence became, in its turn, a source of acute distress to my mother. Even Chertkov's absence had done nothing to calm her jealousy. She now suspected the two men of meeting secretly. And as result she took to following her husband about wherever he went.

On August 5th Tolstoy wrote in his 'boot' diary: 'My abstention from all contact with Chertkov troubles me; it is shameful, ridiculous, and sad. Yesterday I felt such pity for Sofia Andreyevna. No ill feeling on my side. That makes me so happy. It is easy for me to feel sorry for her and love her when she is suffering but not making others suffer.'

But next day: 'I have just run into Sofia Andreyevna. She was walking very quickly, horribly agitated. A feeling of great pity came over me. Back at the house I told them someone ought to follow her and see where she was going. Alexandra claims that the walk had a purpose, that she is keeping watch on me. I felt less pity for her then. There is an element of badness there, and I could not manage to make myself not care with deliberate wickedness involved. I am thinking of going away and leaving a letter, but I recoil from it, even though I believe it would be better for her.'

'It would be better for her.' That was one of the reasons behind my father's departure several weeks later. He thought that it would be for the patient's good. And secondly, the frivolity inherent in life at Yasyana Polyana, a life quite inadmissible as far as he was concerned ever since his 'second birth', had become quite intolerably distressing now that he was an old man of eighty-two no longer interested in anything but the most abstract religious problems.

On August 20th 1910 he noted: 'The sight of this manorial estate causes me such torment that I dream of escaping from it, of disappearing.' He often spoke enviously of the way in which Hindu men, when they become old, withdraw from society and live in solitude. He had been harbouring a secret dream for a long while now, that of spending his last days in material poverty, surrounded by the peasants and workers he loved. The scales dipped now this way now that under the weight of his contradictory resolves, but toward the end it was the desire to leave that was weighing daily heavier.

In August I went over to fetch my father for a stay with me at Kotcheti. I wanted him just to live quietly for a while with me and my family so that he could rest from the stresses of recent months. As soon as I arrived at Yasnaya Polyana my mother began using every weapon in her armoury to ensure that she came back to Kotcheti with us. Sometimes she used her illness as an argument, at others she waxed indignant at the notion that anyone should want to take her husband from her so that he could *have a rest* away from her. 'Have a rest from what?' she demanded. 'A rest from my love, is that what you mean? From all the care I take of him? What would you say if I took your husband away so that he could *have a rest* away from you?' In the end she resorted to the ultimate persuasion. One day when I was with my father in his study she came in, burst into floods of tears, and begged us to take her with us. She was afraid of being left alone. She gave her solemn promise that she would leave him in peace. The result was a foregone conclusion. We took pity on her and said yes. That day, August 10th 1910, my father noted: 'Things are going from bad to worse. She didn't sleep all night. Toward morning she suddenly sat up: "Who are you talking to?" Then she came out with a spate of horrors . . . I will bear it. May God come to my aid! She has reduced everyone to exhaustion, herself most of all. She is coming with us.'

Eventually six of us left: my father, my mother, my sister Alexandra, Dr Makovitski, myself, and my father's last secretary, V. T. Bulgakov. Once we had settled in, with my family around us, things improved. After two weeks my mother had to return to Yasnaya Polyana on estate business. My father recorded her departure as follows:

'She was very touching as she said goodbye. She asked everyone's forgiveness. The pity I feel for her makes me love her so much. I wrote her a little letter.'

Here is that letter: 'You touched me so deeply, dear Sonya, as you were leaving, with your good, sincere words. If you could manage to overcome in yourself that . . . how can I put it? . . . that in yourself that is the cause of your self-torture! How good that would be for you and for me. I was sad all evening, depressed. I don't stop thinking of you. I am writing what I feel, without adding anything. Write to me, I beg you. Your husband who loves you. L.T.'

The day after her departure he noted that he was sad without her, as well as afraid for her and worried.

Even though my mother had gone, my father did not lack news of her. The copy made of his diary was sent over to Kotcheti, and certain people at Yasnaya and Telyatinki saw fit to include in the package an account of all that his wife had been saying and doing. 'Thanks be to God, it is of no importance to me, but it has a bad effect on my feelings for her. It ought not to be happening.' That was his first reaction. And as the accusations continued, here is the second: 'I have received a letter and an extract from Goldenweiser that have horrified me. The letters from Yasnaya are frightful.' My mother asked her husband to come home for their forty-eighth wedding anniversary. He agreed, and arrived back at Yasnaya on September 23rd during the night. The last entry in his first boot diary dates from the day before that: 'I am leaving for Yasnaya and am seized with terror at the thought of what awaits me there. The essential thing is to maintain silence and not to forget that there is a soul within her—God.' Those are the words with which the first little notebook of Leo Tolstoy's secret diary comes to an end.

Alas, no sooner was my father back at Yasnaya Polyana than he was plunged once more into the same torments he had endured during the previous months. My mother, continuing her relentless search, finally managed to lay hands on a tiny notebook: it was the secret diary. She removed and hid it. My father assumed that he had lost it and continued in another notebook. On September 24th he wrote in it:

'During lunch conversation on D.M. (*Dyetskaya Mudrostzh*, the Wisdom of Childhood, an article my father was writing). Chertkov, magpie that he is, has made off with the manuscript. What will he do with all these manuscripts after my death? I begged fairly energetically to be left in peace. It seemed to be over. But after dinner the reproaches began: I became angry with her when I ought to have pitied her. I said nothing. She went to her room. It's eleven now, she has not come out again and that distresses me. Received a letter from Chertkov full of reproaches and accusations. They are tearing me to pieces. Get away from them all? I think about it sometimes.'

In October I went over to Yasnaya Polyana again. What a frightful state of things I found! My sister Alexandra, as a result of a quarrel with her mother, had moved out to her own little property nearby. My mother was pouring out an unending stream of complaints about everything and everybody. She claimed that she was exhausted by her work on the new edition she was preparing for publication, and by constant allusions on my father's part to the departure he was threatening her with. She also said that she simply didn't know what to do about Chertkov. Should she forbid him the house? Her husband would be disturbed and upset by his absence and blame her for it. But welcome him into her house? She hadn't the strength. The mere sight of his picture brought on a nervous attack. And it was at this point that she went to my father and demanded that all his diaries should be taken out of Chertkov's hands. My father again gave way on this point. But these perpetual struggles were by now driving him to the very limit of his strength.

On October 3rd he had a heart attack that brought on convulsions. My mother thought he was dying. She was so shaken that she suddenly opened her eyes to the truth. Her own guilt became apparent to her, and she realized how far she herself was to blame for her husband's illness. One moment she was hurling herself on to her knees at the foot of his bed, clasping his jerking feet in her arms, the next she was rushing out into the room next door, throwing herself down on the floor, seized with terror, jerkily crossing herself again and again as she murmured beseechingly: 'Oh Lord, Lord! Forgive me. Yes, I am the one to blame. Lord, not yet, not this time! Not this time, oh not yet!'

My father recovered from his attack. But he emerged from it even more bent, the sadness deeper in those pale eyes.

As a result of our father's illness Alexandra came back to live in the house and made things up with her mother, who in her turn, summoning up all her courage, invited Chertkov to resume his visits to Yasnaya. She was a pitiable sight the evening she was expecting his first visit in response to her suggestion. She was in a highly emotional state and visibly in great distress. Her nervous excitation had brought a hectic flush to her face, and she was filling the whole house with her agitation. She kept perpetually glancing at the clock, running to the window, then out into the study where my father was sitting. After Chertkov's arrival she became quite beside herself. There was nowhere in the house she felt able to settle, so she kept constantly rushing from one of the doors of her husband's study to the other. Eventually she rushed in to me. She threw herself on to my neck and burst into bitter sobs. I tried to comfort her, to calm her down. But calm was by then beyond the reach of her sick heart.

From then on things went from bad to worse. On October 25th, three days before his departure, my father wrote:

'Still the same distressing feeling. Suspicions, spying, and a guilty desire for her to give me justification for going. I am so wicked. When I think of my leaving and her situation, I pity her. And yet I cannot...'

That same day he also wrote:

'All through the night I see myself locked in painful struggle with her. I wake, go back to sleep, and it all starts all over again.'

Two more days passed, and then, during the night of October 27th–28th, there came the awaited jolt that led to his leaving Yasnaya Polyana for ever.

Here is how he recorded the event in his diary:

'*October 28th 1910*—I went to bed at half-past one, and slept till three. I woke up, and as on previous nights heard doors opening and footsteps. The other nights I hadn't looked at my door, but this time I did glance over, and through the cracks I saw bright light coming from the study, (and heard) a rustling. It was Sofia Andreyevna searching for something, and presumably reading . . .

'More footsteps, the door stealthily opening, and she went by.

'I don't know why it aroused such an irresistible feeling of disgust and outrage in me. I tried to go back to sleep. I couldn't. I turned over and over in bed for about an hour. I lit my candle and sat up.

'The door opened. She came in asking after my "health", and expressing surprise at the light she had noticed in my room.

'The disgust and outrage increased. I had difficulty breathing, I took my pulse: 97. I couldn't stay in bed and abruptly made a firm resolve to go.

'I wrote her a letter; I began getting together the few things I needed to get away. I woke up Dushan (Makovitski), then Alexandra, and they helped me get my things packed. I was trembling at the thought that she might hear me from her room and come out—scene, hysterical attack—and then no leaving.

'By six everything was more or less packed. I went down to the stables to tell them to harness up . . .

'Perhaps I am wrong to justify myself, but it does really seem to me that it was not Lev Nicolayevich I was saving but that something, however tenuous, that exists within me . . .'

Those last words should perhaps be set alongside a sentence in the draft of a will that Tolstoy copied into his diary on March 27th 1895: 'I have had moments when I have felt myself to be a conductor through which the divine will was passing, and those were the happiest moments of my life.'

I was not at Yasnaya on the 27th and 28th of October. On the 28th, late in the afternoon, I received a telegram from my sister Alexandra: 'Come at once.' I left immediately. When I reached Orel station the porter there, who knew me, handed me two telegrams addressed to my father. The first read: 'Come back quickest, Sacha.' (Sacha is the diminutive of Alexandra.) The other read: 'Don't worry. Ignore all telegrams not signed Alexandra.'

Reading both telegrams together like that, it was easy enough to see what had happened: the first was a forgery.

I arrived at Yasnaya Polyana next morning. Everyone there was in a terrible state. All my brothers except Lev, who was in Paris, were arriving as quickly as they could. My mother's condition was causing great alarm. On the morning of the 28th, after being handed the letter my father had left for her, she had run out of the house, rushed down to the pond, and thrown herself into it. They had pulled her out in time; but since then she had made a variety of further suicide attempts. Then finally, realizing that the constant watch by then being kept on her was going to prevent her achieving her end, she announced that she was going to starve herself to death.

The days that followed were dismal ones indeed. We each wrote to our father. He answered:

October 31st 1910

I thank you, my dear friends, my true friends, Sergei and Tanya, for sharing my grief and for your letters. Yours, Sergei, pleased me particularly: it is clear, short, full of matter, thoughtful and serious, but above all good. I cannot help but feel all the responsibility I bear and be afraid—but I was not strong enough to act otherwise, I have written to Chertkov asking him to have my letter read to my children, I have written everything I felt and still feel—which is that I cannot act otherwise than I am doing.

I have written to her too—to mamma. She will show you my letter. I wrote what I could to her and weighed my words carefully.

We are leaving in a moment. Where for we do not know yet. You will still be able to reach me through Chertkov.

Goodbye and thank you, dear children, and forgive me for being the cause of suffering for you nevertheless. You above all, dearly beloved Tanichka. That's all, I am in haste to leave so that—the thing I fear—mamma does not catch up with me. An encounter with her now would be terrible. So, Goodbye.

L.T. Four in the morning.

No one except Alexandra knew where he was. Alexandra left to join him after giving her word that she would let us know if he fell ill. My brother Sergei returned to Moscow. With him gone everything seemed gloomier still, and what we were anticipating the more fearful. There was no doubt whatever in my mind: this change of life on my father's part was the end.

My mother was also a source of fear. Not only fear for her personally but also because I knew that if she succeeded in taking her life my father would never know peace or happiness again. We brought in a psychiatrist and a sister from a nursing order, so that she was never left for a single instant without someone at her bedside.

Alexandra had been gone for several days when V. T. Bulgakov, who was over at Telyatinki with Chertkov, came to Yasnaya to see me and told me in secret that my father had fallen ill and that Chertkov had left to be with him. 'But where has he fallen ill?'—'Chertkov has forbidden me to say.'—'Is it far away? In Russia? Or abroad?' I pressed Bulgakov with questions he was unable to answer. Chertkov had forbidden it. 'How can Chertkov not understand that it is of the utmost importance to me to know, and why has he forbidden you to tell me?'—'I don't know,' Bulgakov answered. And it was said in a tone that I took to mean: 'I don't understand it myself.' Then he made me swear I wouldn't reveal the secret he'd confided in me to anyone else.

What anxiety I lived through the night after that news! My father was dying somewhere quite close to me, and I didn't know where. I couldn't go to him. I couldn't look after him. And perhaps I would never see him again alive. Would I even be allowed to see him for a single instant on his deathbed? Not a moment's sleep. Genuine torture. All night I could hear my mother weeping, complaining, moaning in her room next to mine. When I got up I still didn't know what to do, what course I could take. But there was one person at least, a stranger to me, who understood and took pity on Tolstoy's family. He telegraphed us: *Lev Nicolayevich at house of Astapovo stationmaster. Temperature* 104°. My gratitude to that man, Orlov, a correspondent of the newspaper *Voice of Russia,* will endure till I die.

I woke up my brothers and mother. We set out for Tula. There was only one train a day to Astapovo. We had missed it. We ordered a special.

At Yasnaya, galvanized by febrile haste, my mother had thought of everything, arranged everything. She had brought everything with her my father might conceivably need, she had forgotten nothing. But despite the lucidity of her mind there was no charity in her heart. And at that moment we, her children, held that against her and passed judgment on her. We could not help but see that she was the cause of everything that had happened, and perceiving not the slightest sign of repentance in her we were incapable at that moment of forgiving her.

At Astapovo our carriage was detached from the engine and shunted into a siding. We settled ourselves in and prepared to live there for as long as proved necessary. In order to prevent our mother going to visit my father we decided that we wouldn't go to see him either. Only my brother Sergei went into his room: summoned by Alexandra he had arrived from Moscow before us. But my father learned by chance that I was nearby and asked why I didn't go to see him. Almost unable to breathe for my emotion I ran over to the stationmaster's house. I was afraid he would ask me questions about my mother. I wouldn't have known what to answer. I had never lied to him, and I knew that at this solemn moment I would be incapable of answering him with an untruth. I found him lying in bed fully conscious. He said a few affectionate words to me, then asked: 'Who has stayed behind to look after mamma?' The phrasing of his question made it possible for me to answer without deviating from the truth. I told him that my mother was being looked after by my brothers and had a doctor and a nurse with her. He questioned me at length, asking for further details. And when I said: 'Are you sure talking about this doesn't upset you?' he interrupted me emphatically: 'Go on, go on, what could be more important to me?' And he went on questioning me about her at length and in great detail.

After that first visit I had free access to him. I had the privilege and the joy of seeing him often during the few days he still had left to live. My keenest desire was that he would ask for my mother to come to him. I longed ardently for a reconciliation between them before he died. Alexandra shared my feelings. But it was clear that he was alarmed at the thought of seeing her. In his periods of delirium he would repeat again and again *'escape, escape . . .'* or: *'. . . after me, after me . . .'* He ordered the curtains to be drawn over the window because he thought he could see a woman outside trying to look in at him. He dictated a telegram to the sons he supposed to be still at Yasnaya with their mother: 'I beg you earnestly to keep mamma there. In my present weak state my heart would not withstand a meeting.'

Once when I was taking my turn to sit with him he said to me: 'So many things are falling on Sonya. We managed things badly.' The emotion I felt made it difficult to breathe. I tried to get him to repeat what he had said so that I could be certain I had heard correctly. I said: 'What was that, papa? So . . . what? Soda?' And he said again: 'Sonya, on Sonya, so many things falling on her.' I asked him: 'Do you want to see her? Do you want to see Sofia?' But he had lost consciousness. I received no reply, no sign of acquiescence, no gesture of refusal. I did not dare to repeat my question. I felt it would have been like blowing on a dying flame to say the words again.

It was difficult to understand my mother. At times she announced that she wasn't insane and didn't have to be told that her going to see him could kill him, at others she said it didn't matter much if it did, since whatever happened she knew she was never going to see him again. At others, in floods of tears, she lamented the fact that she wasn't being allowed to look after him. 'To think that I've lived with him for forty-eight years, and that it's not me looking after him when he's about to die . . .'

We all felt the monstrous horror of the situation deeply. But as long as our father did not ask to see her we held to our decision that her presence at his bedside was an impossibility.

One day I was sitting at my father's bedside holding his hand, that hand I loved so much and never looked at without emotion, without thinking of all it had transmitted to mankind under the orders of that great mind. He was dozing, eyes closed. But suddenly I heard his voice: 'And here is the end, and . . . *nichevo* [it is nothing].' I saw that he had lost all his colour and realized that his breathing was becoming steadily slower.

I told myself that this must really be the end, and in my terror I felt the hair rising on my scalp and the blood slowing in my veins. I couldn't get up and call for someone to come because he was still holding my hand, and when I made a slight movement to withdraw it he strengthened his grip.

At last someone came in and I sent for the doctor. A camphor injection was administered, and I saw the colour come back into his cheeks as his breathing gradually returned to normal again.

Abruptly he raised himself with great energy to a sitting position, and in a loud, clear voice uttered these words:

'I advise you to remember one thing: there are a great many people in the world besides Lev Tolstoy, and you are all concerning yourselves with Lev alone.'

The last few words were uttered more weakly, and he fell back on to his pillows . . .

On November 6th, the day before his death, he called out: 'Sergei!' And when Sergei went over to him he made a tremendous effort and said in a weak voice:

'Sergei! I love Truth . . . very much . . . I love Truth.'

Those were his last words.

As a very young man he had proudly proclaimed that his idol, that which he loved with all the strength of his soul, was Truth. And right up until that day when he told his eldest son, 'his true friend', in a faltering voice that he loved Truth, he was never unfaithful to that Truth.

'And ye shall know the Truth, and the Truth shall make you free.' He knew that, and he served that Truth until death.

That same day, at ten in the evening, my brother Sergei came into our carriage and told us that our father was worse. We didn't know whether to tell our mother or not. We each gave our opinion, then decided that we ought first to check on our father's condition again, then either call our mother to him or not according to what we found. But Sergei and I did not even have time to reach his bedside: our mother had followed us. We went in. My father was unconscious. The doctors told us that it was the end. My mother went over, sat down beside his bed, and leaning over him murmured words of affection, saying goodbye to him and begging him to forgive her for all she had done wrong. A few deep sighs were all the answer she received.

That was how my father died, taken in by a stationmaster, in the wintry wastes of Riazan. I say 'how my father died' because it is solely as a daughter that I have been speaking. Tolstoy, the great writer, belongs no more to me than to anyone else. For my part I have simply tried to tell what I believe to be the humble truth about two beings I have loved, about their hearts, their sufferings, and their joys, in a word about their life.

My mother lived for another nine years. She died at Yasnaya Polyana, also in November, and also, like her husband, of pneumonia. She died surrounded by her children and grandchildren. She had the joy of being nursed to the end with extraordinary tenderness by her daughter Alexandra, with whom she had earlier had such deep disagreements. She knew that she was dying. And she submitted to death, welcomed it even, with humility. Calm had come to her during her final years. Her husband's dream for her had in part come true, that transformation for which he would have sacrificed all his fame. My father's ideas had become less alien to her. She had become a vegetarian. She was kind to those around her. But she had retained one weakness: she was still afraid of what people would say and write about her when she had gone, she feared for her reputation. As a result she never let slip the slightest opportunity of justifying her words and actions. There was no weapon she would not use in her campaign of self-defence: she was warding off in advance the attacks she knew would one day be made upon her. And she knew by whom.

Toward the end she often talked about the little son she had lost, and about her husband. She thought constantly of my father, she told me one day. And then added: 'I treated him badly, and it's a torment to me . . .'

Such, in essence, was the life together of these two beings as closely linked by mutual love as they were separated by the divergence of their aspirations. Infinitely close to one another but also infinitely far apart. A particular instance of an eternal struggle: that between the power of the spirit and the dominion of the flesh.

And who will take it upon him to call one of them guilty? Can the spirit refrain from defending its liberty? Can one blame the flesh for its struggle to live? Can one blame my mother for not having been capable of following her husband up to the heights? It was much more her misfortune than her fault, and that misfortune broke her.

And was my father guilty because he tried to preserve that thing 'of which he sometimes felt the trace in him', and because he rescued it at the cost of his life?

I often think of my mother

by Tatyana Albertini

My mother died in Rome, in September 1950, a few weeks after reaching her eighty-sixth birthday. She was the second of Leo Tolstoy's thirteen children, only nine of whom reached adulthood. The only one still alive today is his youngest daughter, Alexandra, now ninety. She never married, and lives now in the United States, where she created the Tolstoy Foundation, an organization that provides assistance for refugees and exiles.

My mother married very late, at thirty-five. However, we know from her private diary that the prospect of marriage had never been far from her mind: she wanted a home, a husband, and above all lots of children. Leo Tolstoy, on the other hand would have liked all his daughters to remain spinsters, and told them so. The idea of seeing them married was very painful to him, and pre-sumably, though he never admitted it to himself, he was jealous of the men who inevitably came between his daughters and himself to some extent. My mother was pretty, flirtatious, and loved balls and entertainments of all kinds. Yet it was only after long hesitation that she did finally make up her mind to marry, in 1899.

Her husband, Mikhail Sukhotin, fifteen years her senior and a widower with six children, was an old friend of the Tolstoy family. In other words my mother suddenly found herself at the head of a family of by no means little children, five boys and a girl. She very quickly succeeded in making them love and even adore her, even though the task was not always an easy one. As for her wish to have several children of her own, that was not granted: I am her only child, born when my mother was forty and had already suffered four miscarriages. It was after one of these miscarriages that Tolstoy wrote telling her to look upon her mis-fortune as a trial sent by God: 'I look at your dear picture,' he added, 'and I read in your face—if you can understand this every now and then—other faces, submerged in sadness, those of your suffering . . .' (31st December 1902).

Tolstoy's three daughters—Tatyana, Marya, and Alexandra—were always closer to their father than his sons were. They all lived with him for a long while, and each in turn helped him with his work, acting as his secretary. During *the first years of his marriage it was his wife who always found the time, despite having her children to look after, to copy out his manuscripts. She did it in the evenings. Tolstoy would then take the fair copy away to his study, and next evening my grandmother would find the manuscript back on her desk, smothered in corrections, sometimes wholly re-written, and had to set to and copy it all over again. Later on it was her daughters who performed this task, first Tatyana, the oldest, then Marya, and finally Alexandra.*

Asked if my mother was the only one of Tolstoy's children who understood their father and mother equally, I would answer yes. She loved her father deeply, admired him, and strove loyally to follow his ideas. Even when still young, at a time when the amusements of 'society' balls and flirtations occupied a large part of her time, she had already grasped their uselessness and vanity, yet would not let herself admit it. She also sensed her father's unspoken disapproval, albeit without clearly understanding the motives for it, and this often distressed her. The love binding her to her father was the feeling that governed her whole life.

This devotion did not prevent her from bestowing an equal love and understanding on her mother, a hypersensitive woman with a difficult character who, while suffering from being unable to share her husband's ideas, also loved him with a passionate and even possessive love that made her jealous of all Tolstoy's 'followers'. Both father and mother, equally aware of the understanding and indulgent love their eldest daughter had for them, frequently took her into their confidence.

Her parents' tragedy never ceased tormenting my mother, even into her old age, when I have heard her say on many occasions: 'If only that old couple had been left to live in peace and resolve their problems themselves, if only no one had interfered . . .' It was because Alexandra, her youngest sister, had allowed herself to become involved in that tragedy as she did that relations between the two sisters were for a long time difficult and strained. It was only toward the end of her life that my mother stopped speaking of Alexandra with bitterness and sadness.

After her marriage, my mother remained in constant contact with her father. He often went over to spend a few days with her at Kotcheti, about a hundred and twenty miles from Yasnaya Polyana, especially at those moments of exhaustion when he felt he needed to escape for a while from his wife's hysterical attacks, Chertkov's despotism, or simply the poisoned atmosphere that reigned in his own home. My mother always found the right words to comfort him, calm him, and prove her affection for him.

As is well known, Tolstoy spent the last days of his life, dying of pneumonia, in the little house of the stationmaster at Astapovo. His wife, as well as my mother and her brothers and sister, hurried there after him. The children, for fear of upsetting their father, forbade their mother to go and see him, and it was not until the very last moment that she was permitted to go into the room where the man who had been her husband for forty-eight years lay dying. She sat down close beside his bed, leaned over him, and murmured words of love and tenderness. Did Tolstoy hear them, understand them? My grandmother was certain he did. My mother, later on, often asked herself whether Tolstoy's children had done the right thing in the circumstances. At the time they were thinking only of their father's welfare and peace of mind, but had they not been too cruel to their mother . . . ?

The last sentence Tolstoy wrote in his diary, in French, was: 'Do what you must, whatever may . . .' His strength failed him before he could add 'befall'. My mother used to say that those seven words, simple and brief as they are, summed up the essence of his teachings and his own ideal: to do one's duty without thinking of the consequences.

A disturbing detail. On October 28th 1910, during the night, at the very moment when Tolstoy was leaving Yasnaya Polyana for ever, my mother woke with a start in her bedroom at Kotcheti. She thought she had heard steps in the corridor, outside her door, and clearly recognized her father's voice. She glanced at the clock: it was three in the morning. If her father had taken the night train that would be just the time he would arrive at Kotcheti. My mother made to get up, but then, thinking that her father might be tired, and probably upset after some new crisis at Yasnaya Polyana, she decided it would be better to leave him to get some sleep. Next morning she asked her maid:

'Is the Count awake yet?'

'Which Count?'

'Why, my father, who arrived last night.'

The maid replied in some surprise that no one had arrived during the night. And not long afterwards my mother learned that at the very moment when she thought she heard him, Tolstoy, on the point of leaving Yasnaya Polyana, had written her a letter: 'My leaving will cause you pain, you more than anyone, my very dearest dove, Tanichka . . .'

My mother enjoyed recounting this odd incident. She regarded it as one more proof of the bonds that linked her so closely to the father whose thoughts had reached her, over all those miles, at the most dramatic moment of his life . . .

After her father's death my mother maintained a cult to his memory. She was always surrounded by his books and innumerable pictures of him. In Rome, where she spent the last twenty years of her life, she created a 'Tolstoy room', which she also referred to as her 'little museum'. It was packed with all Tolstoy's works and all the works of criticism devoted to him, the many editions of his

247

books printed in the Soviet Union as well as translations into every language, copies of which the publishers were always happy to present to her. She cut out anything she found in newspapers or magazines relating to her father, and the articles collected in this way filled a huge series of scrapbooks. Apart from hundreds of photographs, she also had recordings of her father's voice, speaking in English and in Russian, which Tolstoy himself had made on a machine presented to him by Edison. There was also a wooden box in which she kept a few relics brought with her from Russia: a lock from Tolstoy's beard, his paperknife whittled from a piece of oak from Yasnaya Polyana, the satchel in which he kept his manuscripts, and the ring, set with a little ruby, that he had given to his wife as a thank-you for having copied out the manuscript of Anna Karenina *three times.*

My mother was a very talented artist, and as a young girl had attended the Moscow Academy of Fine Arts, where she was the pupil of Repin and other famous Russian painters. The very last portrait of Tolstoy was her work, and many contemporaries considered it to be one of the best likenesses ever achieved.

My mother was very concerned over what was going to happen to her 'treasures' when she was no longer there, for she was not at all afraid of talking about death—a characteristic I seem to have inherited. Being extremely fond of France, because she was so grateful for the welcome she had been given there during the most difficult years of her life, she finally decided to bequeath her archives 'to France'. By the time of her death, however, the question had still not been completely settled. 'To France', yes, but to whom in particular? On the advice of a friend, the French ambassador to Rome, Jacques Fouques-Duparc, I finally decided to entrust them to the Institut d'Etudes Slaves in Paris, whose director, Professor André Mazon, was a great friend of the family. These archives can now be consulted at the Institute's library on the Rue Michelet.

Saying goodbye to everything that linked me to my past and to my grandfather's memory was not something I was able to do without sadness; but in the event I kept only a very few souvenirs of Tolstoy for my children and myself.

My mother and I left Russia in 1925. After a brief stay in Prague with President Masaryk—who had become friendly with Tolstoy and visited him at Yasnaya Polyana—we then spent several weeks in Vienna with the actor Alexander Moissi, through whose good offices we were able to obtain passports. He had visited Moscow in 1923 and played the leading role, with incomparable delicacy and sensibility, in Tolstoy's Living Corpse. *He and his wife had become great friends of ours.*

From Vienna we moved on to Paris, where we met up with many relations and friends, both Russian and French. To make a living, my mother gave lectures about her father, both in France and other countries, while I found employment making artificial flowers. Later, having learned to take shorthand and type in French and English, I worked as a secretary in an American bank. I had always had a passion for the theatre, and in the end my dream came true: I was taken on by Georges and Ludmilla Pitoëff as a member of their troupe. I only played small parts, but I was young, full of enthusiasm, and it was one of the most wonderful times of my life. I often think about it still, remembering with nostalgia that very distinctive backstage smell, and the friendships I struck up with my fellow performers. It was during a tour of Italy with the Pitoëff company that I met Leonardo Albertini, who was to become my husband.

In Paris, as I have said, my mother and I lived on what I could earn and what my mother received for her talks and articles. When all the bills came in at the end of the month things were sometimes very tight, but a great many French friends came to our aid, and that is something I shall never even begin to forget. When my mother wasn't working on her talks she pluckily tackled the housework or sat knitting shawls.

To explain our straitened circumstances I should perhaps recall the fact that Tolstoy had renounced all royalty rights on his works, books and plays alike. He said he didn't want to be paid money in exchange for 'his thoughts and feelings'. My mother never complained, never lamented the consequences of her father's principles or the loss of the fortune those royalties would have represented to her. She shared Tolstoy's ideas totally, and moreover regarded his wishes as sacred.

I only once saw her slightly perplexed. There was a film of Anna Karenina, the one starring Greta Garbo, showing at one of the big Paris cinemas. My mother, a cousin, and I decided to go and see it. But when we arrived at the Gaumont-Palace box-office we had to give up the notion, since the prices were way above our means, and we were forced to trudge sadly home again. When we got back, my mother said with a sweet and disappointed little smile: 'I wonder what papa would have said if he'd seen that. Or the sight of me sweeping the floor, doing my shopping, and not knowing if I'll have enough left to pay the rent . . .' But even then she added immediately: 'Though he was quite right to do what he did . . .'

After my marriage in 1930 I went with my husband to Rome, where his family were living. They were notoriously anti-fascist, and for that reason my father-in-law had been forced to give up the editorship of the Corriere della Sera *and leave Milan. My mother went with me to Rome, but from the very start she announced that she was not going to impose herself on 'the youngsters' and live with them. So for the first time in her life she settled down to living on her own.*

Fenya, the Russian maid she had looking after her, liked to cook Russian delicacies for her, even though my mother could scarcely ever eat them. She had begun to have gall bladder trouble and was consequently on a very strict diet: rice, boiled vegetables, fruit, and a little yoghurt. However, that didn't prevent her retaining her love of good food and taking an interest in what other people ate. Whenever I went to see her I had to give her all the details of what my guests had talked about, how my friends had been dressed, and—the menu!

*She had been a vegetarian for many years—*tolstoyism oblige—*and maintained an indefatigable propaganda campaign on behalf of her beliefs. How many times I have heard her reproaching some unfortunate who had dared to eat a steak for 'turning his stomach into a graveyard', or another who had drunk a cup of beef tea for 'drinking corpse juice'! She was equally opposed to tobacco in all forms and deeply anti-militarist. Influenced by her hatred of everything that smacked of war, I never gave my son 'military' toys. But the day arrived, alas! when we came upon him pointing a pencil at one of his cousins and savagely yelling 'Boom! Boom!' My mother gave me an ironic and slightly disillusioned smile as she said with a sigh: 'What can you expect, it's a man's instinct . . .' Then immediately added: 'But we must fight against it.' She also incited my children to tear up our cigarettes, in order to prevent my husband and me from smoking. The children naturally performed this task with high delight, which never prevented us from buying a fresh supply.*

*My children were very fond of their Baba [from the Russian *babushka, *grandmother], as they called her. Despite principles that could seem very strict, puritanical, and even outlandish in their severity, she was always extremely open-minded with regard to the young generally, and would go to almost any lengths in her desire to help and understand them. She seemed captivated by the presence of young people, and let them talk away to their hearts' content. In conversation she could quite often make herself understood with no more than a single subtle or amused glance. She had gaiety, beyond doubt, but it was a discreet gaiety, despite the fact that she was capable on occasion of bursting into fits of schoolgirlish laughter. And her laughter then was so infectious that my cousins and I would often become helpless with mirth too, sometimes without any idea what we were laughing at.*

My mother had always been deeply interested in the education of young children. Before 1914, during a winter spent in Rome, she had met Maria Montessori and become extremely interested in her method. She took all the Montessori textbooks back with her to Russia, and I still have photographs of the village children and myself learning to read and write by that method.

During the German occupation of Rome, in 1944, my children went to live with their grandmother. If they began squabbling at table my mother would simply get up and very calmly remove herself to the kitchen. Since they wouldn't stop their intolerable quarrelling, she told them, she was going to eat on her own. Whereupon the children naturally rushed over to hug their grandmother and peace was restored. Possessing great self-discipline herself, she was constantly trying to help my children acquire it too, just as she had done from her father. She rarely gave advice because, she said, advice is useless: those who ask for it will only follow it if it is what they wanted to hear. Better to let people act as they choose.

My mother's old age was serene and happy. It was spent in the beautiful city of Rome, which she had loved ever since her first long visit there with her husband in 1903. To give and then to go on giving was what mattered most to her in life. She gave her love, her intelligence, and also her concern to all those who asked for it. And many of them, as often happens in life, later repaid her in kind. She asserted that in growing old she had attained an inner joy such as she had never known in her youth.

A long life teaches one to look for happiness in the present, she would say, to welcome every new day as a gift, to accept joys with gratitude and griefs with resignation. She often quoted her father's words: 'Deep sadnesses and inward struggles are not useless, for they raise you to a higher plane, so that soon you will be soaring far above all that is troubling you today.'

My mother kept up a worldwide correspondence. I have kept the letters she received during her twenty-five years of exile from Russia. Many of them come from members of our family, scattered to the four corners of the earth, others from her colleagues in the Moscow Tolstoy Museum, of which she was once the director, others from writers and academics in many lands: André Maurois, Romain Rolland, George Bernard Shaw, Charles Du Bos, and many others. These latter wrote to her partly because she was Tolstoy's daughter, of course, but even more because she was an intelligent, sensitive woman, open to all problems and always ready to give her help to anyone who asked for it.

However, my mother accepted that she had not inherited her father's gift for writing, and she dreaded sitting down to write. Often, when she had an important or even an urgent letter to write, I would find her busy boiling jam, making Russian dolls, darning her espadrilles, or knitting one of her beautiful shawls. 'Mummy! What about your letter?' I would ask. Then she would look rather hangdog and tell me she was feeling a wee bit tired, so she was doing a few little chores by way of a rest. 'After all, they say a change is as good as a rest, don't they?' Now I look back I'm sorry my mother didn't write more, because she had a real talent as a letter writer. Her letters, which I still have, are all interesting and neatly turned. As for her articles, her reminiscences, and her diary, in my opinion they are certainly worthy of Tolstoy's daughter.

But however much my mother jibbed at writing, like the true Russian she was, she adored company. It wasn't frivolous gossip—what she called 'shaking the air'—that interested her, but heart to heart conversations with her visitors. She would listen to them, give her opinion, find just the right words of consolation or encouragement. Often people came to see her to hear her talk about her father, a desire she always gratified with great good grace. She would tell them the story of Tolstoy's life and his conjugal tragedy. These explanations she regarded as due to her father's memory; she 'owed it to herself' to do that for him.

I have already said that as far as such a thing is possible my mother was not afraid of death. She spoke of it often with serenity, and always wanted to hear about the last moments of people she had known. Moreover, despite the great pain she was sometimes in because of her gallstones, she always refused to take any form of painkilling drugs, saying that she wanted to die in a state of full awareness. She made me promise that even if she was in great pain at the end I would refuse permission for any morphine or other injection that might impair her consciousness. I was greatly worried by my promise, but happily that painful dilemma never arose. My mother faded away very peacefully, without pain.

She had suffered several attacks that had weakened her and obliged her to take to her bed, but she remained lucid and gentle, her heart still as young and brimming with enthusiasm as ever. She herself had once said in fact that she was 'a little girl disguised as an old lady'. One day she said to me: 'Thanks to you I have been happy in my old age, and I have no wish to die. These last few days, however, I have been looking death in the face. We've become acquainted, and even shaken hands.' She confessed that she was curious 'to find out'. A few weeks before her end, one day when her condition had taken a slight turn for the better, she told me with a half smile: 'It is a nuisance, you know. I'd prepared myself for death so well, and now it hasn't come. So now I shall have to re-prepare myself . . .'

The English say: 'Old parents don't die—they fade away' (sic), That is what happened in my mother's case, she faded away, with her hand in mine. There was no knowing if she even knew she was dying. Her face was beautiful and serene. She who shared her father's ideas, and was not a practising Christian, had nevertheless sent for the Orthodox archimandrite of Rome, who had spent a long while with her. There had been many occasions before that, during his visits to take tea with her, when she had said: 'Father Semyon, it will be you who will bury me.' And so it turned out. She lies in the foreigners' cemetery in Rome, near the pyramid of Cestius. The cemetery, very shady and full of flowers, is like a lovely garden. The words on her gravestone read: Tatyana Sukhotin-Tolstoy, born October 4th 1864, died September 21st 1950.

Appendix

Notes to *Childhood at Yasnaya Polyana*

1 Russian names are made up of three elements: the forename (Lev—Leo—, the diminutive of which is Lyova); the patronym (Nicolaye-vich—son of Nicholas—or Nicolayevna—daughter of Nicholas): and the family name (Tolstoy).

2 The diminutive of Sergei. Born in 1863, he was to die in 1947 without ever leaving Russia. He assisted in the editing of his father's works and contributed generally to the field of Tolstoy studies.

3 Tatyana Andreyevna Behrs (1846–1925), younger sister of Tolstoy's wife, who was to marry Alexander Kuzminski. She has left an interesting set of reminiscences: *My life at home and at Yasnaya Polyana,* published in three volumes by Sabashnikov, Moscow.

4 A very affectionate diminutive of Lev (Leo).

5 Brandt was a landowner whose estate, Kaburino, bordered on Yasnaya Polyana.

6 German tutor of Grisha, Sergei Tolstoy's son. Leo Tolstoy had brought him back from Jena in 1861.

7 Doctor Behrs died in 1868.

8 Seryozha was in fact five.

9 The author mistakenly wrote Hannah Jarsey.

10 Also frequently known as Sonya.

11 Diminutive of Marya (1871–1906).

12 Diminutive of Alexandra. Born in 1884, she is now at ninety-three Tolstoy's only surviving child. She lives in the United States and has written two books about her father: *My life with my father,* and *Tolstoy, my father.*

13 1866–1933. He emigrated to the United States, where he was involved in the film made there of Tolstoy's *Resurrection.* He also wrote a book called *Reminiscences of Tolstoy,* Chapman and Hall, London, 1914.

14 I have rarely met a woman as physically strong as myself, and I think many men would have been forced to concede me points on that score. It is something that has brought me great pleasure throughout my life. Whether doing manual work, riding, driving a carriage, or skating, it was always enjoyable being aware of such a reserve of physical strength, since it meant that any form of

exercise, far from being an effort, was on the contrary easy and agreeable. (*Author's note.*)

15 Pierre Fedorovich Samarin (1830–1901) was a local landowner and marshal of the nobility in the Tula provincial government.

16 Afanassi Afanassyevich Shenshin, better known under his pseudonym Fet (1828–91). A poet (*The Lyric Pantheon, Poetry, Evening fires*) and biographer (*Memories of Tolstoy,* 1890).

17 Founder of the Society for the Encouragement of Religious and Moral Reading.

18 The Arsenyev family lived on their estate, Sudakov, about six miles from Yasnaya Polyana. Some years before his marriage, Leo Tolstoy had been more or less in love with Valerie Arsenyev.

19 Diminutive of Lev, or Leo (1869–1945). He emigrated and lived in the United States, Italy, France and Sweden. He wrote two books: *The truth about my father* and *Leo Tolstoy seen by his son.*

20 Eight more children were to follow.

21 Mikhail Alexandrovich Stakhovich (1861–1923), a landowner, member of the Duma, and of the Council of the Empire in 1907.

22 Site of a famous ikon, the Iberian Virgin, which stood at the entrance to Moscow's Red Square.

23 (1830–1912). She married her cousin, Valerian Petrovich Tolstoy in 1847. In 1857 she separated from her husband, whose excesses of behaviour had by then become notorious. She had three children by him: Nicolai, Varya and Lisa. Valarian died in 1865. After that Marya entered into a liaison with a Swedish nobleman, the Viscount Hector de Kleen. Later she entered the convent of Chamardino.

24 In January 1873 he wrote to a friend, K. D. Golokhvostov: 'Since the summer I have been in an abnormal, very distressing state. I torment myself, I worry, I am filled with fear at the thought of the future, I despair, I start to hope again, and then come to the conclusion that there is nothing ahead for me but suffering . . . I find it hard to put up with myself, so I must be quite intolerable to others.'

Notes to *Adolescence*

1 Marya Kuzminski, who was later known as Big Masha (in English) to distinguish her from Tolstoy's daughter who was called Little Masha.

2 Dmitri Ilovayski (1834–1920) was a professor at the University of Moscow. He was a famous historian of that day and wrote a number of works including a six-volume *History of Russia* that appeared between 1876 and 1905.

3 Four-wheeled carriage for long journeys, usually closed.

4 Carriage with a single seat running from back to front.

5 A peasant vehicle, a cross between a carriage and a cart.
6 A cossack chieftain (1630–71). Headed the great peasant revolt of 1667–70 and eventually hanged, drawn and quartered in Moscow. Subject of a great many folk songs.
7 The Bashkirs are Moslems. The mullah exercised both religious and judicial functions.
8 Statistics indicate that the majority of disappearances, suicides, and even murders, occur among adolescents between the ages of thirteen and sixteen. (*Author's note.*)

Translation of poem on page 145

Oh conjugal love, sweet bond of our souls,
Wellspring and source of all we hold sweet,
May your heavenly flame never fade in our hearts
And crown our desires in a haven of peace!

From the heavens I ask neither fame nor great wealth,
This quiet existence is all I desire,
As long as my spouse, his love never failing
Is always happy as he is beloved.

May our life like a stream flow peacefully on
Leaving no traces except among flowers,
May our pleasure in loving ever increase
And fix fleeting joy for aye by our side.

Yes, my heart tells me, this fate that men crave
Heaven in its goodness has decreed for us twain,
And those names intertwined, Nicolas and Marie,
Will forever denote twin beings in bliss.